THE PROPHET
ISAIAH

EXPOSITORY NOTES ON
THE PROPHET
ISAIAH

By

H. A. IRONSIDE, Litt.D.

Author of NOTES ON JEREMIAH AND LAMENTATIONS;
NOTES ON EZEKIEL THE PROPHET; LECTURES ON DANIEL THE PROPHET;
NOTES ON THE MINOR PROPHETS, etc., etc.

1952

LOIZEAUX BROTHERS
Neptune, New Jersey

FIRST EDITION, OCTOBER 1952
TENTH PRINTING, MAY 1974

COPYRIGHT 1952

BY

LOIZEAUX BROTHERS, Inc.

PRINTED IN THE UNITED STATES OF AMERICA

FOREWORD

For several years Dr. H. A. Ironside had it on his heart to write an exposition of the Book of Isaiah. His extremely busy preaching and teaching schedule, and later his failing sight, seemed to prevent his making headway on the exposition. Then, when he had progressed part way in this work, the Lord took him to be with Himself. It seemed as if the planned volume were doomed to be left uncompleted.

But God had planned otherwise. Surely the events that transpired to produce this volume are of God. We have asked Mrs. Ironside to tell a little about the way this exposition on Isaiah has come to fulfillment, believing that readers of this volume will be thrilled, as we were, to see how God arranges men's affairs so that their work for Him can never be thwarted.

In December 1949, Dr. Ironside gave lectures on the Book of Isaiah at Dallas Theological Seminary. One of the students, Ray C. Stedman, made wire recordings of the classroom lectures.

Mr. Stedman also did a great deal of secretarial work for Dr. Ironside during his stay at the seminary. He was so efficient and helpful that Dr. Ironside asked him if he would be willing to travel with us during the summer, and help with the writing of his exposition of the Book of Isaiah, which had long been delayed on account of his failing sight.

Mr. Stedman joined us in June 1950, after his graduation from the seminary, and for two months served not only as chauffeur, secretary, and companion, but as a "brother beloved" was so helpful in all the varied activities of the itinerant ministry that we came to love him as a son. Without his help and cooperation the publication of Dr. Ironside's "Isaiah" would have been impossible.

Traveling constantly, Dr. Ironside's reference library consisted of M. A. Vine's *Isaiah—Prophecies, Promises, and Warnings;* F. C. Jennings' *Isaiah;* a one-volume Bible encyclopedia; and J. N. Darby's New Translation of the Holy Scriptures.

As Dr. Ironside was unable to read at all during this time, except with the aid of a powerful magnifying glass, his method of working under this handicap may be of interest. Mr. Stedman writes:

"In general our procedure was as follows: I would read to him the portion chosen for comment, out of the Authorized Version—a portion which had previously been read to him and over which he had been meditating. He would take a moment or two to gather his thoughts and then would begin dictating, seldom pausing for rephrasing or changes. I would then read the next section and he would dictate on that until an entire chapter had been covered. After that I would read through the next chapter, usually from Darby's "New Translation" and also the corresponding portion from Jennings and Vine. This would form the basis for his meditation in preparation for the next day's dictation.

"Occasionally we would discuss interesting sections of the chapters together and he would ask me to look up certain words in a one-volume Bible encyclopedia he carried. I was always amazed at the way he kept his comments from simply being a "rehash" of Vine and

Jennings, but always managed to bring out some interesting sidelight which the others had overlooked."

When Mr. Stedman left us to go to the pastorate of the Peninsula Bible Fellowship at Palo Alto, California, the first thirty-five chapters of Isaiah were completed and typed.

After the operation on Dr. Ironside's eyes in September 1950, which entirely restored his sight, he edited the manuscript and left it with Loizeaux Brothers before our departure for New Zealand. Chapters 35-39 were written by Dr. Ironside in his characteristic scrawl during December 1950 and were copied in longhand by his wife, who was his only secretary on the trip.

When he went to be with the Lord from Rotorna, New Zealand, on January 15, 1951, he had only completed chapter 39.

As to chapters 40-66, Ray Stedman writes: "I had taken them on wire recordings at the time of his lectures in Dallas. Unfortunately, I did not have enough wire to take the whole series. I did record the early chapters, too, but had to wipe them off and use that same wire for the later chapters, which I saved. Upon the request of one of the students, I copied off on Soundscriber discs the entire series from chapter 40 on. It was these discs which were sent Loizeaux Brothers for transcription. . . . It certainly was the hand of the Lord that I should have retained the lectures beginning with the very one where Dr. Ironside left off and that they should be on Soundscriber discs, ready for immediate transcription. The wire originals are a precious heritage to me, and have already proven of wide blessing wherever they have been played."

Chapters 40-66, after having been transcribed from

the Soundscriber discs, have been edited by Miss Emily Farmer,* who edited in the past, most of Dr. Ironside's manuscripts when his works were being prepared for publication. We are most grateful for her careful and efficient work as unto the Lord.

It has been a joy to each of us to have a part in the publication of this book. May God continue to bless the written ministry of "H.A.I.," who, being dead, yet speaketh.

ANN HIGHTOWER IRONSIDE

Thomaston, Georgia, 1952

Publishers' Note: Miss Emily Farmer came to Loizeaux Brothers from Colchester, England, in 1907. From that time until her retirement in 1947 she was invaluable as an accurate proofreader and an able editor with a wide knowledge and deep appreciation of the truths of Scripture.

Dr. Scofield borrowed the services of Miss Farmer to give editorial assistance in preparing notes for the Scofield Bible in their final form. The excellence of the Scofield Bible today is attributable in no small measure to Miss Farmer's keen discernment of sound doctrine.

In her work on Dr. Ironside's ISAIAH, Miss Farmer has had to accomplish this while lying in her bed and it has thus been a real labor of love on her part, for which the Publishers wish to express their heartfelt thanks.

CONTENTS

THE PROPHET
ISAIAH

INTRODUCTION

ISAIAH'S "wild measure" has ever been a portion of God's Holy Word in which spiritually minded believers have found much to exercise their hearts and lead out their souls in glad anticipation of the coming day when Immanuel, of whom this prophet speaks, will take His great power and reign.

Longer than any other prophetic book, it contains the fullest Messianic predictions to be found in the Old Testament, testifying in no uncertain way to "the sufferings of Christ, and the glory that should follow."

Of late, like all other books of the Bible, it has suffered much at the hands of unbelieving and haughty critics, who have done their best to undermine the faith of the simple in the integrity and unity of the Bible, but all that is settled for those who have faith by the Lord Jesus. When here on earth He placed the seal of his divine approval upon it in its entirety. And from this book the apostles drew again and again in their ministry after the ascension of the Saviour, all by the direct guidance of the Holy Spirit, giving it a place of unquestionable authority as the very word of Jehovah.

Isaiah himself was a man of wealth, rank, and learning, if we may give any credence to Jewish tradition respecting him. He is supposed to be the one referred to in Hebrews 11:37, who was "sawn asunder" by the enraged rejecters of his prophetic ministry. If this be so, it occurred at the close of a long and honored life, for his public service extended over at least half a century. As he tells us in the opening verse, he prophesied "in the days of Uzziah, Jotham, Ahaz, and Hezekiah." In all likelihood he did not appear in the prophetic office until the last year of Uzziah's long reign (Isa. 6:1).

Chapter six records his divine commission, and it is questionable if he had uttered the burdens of the previous chapters ere the vision there portrayed, which took place "in the year that King Uzziah died": that is, not necessarily after he died but in the same year as that solemn event. We know he continued to give forth the word of the Lord later than the fourteenth year of Hezekiah's reign, for it was then that he was commissioned to make known to the stricken monarch that fifteen years were to be added to his life. He was, therefore, contemporary with Hosea throughout, and possibly with Amos for a very brief season, though it is more likely the herdman-prophet had passed off the scene before Isaiah began to make known the mind of God. Micah also held the prophetic office during the reigns of the last three kings mentioned. So Isaiah would be the chief among a goodly little company, who had the secret of the Lord in a day when formalism and hypocrisy largely prevailed.

That there was but one Isaiah, not two, is evident from the testimony given by the inspired writer of the Gospel of Luke. He tells us that on the occasion of the Lord's first public visit to the synagogue at Nazareth, "there was delivered unto Him the book of the prophet Esaias," (not of "the great unknown"), and from it He preached His gospel of deliverance to the captives and the acceptable year of the Lord. The glorious predictions of Isaiah 61:1,2 the Lord cited as inspired Scripture and written by Isaiah, not as the writing of an unknown poet of the Maccabean or a later period.

The book as it stands bears every evidence of being preserved in its divinely arranged order. It is only unbelieving ignorance coupled with amazing egotism, that could lead any to think to rearrange and dissect it in the manner of modern critics, of which George Adam Smith's "Isaiah" in the *Expositor's Bible* series is the most commonly known specimen. It is a virtual denial of inspiration and a biased attempt to destroy the true prophetic character of the Messianic portions of this magnificent "golden prophecy."

Unbelief finds difficulties where faith bows with adoring reverence. As I write not for sceptics, but for those who truly know Christ whose sufferings and glories Isaiah foretold, I shall pay but slight attention to the objections of those unbelieving, natural men, albeit distinguished in the world of letters and in the Christless religious circles of the day.

Many professing Christians pay little or no attention to the prophetic word, but in neglecting that which formed so large a part of the Holy Scriptures, they wrong their own souls and dishonor Him who gave His Word for our edification and comfort. The real value of prophecy is that it occupies us with a Person, not merely with events. That Person is our Lord Jesus Christ who came once to suffer and is coming again to reign. Of both these advents Isaiah treats, and that in a way more plain and full than do any of the other Old Testament seers.

It should be borne in mind, however, that prophecy is not simply the foretelling of future events, but is rather the *forth-telling* of the mind of God for the moment. When both the priesthood and the monarchy had failed completely in Israel and Judah, God continued to minister to His people through the prophets. These were men to whom special insight was given into holy things, and who were sent of God to call an erring people to repentance. It was their responsibility to put before the people not only the coming glories into which they were to enter in Messiah's day, but also to impress upon them the necessity of preparing the way of the Lord by turning from sin to righteousness, and from their idolatrous vanities to the living God who had so wonderfully manifested His power on their behalf throughout Israel's history.

Those who are interested in the curious things of Scripture have noticed long since that Isaiah, in one sense, comprises a miniature Bible. The Bible consists of sixty-six books: Isaiah has sixty-six chapters. The Bible is divided into two Testaments, Old and New: Isaiah is also divided into two parts, the first having to do largely with Israel's past condition and the promise of Messiah's coming, and the second dealing particularly with their future deliverance. The Old Testament has thirty-nine books: the first half of Isaiah has thirty-nine chapters. The New Testament has twenty-seven books: the second part of Isaiah has twenty-seven chapters. This, of course, is a mere coincidence because it was not the Spirit of God but human editors who divided the book in this way; nevertheless it is interesting and quite suggestive when we realize that Isaiah deals in a very definite way with that which is the outstanding theme of all the Scriptures—God's salvation as revealed in His blessed Son.

There are many things in the writings of Isaiah which are perhaps beyond our present comprehension even as they were beyond the comprehension of the writer himself. Like the other prophets, Isaiah wrote at the command of the Lord, and then searched his own scriptures, the scriptures then available, as to what manner of time the Spirit of Christ that was in him did prophesy when he testified beforehand concerning the sufferings of Christ and the glories that should follow. The portions that deal with the sufferings of Christ which took place at His first advent have become amazingly clear in the light of the New Testament Gospels. Those that have to do with the glories that shall follow at His second advent, while linked with all prophecy as to that glorious advent, will never be fully understood until the day of fulfillment arrives. Even though at times, as we study this book, we may seem to see through a glass darkly, we may be assured of real blessing as we weigh carefully before God that which He commissioned Isaiah to proclaim.

The divisions of the book would seem to be as follows.

There are three great divisions, though these again readily subdivide: Part I is chiefly ministry to the conscience of Israel and Judah, suffering under God's hand in government, with Messiah's coming as the goal of blessing before them. It consists of chapters one to thirty-five, and is an orderly, connected series of messages or burdens, evidently uttered by Isaiah before the illness of Hezekiah. Part II is historical, though of a prophetical, and typical character, showing how, for Judah, all blessing is bound up with a Son of David who goes down to death but is raised up by omnipotent power. It consists of chapters thirty-six to thirty-nine, and is almost identical with 2 Kings 18:13 to 20:19, and also as to the main points with 2 Chronicles 32. Isaiah himself doubtless was the recorder of the portion of the book of Kings written during his ministry, and by divine direction he introduces the parts specified into the book bearing his name. Part III concludes the prophecy, embracing chapters forty to sixty-six. It sets forth the utter failure of the first man and the bringing in of the Second, the Lord from heaven. Israel as the servant of God is shown to be unfaithful in every particular and is set aside that the True Servant, the Elect of Jehovah, may be manifested.

Through Him, all God's counsels shall stand and His glory be established, and that forevermore. Prophecy, however, does not go beyond this earth, so it is "as long as the sun and moon endure." But we know from the later revelation that He, the Eternal Son of the Father, will be the One in whom all the fullness of the Godhead shall be displayed forever.

With these preliminary thoughts before us, we turn then to the consideration of the book itself, assured that like all other Scriptures, we shall find it profitable for teaching, for reproof, for correction, and instruction in righteousness.

CHAPTER ONE

THE CALL TO HEAR

The vision of Isaiah the son of Amoz, which he saw concerning Judah and Jerusalem in the days of Uzziah, Jotham, Ahaz, and Hezekiah, kings of Judah. Hear, O heavens, and give ear, O earth: for the Lord hath spoken, I have nourished and brought up children, and they have rebelled against me. The ox knoweth his owner, and the ass his master's crib: but Israel doth not know, my people doth not consider. Ah sinful nation, a people laden with iniquity, a seed of evildoers, children that are corrupters: they have forsaken the Lord, they have provoked the Holy One of Israel unto anger, they are gone away backward. Why should ye be stricken any more? Ye will revolt more and more: the whole head is sick, and the whole heart faint. From the sole of the foot even unto the head there is no soundness in it; but wounds, and bruises and putrifying sores: they have not been closed, neither bound up, neither mollified with ointment (verses 1-6).

ABRUPTLY the voice of the Lord breaks in upon the ears of men who prided themselves upon their religiousness and trusted in their formal observance of the legal ritual, "Hear, O heavens, and give ear, O earth: for the Lord hath spoken, I have nourished and brought up children, and they have rebelled against Me. The ox knoweth his owner, and the ass his master's crib: but Israel doth not know, My people doth not consider." There is something sublime in the very simplicity of this challenge to obedience. Heaven and earth, ever subject to His will, are called to witness the base ingratitude of Jehovah's people. The objects of His solicitous care

9

from their childhood in Egypt to the moment then present, they had never, as an entire nation, given Him that loving obedience which was His due.

Individual faithfulness there ever was; but nationally, as later in the case of the Church viewed as a collective body, failure had come in almost at the very beginning and there had never been recovery.

Ox and ass know their owner or their master's crib because of his care for them. May we not well challenge our hearts as to how far we really *know* our Owner? To what extent do we sanctify Christ as Lord? He is our Owner now. Other lords have had dominion over us, but by Him only will we now make mention of the ineffable Name. The kingdom of God for us is that of the Son of His love. To the Crucified we owe unswerving allegiance. Our Master's crib is the Word of God, a part of which we have now before us. Do we really *know* it? Does hunger ever drive us to it; or, are we often found foolishly sniffing the desert air, following the wind like the wild ass, our backs on God's well-filled storehouse, vainly seeking a satisfactory portion in the world we have professed to judge? Solemn questions these, not to be evaded or ignored, but faced in the presence of the Lord: lest a day come when, of us too He shall have to say, "Ah sinful nation, a people laden with iniquity, a seed of evildoers, children that are corrupters: they have forsaken the Lord, they have provoked the Holy One of Israel unto anger, they are gone away backward" (verse 4).

There is no breach of relationship suggested here. Judah was still owned of God, but her moral state was such as demanded discipline. Yet that discipline she had despised until it seemed to be useless to chasten her further. The sore seemed too deep to be healed; the whole head was sick and the heart faint. Everywhere the evidences of inward corruption were manifest. Soundness, there was none; nor had their hearts turned to Him that He who had smitten might bind them up in His grace and longsuffering.

Your country is desolate, your cities are burned with fire: your land, strangers devour it in your presence, and it is desolate, as overthrown by strangers. And the daughter of Zion is left as a cottage in a vineyard, as a lodge in a garden of cucumbers, as a besieged city. Except the Lord of hosts had left unto us a very small remnant, we should have been as Sodom, and we should have been like unto Gomorrah. Hear the word of the Lord, ye rulers of Sodom; give ear unto the law of our God, ye people of Gomorrah. To what purpose is the multitude of your sacrifices unto me? saith the Lord: I am full of the burnt-offerings of rams, and the fat of fed beasts; and I delight not in the blood of bullocks, or of lambs, or of he goats. When ye come to appear before me, who hath required this at your hand, to tread my courts? Bring no more vain oblations; incense is an abomination unto me; the new moons and sabbaths, the calling of assemblies, I cannot away with; it is iniquity, even the solemn meeting. Your new moons and your appointed feasts my soul hateth: they are a trouble unto me; I am weary to bear them. And when ye spread forth your hands, I will hide mine eyes from you: yea, when ye make many prayers, I will not hear: your hands are full of blood. Wash you, make you clean; put away the evil of your doings from before mine eyes; cease to do evil; Learn to do well; seek judgment, relieve the oppressed, judge the fatherless, plead for the widow. Come now, and let us reason together, saith the Lord: though your sins be as scarlet, they shall be as white as snow; though they be red like crimson, they shall be as wool. If ye be willing and obedient, ye shall eat the good of the land: but if ye refuse and rebel, ye shall be devoured with the sword: for the mouth of the Lord hath spoken it (verses 7-20).

Prophetically, Isaiah beholds the sad result of all this cold-hearted indifference to the message he brought. Their country was soon to be desolate and their fair cities were to be destroyed by conflagration. Strangers should dwell in their land and but a feeble remnant be left as a workman's hut in a vineyard or a keeper's lodge in a cucumber field. The prophet speaks of things not seen as yet, in the present sense, for faith's eye can see all that God has declared as though already fulfilled. It is here he uses the words quoted by the Apostle Paul in Romans 9:29: "Except the Lord of hosts had left unto us a very small remnant, we should have been as Sodom, and we should have been like unto Gomorrah" (verse 9). That remnant alone could be owned of God. Because of it, He would not utterly cast off His people, and it will be observed that throughout the balance of the book, the remnant is ever given the place of the nation. The mass are already rejected—"children in whom is no pleasure." In verses 10-20 it is this evil majority who are before God. No link of relationship does He acknowledge with them. They are in very deed as Sodom and Gomorrah, and as such He designates them and calls them to repentance. Rulers and people alike were evil; and in their unholy, unregenerate state, they could have no place before Him. For such as these to offer sacrifice was but to mock and insult His holiness. He found no delight in their offerings, nor could He complacently behold them treading His courts.

What a scathing rebuke have we here for any who would profess to draw near to God by sacramental observances while not born of His Spirit and broken before Him! Ritualism is an offence; religious exercises, as they are called, are filthy in His sight, if there be no true recognition of guilt and the need of atonement whereby iniquity may be purged. From all their solemn feasts and sacred seasons, Jehovah turned away in disgust. He would hide His face and close His ears, for the proof of their defiled condition was in their hands.

What was needed? The application of the Word of God to heart and conscience, evidencing genuine faith in Him whose voice to man it is, resulting in purged ways and a clean life. "Wash you, make you clean," He cries; "Put away the evil of your doings from before Mine eyes; cease to do evil; learn to do well; seek judgment, relieve the oppressed, judge the fatherless, plead for the widow. Come now, and let us reason together, saith the Lord." Observe the order here. There is no promise of gospel blessing until the Word of God be bowed to. Nor is it making grace to wait on works, or salvation dependent on human effort or upon advancement in righteousness. But God has no blessing either for time or eternity for the man who persists in sin and refuses to judge himself in the light of His revealed Word. Where faith is truly present, contrition for sin will be manifest and amendment will follow inevitably.

It is to the self-judged, therefore, that the glorious Word comes in power; "Come now, and let us reason together, saith the Lord: though your sins be as scarlet, they shall be as white as snow; though they be red like crimson, they shall be as wool" (verse 18). No more blessed proclamation of full amnesty is found in all the Bible than in this lovely verse. It is the offer of full judicial cleansing for every repentant soul, no matter how grievous his record may have been. Well may Isaiah be called "the evangelical prophet." A wondrous gospel pervades all his pages, though warnings of judgment are ever before us.

Cleansed and forgiven, the delivered soul is then called to tread the path of obedience and subjection to the One who has justified from all things. Dispensationally, it may be remarked, justification had to await the revelation of the gospel of the glory of the blessed God, announced in New Testament times only; but, actually, every soul in every age who heard the Word in faith was cleared of every charge.

The obedience here indicated was of a decidedly legal character as befitting the age of law and the reward in keeping. "If ye be willing and obedient, ye shall eat the good of the land." But in this age of grace there is a land, unknown to sight but seen and enjoyed by faith, of whose goodly fruits each subject soul eats in abundance through the Spirit's gracious ministry.

On the other hand, where the Word of life and blessing is refused and a rebellious spirit is manifested, in place of one of contrition and brokenness, the sword, whether as here of a human enemy or as more clearly made known in the New Testament, of divine judgment, must devour the gainsayer, "for the mouth of the Lord hath spoken it." This whole section is deeply instructive and should be carefully weighed in the light of eternity, by every soul to whom it comes, "For God shall bring every work into judgment, with every secret thing, whether it be good or whether it be evil."

Another section begins with verse 21 and goes on to the end of the chapter. It has in view Jerusalem, once the faithful city, now corrupt and adulterous: in itself, the exemplification of all the evils that afflicted the land. In dirge-like measure the prophet bewails its fallen estate; but the Spirit of grace distinguishes a remnant still and so he sings of mercy and of judgment.

How is the faithful city become an harlot! it was full of judgment; righteousness lodged in it; but now murderers. Thy silver is become dross, thy wine mixed with water: thy princes are rebellious, and companions of thieves: every one loveth gifts, and followeth after rewards: they judge not the fatherless, neither doth the cause of the widow come unto them. Therefore saith the Lord, the Lord of hosts, the mighty One of Israel, Ah, I will ease me of mine adversaries, and avenge me of mine enemies: and I will turn my hand upon thee, and purely purge away thy dross, and take away all thy tin: and I will restore thy judges as at the first, and thy counsellors as at the beginning: afterward thou shalt be called, The city of righteousness, the faithful city. Zion shall be redeemed with judgment, and her converts with righteousness. And the destruction of the transgressors and of the sinners shall be together, and they that forsake the Lord shall be consumed. For they shall be ashamed of the oaks which ye have desired, and ye shall be confounded for the gardens that ye have chosen. For ye shall be as an oak whose leaf fadeth, and as a garden that hath no water. And the strong shall be as tow, and the maker of it as a spark, and they shall both burn together, and none shall quench them (verses 21-31).

The city in whose devotedness Jehovah had once found such delight, which once bore the name of the holy, had become an harlot, following after other lovers who could not save. Once full of discretion and the home of righteousness, it had become a lodging-place for men of blood. In place of silver, speaking of atonement (*cf.* Exodus 30:11-16), was the dross of complacent self-sufficiency; and the wine of joy was diluted with the foul water of earth's broken cisterns (verses 21, 22). The leaders of the people, who should have set an example of subjection to the Word of God, were rebellious and bribe-lovers. Righteous judgment was forgotten in the base desire for gain.

Because of all this, the Lord Himself would awake to judgment, and pour out His vengeance upon those who, posing as His friends, were in reality at enmity with Him. But unmixed judgment it could not be, for they were His covenant people still. He would correct in

measure. His discipline would have the effect of remov-
ing the unjust and unholy, purging the nation from its
dross and sin, from all that was base and unpleasing to
God, after which He would restore their judges as at
the first and their counselors as of old. Then, redeemed
with judgment, Zion shall be called once more The city
of righteousness, The faithful city (verses 25-27). This
will be their final blessing as other Scriptures show us,
after the long years of their dispersion and the bitterness of the last great tribulation have come to an end.

Their sufferings must go on until the unrepentant
transgressors and wilful sinners shall be utterly destroyed, and those that remain—a weak but faithful
remnant—shall loathe themselves for their past sins
and be ashamed of the many false gods who have
allured them, as a nation, away from the God of their
fathers. Beautifully, we see this spirit exemplified in
three ninth chapters of our Bible: namely, Ezra,
Nehemiah, and Daniel; all remnant books, where faithful men judge their people's sin as their own sin, but
from it turn with abhorrence, to seek the Lord with all
their hearts.

All who do not repent shall be consumed together by
the fierce anger of Jehovah as a withered oak, a water-
less garden, and as tow to which the Lord shall apply
the spark.

Nor have the words of this section a voice for the
Jew alone. They are also written for our admonition
upon whom the ends of the ages have arrived. The
failure of the professing Church has been even greater
than that of Jerusalem, because of the greater light
against which we have sinned. Soon must the Holy and
the True, disgusted with such corruption, vomit out of
His mouth all that is unreal and opposed to His Word.

But He stands knocking at the door, and whenever there is reality and a heart for Himself, He will come in and sup there in hallowed, blest communion, though the doom of guilty Christendom is so near.

CHAPTER TWO

ZION'S FUTURE GLORY

The word that Isaiah the son of Amoz saw concerning Judah and Jerusalem. And it shall come to pass in the last days, that the mountain of the Lord's house shall be established in the top of the mountains, and shall be exalted above the hills; and all nations shall flow unto it. And many people shall go and say, Come ye, and let us go up to the mountain of the Lord, to the house of the God of Jacob; and he will teach us of his ways, and we will walk in his paths: for out of Zion shall go forth the law, and the word of the Lord from Jerusalem. And he shall judge among the nations, and shall rebuke many people: and they shall beat their swords into plowshares, and their spears into pruninghooks: nation shall not lift up sword against nation, neither shall they learn war any more. O house of Jacob, come ye, and let us walk in the light of the Lord (verses 1-5).

THE four chapters that now demand our attention form a connected discourse, a soul-stirring message addressed to Judah and Jerusalem, at a time unspecified. The parable of the vineyard in chapter five is a lovely, yet solemn epitome of it all, and forms really the prophet's text, that which precedes being introductory, and what follows is a fitting conclusion, pronouncing the woes of the Lord upon the vine that brought forth but wild grapes.

The opening verses of chapter two (verses 2-4) are almost identical with those of Micah 4:1-3. There is no need to suppose plagiarism or a scribe's blunder, in transferring the words of one prophet to the book of another. Rather is it a blessed evidence that one Spirit inspired each speaker, or writer. The double testimony is but added assurance that the thing spoken cannot fail.

It tells in language too plain to be misunderstood, that in the last days God will again take up His ancient people, Israel, restoring them to their land, and making Jerusalem His throne-city, from which His laws will go forth to the ends of the earth. "The mountain of the Lord's house shall be established in the top of the mountains, and shall be exalted above the hills." The mountain is the city itself. This is a common prophetic symbol. Mountains signify governments and throne-cities; and Jerusalem will be "the city of the great King," and "all nations shall flow unto it." This will be fulfilled literally in the coming age, after God's present work of grace has come to an end. He is now, as James points out in Acts 15:14, visiting the Gentiles to take out of them a people for His Name. But when this special work is completed He will "build again the tabernacle of David," and through restored Israel, bless all the nations. Then will be the time when "Many people shall go and say, Come ye, and let us go up to the mountain of the Lord, to the house of the God of Jacob; and He will teach us of His ways, and we will walk in His paths." For in that day of His power, the law will go forth from Zion and His word from Jerusalem. He will rule all the nations in equity and put down every opposing thing.

It is not in this dispensation that Israel will thus be saved, and, through them, the nations brought to own Immanuel's sway. Therefore, those who expect to see all wars ended and righteousness everywhere established in this age are doomed to bitter disappointment.

It is not now, while the King is sitting as the earth's rejected One upon His Father's throne, that the nations "shall beat their swords into plowshares, and their spears into pruninghooks." But when He returns to this world and takes His own throne—the throne of His father, David—then "nation shall not lift up sword against nation, neither shall they learn war any more." It is in view of this glorious fulfillment of Israel's Messianic hopes that the exhortation of verse 5 comes in, "O house of Jacob, come ye, and let us walk in the light of the Lord." The house of Jacob, so long blinded because of their rejection of Christ when He came the first time, will then have their eyes opened to see the light which has been hidden from them.

Therefore thou hast forsaken thy people the house of Jacob because they be replenished from the east, and are soothsayers like the Philistines, and they please themselves in the children of strangers. Their land also is full of silver and gold, neither is there any end of their treasures; their land is also full of horses, neither is there any end of their chariots: their land also is full of idols; they worship the work of their own hands, that which their own fingers have made: and the mean man boweth down, and the great man humbleth himself: therefore forgive them not. Enter into the rock, and hide thee in the dust, for fear of the Lord, and for the glory of his majesty. The lofty looks of man shall be humbled, and the haughtiness of men shall be bowed down, and the Lord alone shall be exalted in that day. For the day of the Lord of hosts shall be upon every one that is proud and lofty, and upon every one that is lifted up; and he shall be brought low: and upon all the cedars of Lebanon, that are high and lifted up, and upon all the oaks of Bashan, and upon all the high mountains, and upon all the hills that are lifted up, and upon every high tower, and upon every fenced wall, and upon all the ships of Tarshish, and upon all pleasant pictures. And the loftiness of man shall be bowed down, and the haughtiness of men shall be made low: and the Lord alone shall be exalted in that day. And the idols he shall utterly abolish. And they shall go into the holes of the rocks, and into the caves of the earth, for fear of the Lord, and for the glory of his majesty, when he ariseth to shake terribly the earth. In that day a man shall cast his idols of silver, and his idols of gold, which they made each one for himself to worship, to the moles and to the bats; to go into the clefts of the rocks, and into the tops of the ragged rocks, for fear of the Lord, and for the glory of his majesty, when he ariseth to shake terribly the earth. Cease ye from man, whose breath is in his nostrils: for wherein is he to be accounted of? (verses 6-22).

It is very evident that the verses we have been considering are parenthetical, for there is no apparent connection between verse 6 and what has gone before. But if this verse be read as immediately following the last verse of the first chapter it fits perfectly.

Wealth and luxury will not avail to avert the wretchedness that is to be the portion of all who forsake the Lord and turn aside to false gods who are powerless to deliver those who put their trust in them.

In verses 10-22 the prophet speaks of the Day of the Lord when God shall arise in His might and His indignation to deal with wickedness and corruption wherever found. As depicted in the judgment of the sixth seal in Revelation 6, men may seek to enter into the rocks and hide in the ground, but their hope of escaping the fierce anger of the Lord will be in vain, for "the lofty looks of man shall be humbled, and the haughtiness of men shall be bowed down, and the Lord alone shall be exalted in that day" (verse 11).

The day of the Lord is in contrast to the day of man, this present evil age when God is permitting men to take their own way and to try out their own plans independently of His authority. In that coming day high and low, rich and poor, learned and ignorant, all alike shall be brought low before the God they have defied or forgotten.

That judgment will be like a tremendous storm or a forest fire sweeping over the mountains of Lebanon, devouring the great cedars and oaks and destroying lesser trees of the forest, then reaching down the mountain slopes and consuming the farmhouses and villages and even spreading across the plains to the shipping ports, destroying all the ships of Tarshish and all objects of art, for God has decreed that "the loftiness of man shall be bowed down, and the haughtiness of men shall be made low: and the Lord alone shall be exalted in that day" (verse 17). All that men have put in the place of God shall be abolished, and in their terror men shall hide in the holes of the rocks and in the caves of the earth, hoping thereby to find shelter from the wrath of an offended God (verse 19).

Casting away all in which they have trusted vainly, they will find themselves bereft of all confidence and will seek shelter in vain in the most inaccessible places as they endeavor to flee from the majestic glory of Jehovah "when He ariseth to shake terribly the earth" (verse 21). Such will be the end of man's boasted civilization, of his effort to make this world a place of rest and security while ignoring the claims of Him who created all things for His own glory.

And so the section closes with the solemn admonition: "Cease ye from man, whose breath is in his nostrils: for wherein is he to be accounted of?" (verse 22).

CHAPTER THREE

JUDAH'S FALLEN CONDITION

For, behold, the Lord, the Lord of hosts, doth take away from Jerusalem and from Judah the stay and the staff, the whole stay of bread, and the whole stay of water, the mighty man, and the man of war, the judge, and the prophet, and the prudent, and the ancient, the captain of fifty, and the honourable man, and the counsellor, and the cunning artificer, and the eloquent orator. And I will give children to be their princes, and babes shall rule over them. And the people shall be oppressed, every one by another, and every one by his neighbour: the child shall behave himself proudly against the ancient, and the base against the honourable. When a man shall take hold of his brother of the house of his father, saying, Thou hast clothing, be thou our ruler, and let this ruin be under thy hand: in that day shall he swear, saying, I will not be an healer; for in my house is neither bread nor clothing: make me not a ruler of the people. For Jerusalem is ruined, and Judah is fallen: because their tongue and their doings are against the Lord, to provoke the eyes of His glory. The shew of their countenance doth witness against them; and they declare their sin as Sodom, they hide it not. Woe unto their soul! for they have rewarded evil unto themselves. Say ye to the righteous, that it shall be well with him: for they shall eat the fruit of their doings. Woe unto the wicked! it shall be ill with him: for the reward of his hands shall be given him. As for my people, children are their oppressors, and women rule over them. O my people, they which lead thee cause thee to err, and destroy the way of thy paths. The Lord standeth up to plead, and standeth to judge the people. The Lord will enter into judgment with the ancients of his people, and the princes thereof: for ye have eaten up the vineyard; the spoil of the poor is in your houses. What mean ye that ye beat my people to pieces, and grind the faces of the poor? saith the Lord God of hosts (verses 1-15).

THIS third chapter continues along the same line as chapter two, but makes it very definitely clear that it is Jerusalem and Judah which God has in view above all others when He speaks of coming desolation and unsparing judgment.

The covenant people and the one-time holy city had gone so far from the path of obedience that God Himself prepared them for the vengeance decreed by weakening their means of defence. Children were their princes and babes ruled over them. Their leaders, in other words, were like infants unable to control themselves, much less to guide others aright, so disorder and confusion prevailed in place of orderly government. When God is dethroned, anarchy always results.

In their desperation, men were ready to follow anyone who might seem to be able to point out a way of escape from the present misery and might promise to bring order out of the chaotic condition prevailing. But those to whom they turned for guidance were in utter bewilderment themselves, and so refused to take the responsibility of seeking to rectify the abuses which were affecting the nation so adversely (verses 5-7).

The root-cause of all the trouble is indicated in verse 8, "Jerusalem is ruined, and Judah is fallen: because their tongue and their doings are against the Lord, to provoke the eyes of His glory." Thus they had brought down judgment upon their own heads, and so we hear the solemn "woes" pronounced against them—two in this chapter (verses 9 and 11) ; and six in chapter five (verses 8, 11, 18, 20, 21, 22).

First we read, "Woe unto their soul! for they have rewarded evil unto themselves." Then in verse 11,

"Woe unto the wicked! it shall be ill with him: for the reward of his hands shall be given him." As for the righteous remnant, God will care for them, protecting them in the day of storm and stress (verse 10).

Alas, the great majority of the people were oblivious to their danger and were content to go on with children as their oppressors and women ruling over them, as we have seen; a weak and powerless leadership that could not lift them above the existing confusion.

The Psalmist prayed, "Enter not into judgment with Thy servant: for in Thy sight shall no man living be justified" (Ps. 143:2). There is none now to plead for the guilty leaders in Judah; rather, the Lord Himself stands up to plead against them and to enter into judgment with them. Because of the way they have misled His people and abused their confidence, He will hold them accountable for all their waywardness.

Moreover the Lord saith, Because the daughters of Zion are haughty, and walk with stretched forth necks and wanton eyes, walking and mincing as they go, and making a tinkling with their feet: therefore the Lord will smite with a scab the crown of the head of the daughters of Zion, and the Lord will discover their secret parts. In that day the Lord will take away the bravery of their tinkling ornaments about their feet, and their cauls, and their round tires like the moon, the chains, and the bracelets, and the mufflers, the bonnets, and the ornaments of the legs, and the headbands, and the tablets, and the earrings, the rings, and nose jewels, the changeable suits of apparel, and the mantles, and the wimples, and the crisping pins, the glasses, and the fine linen, and the hoods, and the vails. And it shall come to pass, that instead of sweet smell there shall be stink; and instead of a girdle a rent; and instead of well set hair baldness; and instead of a stomacher a girding of sackcloth; and burning instead of beauty. Thy men shall fall by the sword, and thy mighty in the war. And her gates shall lament and mourn; and she being desolate shall sit upon the ground (verses 16-26).

The vain women too who have given themselves to folly come in for a stern rebuke. In their pride and empty-headedness, their one great concern has been personal adornment. Vain of their beauty, they sought to add to it by every device known to women of fashion. But God was about to smite them with sore diseases that would disfigure them and make them to be loathed by their former admirers. It may seem strange to observe that God took note of all the ornaments and apparel that they relied upon to make themselves attractive, but we need to remember that in the New Testament careful instruction is given to women that their adorning be not that which is outward, such as wearing of jewels, putting on of apparel and wearing the hair attractively, but rather that meekness and grace which is the adornment of the heart. It is well for Christian women to pay careful attention to that which is here set forth, as becoming to women professing godliness. Pride and vanity are alike hateful to God, whether manifested in men or in women. In due time such behavior must be dealt with by Him in judgment if there be no repentance.

CHAPTER FOUR

WHEN THE LORD RETURNS TO ZION

And in that day seven women shall take hold of one man, saying, We will eat our own bread, and wear our own apparel: only let us be called by thy name, to take away our reproach. In that day shall the branch of the Lord be beautiful and glorious, and the fruit of the earth shall be excellent and comely for them that are escaped of Israel. And it shall come to pass, that he that is left in Zion, and he that remaineth in Jerusalem, shall be called holy, even every one that is written among the living in Jerusalem: When the Lord shall have washed away the filth of the daughters of Zion, and shall have purged the blood of Jerusalem from the midst thereof by the spirit of judgment, and by the spirit of burning. And the Lord will create upon every dwelling place of mount Zion, and upon her assemblies, a cloud and smoke by day, and the shining of a flaming fire by night: for upon all the glory shall be a defence. And there shall be a tabernacle for a shadow in the daytime from the heat, and for a place of refuge, and for a covert from storm and from rain (verses 1-6).

THE fourth chapter, though very brief, depicts conditions which were to prevail, not only in the days following the threatened Babylonian captivity, but also in the dark days of the great tribulation; for Isaiah looked far beyond his own age to days yet to come.

As so often happens in times of prolonged warfare, the proportion of women to men would become very great, so much so, that seven women should take hold of one man and seek to claim him as an husband in order to take away their reproach. Such polygamous suggestions followed the recent world wars, as many will remember.

When times are darkened, deliverance will come through the Branch of the Lord, the promised Messiah of Israel, and the loveliest of the sons of men. Those left in Zion and remaining in Jerusalem will be the special objects of His favor and will be set apart to the Lord who will wash away their filth in His own blood and cleanse their hearts with the spirit of burning, in accordance with the promises made through many other prophets.

Then Mount Zion and Jerusalem will become a center of blessing to the whole earth, and the glory of the Lord that once was seen over the sanctuary of old will be as a cloudy pillar over all the homes of the redeemed city, both as a glory and a defence. "And there shall be a tabernacle for a shadow in the daytime from the heat, and for a place of refuge, and for a covert from storm and from rain" (verse 6). Thus, like Israel in the wilderness so long ago, will the restored nation be under Jehovah's gracious care when He has cleansed them from their iniquities and turned their hearts back to Himself.

CHAPTER FIVE

THE PARABLE OF THE VINEYARD

Now will I sing to my wellbeloved a song of my beloved touching his vineyard. My wellbeloved hath a vineyard in a very fruitful hill; and he fenced it, and gathered out the stones thereof, and planted it with the choicest vine, and built a tower in the midst of it, and also made a winepress therein: and he looked that it should bring forth grapes, and it brought forth wild grapes. And now, O inhabitants of Jerusalem, and men of Judah, judge, I pray you, betwixt me and my vineyard. What could have been done more to my vineyard, that I have not done in it? wherefore, when I looked that it should bring forth grapes, brought it forth wild grapes? And now go to; I will tell you what I will do to my vineyard: I will take away the hedge thereof, and it shall be eaten up; and break down the wall thereof, and it shall be trodden down: and I will lay it waste: it shall not be pruned, nor digged; but there shall come up briers and thorns: I will also command the clouds that they rain no rain upon it. For the vineyard of the Lord of hosts is the house of Israel, and the men of Judah his pleasant plant: and he looked for judgment, but behold oppression; for righteousness, but behold a cry (verses 1-7).

CHAPTER five completes the prophet's address. In the parable of the vineyard, God rehearses His ways with Israel and emphasizes their lack of response to His love and patience. This "Song of the Vineyard" links intimately with our Lord's parable concerning the same subject, which He put before the scribes and Pharisees shortly before His arrest and crucifixion.

We might well speak of verses 1-7 of this chapter as

the vineyard-poem as we hear in what graphic and touching terms the prophet sings a song of the vineyard. God Himself, of course, is the real Speaker, and when He says, "My wellbeloved hath a vineyard in a very fruitful hill," we cannot but realize that He has His own blessed Son before Him, for He is the Messiah of Israel as well as the Saviour of the world.

This vineyard represents Israel as God viewed them at the beginning of their Palestinian history. Having brought them out of Egypt, He planted them in the land of promise, and there cared for and protected them from the ravages of their enemies.

He fenced His vineyard about, gathered out the stones and planted it with the choicest vine. He built a tower in the midst of it, we are told, and also made a winepress therein, only to find that there was no fruit suitable to His holy desires. "He looked that it should bring forth grapes, and it brought forth wild grapes." That is, instead of bearing fruit for God, Israel brought forth that which only grieved His heart and dishonored His holy Name.

And so, addressing Himself directly to the inhabitants of Jerusalem and the men of Judah, He asks, "Judge, I pray you, betwixt Me and My vineyard. What could have been done more to My vineyard, that I have not done in it? Wherefore, when I looked that it should bring forth grapes, brought it forth wild grapes?" After all the care He had lavished upon Israel, His loving provision for their needs, His gracious forgiveness extended to them over and over again when they failed, how could it be possible that there would be no suitable fruit for Him? Why should they produce only that which was worthless and useless? Alas, it was but the manifestation of a heart that had departed from the living God.

And so, after giving them one opportunity after another to repent and judge themselves in His sight, He finally decided to give them up, saying, "I will tell you what I will do to My vineyard: I will take away the hedge thereof, and it shall be eaten up; and break down the wall thereof, and it shall be trodden down: and I will lay it waste: it shall not be pruned, nor digged; but there shall come up briers and thorns: I will also command the clouds that they rain no rain upon it."

That we are not mistaken in the application made of the parable is clear from verse 7, where we are told definitely, "The vineyard of the Lord of hosts is the house of Israel, and the men of Judah His pleasant plant: and He looked for judgment, but behold oppression; for righteousness, but behold a cry." This is confirmed in Psalms 80, 81; and also in Hosea 10:1.

Woe unto them that join house to house, that lay field to field, till there be no place, that they may be placed alone in the midst of the earth! In mine ears said the Lord of hosts, Of a truth many houses shall be desolate, even great and fair, without inhabitant. Yea, ten acres of vineyard shall yield one bath, and the seed of an homer shall yield an ephah. Woe unto them that rise up early in the morning, that they may follow strong drink; that continue until night, till wine inflame them! And the harp, and the viol, the tabret, and pipe, and wine, are in their feasts: but they regard not the work of the Lord, neither consider the operation of his hands. Therefore my people are gone into captivity, because they have no knowledge: and their honourable men are famished, and their multitude dried up with thirst. Therefore hell hath enlarged herself, and opened her mouth without measure: and their glory, and their multitude, and their pomp, and he that rejoiceth, shall descend into it. And the mean man shall be brought down, and the mighty man shall be humbled, and the eyes of the lofty shall be humbled: but the Lord of hosts shall be exalted in judgment, and God that is holy shall be sanctified in righteousness. Then shall the lambs feed after their manner, and the waste places of the fat ones shall strangers eat. Woe unto them that draw iniquity with cords of vanity, and sin as it were with a cart rope: that say, Let him make speed, and hasten his work, that we may see it: and let the counsel of the Holy One of Israel draw nigh and come, that we may know it! Woe unto them that call evil good, and good evil; that put darkness for light, and light for darkness; that put bitter for sweet, and sweet for bitter! Woe unto them that are wise in their own eyes, and prudent in their own sight! Woe unto them that are mighty to drink wine, and men of strength to mingle strong drink: Which justify the wicked for reward, and take away the righteousness of the righteous for him! Therefore as the fire devoureth the stubble, and the flame consumeth the chaff, so their root shall be as rottenness, and their blossom shall go up as dust: because they have cast away the law of the Lord of hosts, and despised the word of the Holy One of Israel. Therefore is the anger of the Lord kindled against his people, and he hath stretched forth his hand against them, and hath smitten them: and the hills did tremble, and their carcases were torn in the midst of the streets. For all this his anger is not turned away, but his hand is stretched out still (verses 8-25).

Here we have the six woes to which reference has been made already. In verse 8 He pronounces a woe upon them "that join house to house, that lay field to field, till there be no place, that they may be placed alone in the midst of the earth." In other words, the judgment is pronounced on those who selfishly seek to accumulate houses and lands for themselves, showing no consideration for the poor and the needy. Such shall eventually be desolate and their holdings destroyed; their fields will fail to bear, and their hope of gain will be disappointed.

Then in verse 11 He pronounces a woe upon those who give themselves over to voluptuousness and sensual pleasure, who "rise up early in the morning, that they may follow strong drink; that continue until night, till wine inflame them!" They seek to delight themselves with beautiful music and other worldly pleasures, but regard not the work of the Lord, neither consider the operation of His hands. Because of this they shall go into captivity. They have acted as those who are without knowledge; and the leaders among them, who should have been honorable men, have proven themselves but fools. So "hell hath enlarged herself." That is, the unseen world has opened her mouth without measure, and they and all they have delighted in, go down into the pit. The mean man shall be brought down, and the mighty man shall be humbled and the eyes of the lofty shall be humbled also. But the Lord of hosts whom they have despised, shall be exalted in judgment, and God, the infinitely Holy One, shall be sanctified in righteousness when He visits with judgment those who have grievously offended.

The third woe, in verse 18, is upon those who "draw iniquity with cords of vanity, and sin as it were with a cart rope." They openly defy the God of Israel and brazenly insist on taking their own way in opposition to His Holy Word, ridiculing the message of His prophet and spurning His commands.

The fourth woe, verse 20, is upon those who fail to distinguish between good and evil, righteousness and unrighteousness. They put darkness for light and light for darkness; they put bitter for sweet and sweet for bitter. In other words, they make no distinction between that which honors God and that which dishonors Him. Like Laodicea in a later day, they are neither cold nor hot but utterly indifferent to divine truth.

The fifth woe, verse 21, is upon those who are wise in their own eyes and prudent in their own sight; and "pride goeth before destruction, and an haughty spirit before a fall." Pride, so natural to the human heart, is hateful to God, and if persisted in it will eventually bring destruction.

The sixth woe is for those who, inflamed by wine, lose all sense of righteousness in judgment, that "justify the wicked for reward, and take away the righteousness of the righteous from him!" Therefore the Lord declares that, "As the fire devoureth the stubble, and the flame consumeth the chaff, so their root shall be as rottenness, and their blossom shall go up as dust: because they have cast away the law of the Lord of hosts, and despised the Word of the Holy One of Israel." Because of these things the anger of Jehovah was kindled against His people, and His hand stretched out against them. He had smitten them so that the very hills would tremble. But they, themselves, persisted in their iniquity, their hearts unmoved by all His dealings with them; therefore, greater judgments are yet to come, as we shall see as we go on in the study of this book.

And he will lift up an ensign to the nations from far, and will hiss unto them from the end of the earth: and, behold, they shall come with speed swiftly: none shall be weary nor stumble among them; none shall slumber nor sleep; neither shall the girdle of their loins be loosed, nor the latchet of their shoes be broken: Whose arrows are sharp, and all their bows bent, their horses' hoofs shall be counted like flint, and their wheels like a whirlwind: Their roaring shall be like a lion, they shall roar like young lions: yea, they shall roar, and lay hold of the prey, and shall carry it away safe, and none shall deliver it. And in that day they shall roar against them like the roaring of the sea: and if one look unto the land, behold darkness and sorrow, and the light is darkened in the heavens thereof (verses 26-30).

The Lord Himself had summoned the nations of the East to overrun the land of Israel. Already the kingdom of the North had felt the power of Assyria and had been carried away. Soon the kingdom of the South will be destroyed by the might of Babylon.

No effort on Judah's part would enable them to turn back the power of the enemy when the appointed hour had come for the destruction so long predicted. Like a roaring lioness with a litter of young lions, would the eastern nations rush upon their prey and carry it away triumphantly; and in that hour of distress, they should cry to the Lord in vain, for darkness and sorrow were destined to be their portion and the light should be darkened in the heavens above them.

CHAPTER SIX

THE PROPHET'S CLEANSING AND COMMISSION

In the year that king Uzziah died I saw also the Lord sitting upon a throne, high and lifted up, and his train filled the temple. Above it stood the seraphims: each one had six wings; with twain he covered his face, and with twain he covered his feet, and with twain he did fly. And one cried unto another, and said, Holy, holy, holy, is the Lord of hosts: the whole earth is full of his glory. And the posts of the door moved at the voice of him that cried, and the house was filled with smoke. Then said I, Woe is me! for I am undone; because I am a man of unclean lips, and I dwell in the midst of a people of unclean lips: for mine eyes have seen the King, the Lord of hosts. Then flew one of the seraphims unto me, having a live coal in his hand, which he had taken with the tongs from off the altar: and he laid it upon my mouth, and said, Lo, this hath touched thy lips; and thine iniquity is taken away, and thy sin purged (verses 1-7).

ISAIAH here goes back over the years and tells us how he was brought into the knowledge of cleansing from sin, and how he heard and responded to the call of God to be His messenger to a rebellious and gainsaying people.

It is always of interest when one is privileged to get a personal and intimate account of the revelation of God to a human soul. In this chapter Isaiah lets us into the secret of his wonderful power and equipment for service. He takes us into the sanctuary, shows us how the Lord was revealed to him, and lets us know the circumstances of his call to the prophetic office. This was the real starting point of his effective ministry. We know from chapter 1:1, that he began to witness for God in the days of King Uzziah.

As the experience recorded here took place in the year King Uzziah died, it may be that it was subsequent to the prophetic testimony which we have been considering already but, as suggested before, there seems to be no proof of this, for it may have been during the last year of Uzziah that Isaiah began his ministry, and that he is here telling us of his original call to the prophetic office. It is true that many servants of God have preached to others before having a clear, definite experience with the Lord for themselves. John Wesley is a case in point. He tells us in his *Journal*, that while in Georgia he learned that he who came to America to convert the Indians, had never been converted himself. It is true that in later years he doubted whether he had diagnosed his own case aright, but he certainly preached to others for several years before he had that heart-warming experience in London when he knew definitely that he was born of God. And one could tell of many others, even D. L. Moody among them, who began to preach before having the clear understanding of salvation by grace and the enduement of the Holy Spirit. So, while it seems unlikely, there is still the possibility that the stirring message of chapters one to five was proclaimed before the revelation of the divine holiness and of Isaiah's own corrupt heart had come to him as narrated here. But it seems more probable that after he had recorded his burden of the preceding chapters, he then undertook to tell the story of his own meeting with God and his divine commission as God's messenger to the people of his day. This was not, as some would have it, Isaiah's "second blessing." It was rather a part of God's dealings with him in order that he might be prepared to give out the Word to others because of knowing for himself the reality of having to do with God.

He tells us, "In the year that king Uzziah died I saw also the Lord sitting upon a throne, high and lifted up, and His train filled the temple." That word "also" is significant. Was it a sight of God that brought the leprosy out on Uzziah's forehead? The same God revealed Himself to Isaiah while he was attending a service in the Temple at Jerusalem; however, it was not in judgment but in grace that He showed Himself as the infinitely Holy One. Others may have thronged the temple courts at this time, but none but Isaiah saw the glorious vision. In an ecstatic state he became blind to all about him, but his awakened intelligence was fully occupied with the glory that had been revealed to him.

Above the throne he beheld the seraphim, an order of angels apparently, each with six wings. We may drop the *s* from the word "seraphims" as the *im* is the Hebrew plural. These glorious beings seem to be messengers of grace, as distinguished from the cherubim, who speak rather of righteousness and judgment.

They cried one to another, "Holy, holy, holy, is the Lord of hosts: the whole earth is full of His glory." It is an ascription of praise and adoration to the Triune God, whose glory is manifested in all creation.

As the song of worship sounded forth, the very posts of the doors were moved and the house was filled with the fragrant smoke of the burning incense. Strange that inanimate pillars should thus be moved while the hearts of men remained obdurate and motionless! But one man there was who did respond and that in a very definite way.

Isaiah cried, "Woe is me! for I am undone: because I am a man of unclean lips, and I dwell in the midst of a people of unclean lips." The effect of beholding God is to make one realize his own unworthiness and the corruption of his own heart. Isaiah saw himself in the light of Jehovah's infinite holiness. It is ever thus when man is brought consciously into the presence of God. When Job saw the Lord, he cried, "I repent in dust and ashes." When Simon recognized in Jesus the Creator of the fish of the sea, he fell at His feet and cried, "Depart from me, for I am a sinful man, O Lord." And so with our prophet. When he saw himself in the light of the holiness of God, he at once acknowledged his own sinfulness; and moreover, he recognized the fact that he was surrounded by men, who, like himself, were of unclean lips: for "out of the abundance of the heart the mouth speaketh."

In response to Isaiah's confession, we read, "Then flew one of the seraphim unto me, having a live coal in his hand." He had taken the live coal with the tongs from off the altar. It was the altar of sacrifice, which prefigured the Cross. That live coal told of the fire of judgment having burned itself out upon the offering. The representative of the grace of God to needy men flew swiftly to tell of His saving favor, based upon the atoning sacrifice. With two of their wings the seraphim hid their faces as they worshiped the infinitely Holy One. With two they covered their beautiful feet, and with two they hastened forth in loving service. The cherubim are said to have four wings (Ezek. 1:6). The "living creatures" of Ezekiel 1 are identified as the "cherubim" in chapter ten. May not the six wings of the seraphim tell us how mercy rejoiceth against judgment (Jas. 2:13)?

As the coal touched his lips, Isaiah heard the comforting words, "Thine iniquity is taken away, and thy sin purged." The divinely-sent messenger proclaimed the good news of redemption and purification from sin through Him whose one offering was pictured in the sacrifice of the altar.

We would re-emphasize the fact that it was from the altar of burnt offering the coal was taken, not from the golden altar, where only incense was burned. That live coal was witness of the fire, ever burning, which was never to go out (Lev. 6:13). It constantly foreshadowed the work of the Cross. Through that sacrifice alone could iniquity be purged and sin be put away (Heb. 9:13, 14).

Also I heard the voice of the Lord, saying, Whom shall I send, and who will go for us? Then said I, Here am I; send me. And he said, Go, and tell this people, Hear ye indeed, but understand not; and see ye indeed, but perceive not. Make the heart of this people fat, and make their ears heavy, and shut their eyes; lest they see with their eyes, and hear with their ears, and understand with their heart, and convert, and be healed. Then said I, Lord, how long? And he answered, Until the cities be wasted without inhabitant, and the houses without man, and the land be utterly desolate, and the Lord have removed men far away, and there be a great forsaking in the midst of the land. But yet in it shall be a tenth, and it shall return, and shall be eaten: as a teil tree, and as an oak, whose substance is in them, when they cast their leaves: so the holy seed shall be the substance thereof (verses 8-13).

Following the assurance of forgiveness and cleansing came the call for service. The voice of the Lord was heard crying, "Whom shall I send, and who will go for

Us?" In response to this Isaiah exclaimed, "Here am I; send me."

Who Will Go for Us? It has pleased God to commit the declaration of His truth to men rather than to angels. He is still calling for consecrated men and women to carry the offer of salvation and the warning of judgment to a lost world. Such must know for themselves the cleansing power of the blood of Christ if they would give effective testimony to those still in their sins.

The prophet was commissioned to "Go, and tell this people, Hear ye indeed, but understand not; and see ye indeed, but perceive not. Make the heart of this people fat, and make their ears heavy, and shut their eyes; lest they see with their eyes, and hear with their ears, and understand with their heart, and convert, and be healed." Even though the Word seemed to have no other effect than to harden them in their sins and rebellion, Isaiah was to proclaim the message faithfully.

The servant of God is responsible to the Lord Himself. Having received his commission, he is to go forth in the name of the One who sends him, declaring the message committed to him. The results must be left with God. Whether men hear or whether they forbear (Ezek. 2:3-5), he who proclaims the Word faithfully has delivered his soul. The Apostle Paul entered into this when he spoke of being a sweet savor of Christ unto God both in them that are saved and in them that perish (2 Cor. 2:15). God is honored when His truth is preached, no matter what attitude the hearers take toward it, and that Word will not return void, but will accomplish the divine purpose (Isa. 55:11).

Faced with the solemn responsibility of proclaiming so unpopular a message, Isaiah cried, "Lord, how long?" It takes special faith and obedience to continue to preach to an unheeding people who are only hardened by the Word instead of being softened by it. The Lord's answer was that the message must be proclaimed until there were none left to hear.

CHAPTER SEVEN

THE VIRGIN'S SON

And it came to pass in the days of Ahaz the son of Jotham, the son of Uzziah, king of Judah, that Rezin the king of Syria, and Pekah the son of Remaliah, king of Israel, went up toward Jerusalem to war against it, but could not prevail against it. And it was told the house of David, saying, Syria is confederate with Ephraim. And his heart was moved, and the heart of his people, as the trees of the wood are moved with the wind. Then said the Lord unto Isaiah, Go forth now to meet Ahaz, thou, and Shearjashub thy son, at the end of the conduit of the upper pool in the highway of the fuller's field; and say unto him, Take heed, and be quiet; fear not, neither be fainthearted for the two tails of these smoking firebrands, for the fierce anger of Rezin with Syria, and of the son of Remaliah. Because Syria, Ephraim, and the son of Remaliah, have taken evil counsel against thee, saying, Let us go up against Judah, and vex it, and let us make a breach therein for us, and set a king in the midst of it, even the son of Tabeal: thus saith the Lord God, It shall not stand, neither shall it come to pass. For the head of Syria is Damascus, and the head of Damascus is Rezin; and within threescore and five years shall Ephraim be broken, that it be not a people. And the head of Ephraim is Samaria, and the head of Samaria is Remaliah's son. If ye will not believe, surely ye shall not be established (verses 1-9).

WE ARE now to consider a portion which has been the subject of endless controversy throughout the Christian centuries, but which the Holy Spirit makes clear to those who are ready to receive His testimony, because of the way in which this scripture is used in connection with the birth of our blessed Lord. During the reign of King Ahaz, the

grandson of Uzziah, war broke out between Judah and
Israel. Pekah, the son of Remaliah, who was king of
Israel, entered into a confederacy with Rezin, king of
Syria; and these together went up to besiege Jerusa-
lem. Though the siege lasted for some time, they were
unable to subjugate the holy city.

When Ahaz learned of the confederacy against him,
his heart and the heart of his people were moved with
fear, for Ahaz had walked in the ways of the kings of
Israel rather than in those of the house of David. He
had, therefore, little or no reason to expect divine help
against his foes. But God's heart was toward the people
of Judah, for the time had not yet come to deliver them
up to their enemies.

There had been quite a measure of return to the Lord
during the days of Jotham, the father of Ahaz, and God
heard the prayers of His almost distracted people and
sent the prophet Isaiah to meet Ahaz and give him a
word of encouragement. Isaiah took with him his son
Shear-jashub, whose name meant, "The remnant shall
return." All of Isaiah's children seemed to have been
named prophetically in order that they might be signs
to the people of Judah. The message that came to Ahaz
was one of trust and comfort. He was exhorted to take
heed and be quiet, to fear not nor be fainthearted, because of the two kings who had linked their forces
against him. In the sight of God they were but as two
smoking firebrands soon to be extinguished. Their own
wickedness and ungodliness was such that the Lord
was about to deal with them in judgment; and, therefore, would not permit them to overcome Judah or
subdue Jerusalem. It was in vain that they took counsel
together against Ahaz and his people, and sought to
make a breach in the defenses of Jerusalem.

The Lord God declared that their counsel should not stand nor come to pass, but that within a definite period of sixty-five years Ephraim's power would be utterly broken; they would be no longer a people, and Syria would be unable to help them against the king of Assyria, who, in God's own time, was to carry the northern kingdom into captivity.

Moreover the Lord spake again unto Ahaz, saying, Ask thee a sign of the Lord thy God; ask it either in the depth, or in the height above. But Ahaz said, I will not ask, neither will I tempt the Lord. And he said, Hear ye now, O house of David; Is it a small thing for you to weary men, but will ye weary my God also? Therefore the Lord himself shall give you a sign; Behold, a virgin shall conceive, and bear a son, and shall call his name Immanuel. Butter and honey shall he eat, that he may know to refuse the evil, and choose the good. For before the child shall know to refuse the evil, and choose the good, the land that thou abhorrest shall be forsaken of both her kings (verses 10-16).

It was at this time that God gave, through Isaiah, a confirmation of the gospel message in the Garden of Eden. He had declared that the Seed of the woman should bruise the serpent's head. The "Seed of the woman" is a most significant expression and refers to the Virgin Birth of the Messiah. All others born into the world are definitely of the seed of the man, but the great Deliverer was to come only through the woman.

Isaiah told Ahaz to ask for a sign from the Lord in order to confirm the Word the prophet had spoken. Ahaz refused to do this, and his words sound pious enough, "I will not ask, neither will I tempt the Lord." Actually, these were the words that came from an unbelieving heart; he was afraid to ask for a sign lest it should not come to pass.

Isaiah then declared that God Himself should give a

sign and of such a character that men would believe it
impossible to come to pass. "Hear ye now, O house of
David; Is it a small thing for you to weary men, but
will ye weary my God also?" The pretended humility
of Ahaz was hateful to God. He who is all-powerful
might have given any sign that had been asked. Therefore, Isaiah went on to say, "The Lord Himself shall
give you a sign: Behold, a virgin shall conceive, and
bear a son, and shall call his name Immanuel"—
Immanuel, as we know, being interpreted, *God with us.*
The virgin's Son was to be God manifested in the flesh.
It is only unbelief that would try to nullify the force
of this passage by reading in place of "virgin" a
"young woman," and attempting to make that young
woman to be the wife of the prophet, and the son born
to be his son through her. It is perfectly true that the
word rendered *virgin* might also be rendered *maiden*,
but every maiden is presumably a virgin—if not, something is radically wrong—so that the prophecy here
clearly and definitely declared that an unmarried
virgin should become a mother and the child should be
named *God with us.* This is not to say, as Rome does,
that the virgin Mary is herself the mother of God. She
became the mother of the humanity of our Lord Jesus
Christ, but He who was thus born of her was God
manifest in the flesh.

However, this sign was not to be fulfilled during the
days of Ahaz nor yet for some time afterward, for the
prophet immediately added, "Butter and honey shall he
eat, that he may know to refuse the evil, and choose the
good. For before the child shall know to refuse the evil,
and choose the good, the land that thou abhorrest shall
be forsaken of both her kings." Thus, before this child
should come on the scene and grow up to years of ma-

turity, not only the king of Israel but also the king of Judah would have ceased to reign, and the land would be left without a son of David sitting on the throne of Judah, or any representative sitting on the throne of Israel.

The expression "butter and honey shall he eat" is very striking, for it indicates the true humanity of the Child to be born of the virgin. In chapter nine we read of Him again and fuller details are given. While He was to be supernaturally conceived, He would have a real, physical body which would be nourished by proper food as in the case of others. Butter (curds) is the quintessence of animal food, and honey the quintessence of vegetable food. With such as these, therefore, the holy Child was to be nourished that He might grow from infancy to manhood in a normal way. When we turn to the New Testament records we do not read of some remarkably precocious child whose early activities were different from those of other little ones. He increased in wisdom and stature and in favor with God and man. Feeding upon the food provided, He grew from childhood to youth and from youth to manhood.

In the so-called Apocryphal Gospels many curious and weird legends are connected with the boy Jesus. From the very first He is pictured as acting in a supernatural way, even at His very birth taking three steps forward to the amazement of those attending upon His mother, and when playing with other boys He would work strange miracles that amazed them, though, on the other hand, if they failed to appreciate Him He is said to have visited judgment upon them. But this is not the Christ of God, but rather a creature of man's unholy imagination. As babe, growing child,

youth, and man, our Lord's humanity was exactly like
that of others, apart from sin. He was made in all
things like unto His brethren that He might properly
represent us before God as our Kinsman-Redeemer.

The Lord shall bring upon thee, and upon thy people, and
upon thy father's house, days that have not come, from the day
that Ephraim departed from Judah; even the king of Assyria. And
it shall come to pass in that day, that the Lord shall hiss for the
fly that is in the uttermost part of the rivers of Egypt, and for
the bee that is in the land of Assyria. And they shall come, and
shall rest all of them in the desolate valleys, and in the holes of
the rocks, and upon all thorns, and upon all bushes. In the same
day shall the Lord shave with a razor that is hired, namely, by
them beyond the river, by the king of Assyria, the head, and the
hair of the feet: and it shall also consume the beard. And it shall
come to pass in that day, that a man shall nourish a young cow,
and two sheep; and it shall come to pass, for the abundance of milk
that they shall give he shall eat butter: for butter and honey shall
every one eat that is left in the land. And it shall come to pass in
that day, that every place shall be, where there were a thousand
vines at a thousand silverlings, it shall even be for briers and thorns.
With arrows and with bows shall men come thither; because all the
land shall become briers and thorns. And on all hills that shall be
digged with the mattock, there shall not come thither the fear of
briers and thorns; but it shall be for the sending forth of oxen, and
for the treading of lesser cattle (verses 17-25).

Upon Ahaz and his people and his father's house,
God would bring distress and trouble through the coming into the land of the king of Assyria. In fact, Judah
was to be the bone of contention between two great
powers; Assyria on the east, and Egypt on the west.
As they contemplated the increasing might of Assyria
they turned desperately toward Egypt, hoping to find
in that people an ally who would help to protect them
from the eastern power; but they learned in the end
that Egypt was a broken reed. Instead of becoming

helpful she would herself turn against them. As a result of the conflict that would ensue, the day was not far distant when famines and pestilence would sweep through the land. The great cities of Judah would fall; whereas, out of the country places those who remained would exist upon the produce of the soil, and even this in limited quantity, for thorns and briers would soon cover large districts where once had been flourishing industries, plantations, and vineyards. Nevertheless, God would still intervene to protect the poor of the flock and those who waited upon Him, so that in response to their toil the land would once more bear fruit instead of the thorns and briers, and oxen and sheep would again be raised in sufficient quantities to meet the needs of the people.

To some it might seem strange that the prophecy of the virgin's Son, who was also, as we know elsewhere from Scripture, to come into the world as the Son of David, would be given in such an unexpected place, but we need to remember that God ever had Christ before Him and every king of Judah was the anointed of the Lord at that time. Our word "Messiah" simply means "the Anointed," and therefore each of these kings was set by God to prefigure His own blessed Son, who was to come into the world in the fullness of time and be presented to the chosen nation as the anointed One in whom alone deliverance was to be found. Many of these kings failed utterly to picture the Lord Himself. Their behavior shows that they were far removed in spirit from God's thoughts for them. Ahaz had shown himself forgetful of the law of the Lord, and so in the hour of his distress he would not have the courage to count upon God or to expect help from Him. How natural then that under the circumstances God should speak of another king, a Son of David, who was to be born into the world supernaturally and in His own time would show who was the blessed and only Potentate, King of kings and Lord of lords.

CHAPTER EIGHT

MAHER-SHALAL-HASH-BAZ

THIS chapter is remarkable because of the long and, to our ears, outlandish name of another of the prophet's sons. We have met Shear-jashub already and noted his name's significance, "the remnant shall return." Now we are introduced to Maher-shalal-hash-baz, the interpretation of which is, "In making speed to the spoil he hasteneth the prey." The name was given him for a sign but must have caused him no end of annoyance when he mingled with other lads.

> Moreover the Lord said unto me, Take thee a great roll, and write in it with a man's pen concerning Maher-shalal-hash-baz. And I took unto me faithful witnesses to record, Uriah the priest, and Zechariah the son of Jeberechiah. And I went unto the prophetess; and she conceived, and bare a son. Then said the Lord to me, Call his name Maher-shalal-hash-baz. For before the child shall have knowledge to cry, My father, and my mother, the riches of Damascus and the spoil of Samaria shall be taken away before the king of Assyria (verses 1-4).

Some critics have insisted that this was the maiden's son referred to in the previous chapter, and that the young woman was the prophet's wife. But there is no possible identification between Immanuel and Maher-shalal-hash-baz. The one denotes, "God dwelling among men in the Person of His Son" (and this is confirmed in chapter nine), but this young lad with the long name was so called in view of something of an altogether different character. For this purpose the name was given and recorded in the temple records before the child was born. The significance of the name was this: Damascus, the Syrian capital, which had been at enmity with Judah and confederate with Israel was about to be spoiled by the Assyrians, and at the same time Israel was to fall a prey to this great and mighty power. All this would transpire before the child was well grown.

The Lord spake also unto me again, saying, Forasmuch as this people refuseth the waters of Shiloah that go softly, and rejoice in Rezin and Remaliah's son; Now therefore, behold, the Lord bringeth up upon them the waters of the river, strong and many, even the king of Assyria, and all his glory: and he shall come up over all his channels, and go over all his banks: And he shall pass through Judah; he shall overflow and go over, he shall reach even to the neck; and the stretching out of his wings shall fill the breadth of thy land, O Immanuel (verses 5-8).

The allied peoples of Syria and Samaria (or Israel, the northern kingdom) had refused to recognize the value of association with Judah, and so had spurned the waters of Shiloah (that is "peace"), and had joined forces under Rezin the Syrian king, and Pekah the son of Remaliah, the upstart king of Israel, in order to destroy Judah. Therefore the Lord was bringing against them the armies of the king of Assyria which would flow over their lands like a great river and would even reach into Judah also, as we have seen already, thus overspreading Immanuel's land: that is, the land promised by covenant to Abraham and his seed, which seed, as we know, is Christ.

We, as Christians, delight to use the term "Immanuel's land" in a spiritual sense, and we are justified in doing this, but actually, "Thy land, O Immanuel," refers to the land of Palestine, the land Jehovah had claimed as His own when He declared, "The land shall not be sold for ever: for the land is Mine."

To ward off this danger, Ahaz sought an alliance with Egypt, but no such association would avail to avert the threatened judgment. So we read,

> Associate yourselves, O ye people, and ye shall be broken in pieces; and give ear, all ye of far countries: gird yourselves, and ye shall be broken in pieces: gird yourselves, and ye shall be broken in pieces. Take counsel together, and it shall come to nought: speak the word, and it shall not stand: for God is with us. For the Lord spake thus to me with a strong hand, and instructed me that I should not walk in the way of this people, saying, Say ye not, A confederacy, to all them to whom this people shall say, A confederacy; neither fear ye their fear, nor be afraid. Sanctify the Lord of hosts himself; and let him be your fear, and let him be your dread. And he shall be for a sanctuary; but for a stone of stumbling and for a rock of offence to both the houses of Israel, for a gin and for a snare to the inhabitants of Jerusalem. And many among them shall stumble, and fall, and be broken, and be snared, and be taken (verses 9-15).

Instinctively in times of stress and danger men think of confederacies and associations of some kind as the best means of preserving the traditions and conditions which they hold dear. It was so in Judah. It is so in Christendom today. So we have various associations and federations of individuals and of churches which it is hoped will prove to be bulwarks against the on-rushing tide of evil. But again and again it has been demonstrated that all such confederacies tend to deteriorate as time goes by, and afterward the children of those who formed these associations revert to the evils against which their fathers protested.

The only real recourse in a day of evil is to cleave to

the Lord Himself with purpose of heart. No matter
what failure may come in, He remains unchanged and
unchangeable. So the prophet exhorts, "Sanctify the
Lord of hosts Himself; and let Him be your fear, and
let Him be your dread" (verse 13).

When He is given His rightful place He will be as a
sanctuary to those who put their trust in Him, but He
will ever be a stone of stumbling and a rock of offense as He was when He appeared in human form to
both the houses of Israel, and for a trap and a snare to
the inhabitants of Jerusalem (verse 14). These words
are applied definitely to our blessed Lord in the New
Testament; when He, the long-looked-for Messiah came
in lowly grace, the nation stumbled over Him as over a
stumbling stone, and so was broken and scattered as
predicted in verse 15.

God's Word is the sure resource for His obedient
people, and so we read,

> Bind up the testimony, seal the law among my disciples. And I
> will wait upon the Lord, that hideth his face from the house of
> Jacob, and I will look for him. Behold, I and the children whom
> the Lord hath given me are for signs and for wonders in Israel
> from the Lord of hosts, which dwelleth in mount Zion. And when
> they shall say unto you, Seek unto them that have familiar spirits,
> and unto wizards that peep, and that mutter: should not a people
> seek unto their God? for the living to the dead? To the law and to
> the testimony: if they speak not according to this word, it is be-
> cause there is no light in them. And they shall pass through it,
> hardly bestead and hungry: and it shall come to pass, that when
> they shall be hungry, they shall fret themselves, and curse their
> king and their God, and look upward. And they shall look unto the
> earth: and behold trouble and darkness, dimness of anguish; and
> they shall be driven to darkness (verses 16-22).

Just as Paul, after predicting the coming apostasy in

the Ephesian church, said, "I commend you to God, and to the word of His grace" (Acts 20:32), so here Isaiah, speaking in God's behalf exclaims, "Bind up the testimony, seal the law among my disciples." To those who are willing to be taught of God, the Word becomes increasingly precious as the days grow darker.

Verse 17 is the voice of him who takes the place of dependence upon God: "I will wait upon the Lord, that hideth His face from the house of Jacob, and I will look for Him." He may seem to be indifferent to the trials His people are passing through, but actually it is not so. His face may be hidden but His heart is ever toward them.

Isaiah and his family were called to be a testimony to all Israel. "Behold," he says, "I and the children whom the Lord hath given me are for signs and for wonders in Israel from the Lord of hosts, which dwelleth in mount Zion" (verse 18). Part of this verse is quoted in Hebrews 2:13, and is applied to the Lord Jesus and to those who receive life through believing in His Name.

The remaining part of the chapter gives us a solemn warning against what is now known as Spiritualism or any form of necromancy. When urged to seek unto spirit-mediums for light and help, the answer is, Should not a people seek unto their God? Should the living seek unto the dead? All such attempts to get into contact with the spirits of the dead are forbidden in Scripture. (See Deuteronomy 18:9-12 and Leviticus 20:27.) It is a grievous offence in the eyes of God for anyone to turn from His revealed Word to those who profess to have power to summon the spirits of the departed in order to give light and help. Such are either charlatans deceiving those who go to them or else possessed by impersonating demons misleading all who follow them.

God's sure Word abides and if any speak contrary to it, it is because they are in darkness themselves and there is no morning for them. That is, when the day dawns for the eternal blessing of the redeemed, there will be outer darkness for those who spurned the light of truth only to be misled by falsehood.

Such will be exposed at last for what they really are, blind leaders of the blind, who will look in vain for help when those who obeyed the Word of God find light and blessing.

Spiritism is a satanic cult which can only disappoint those who follow the will-o'-the-wisp of its direction and shall at last be driven into the darkness.

CHAPTER NINE

THE PROMISED DELIVERER

A S WE STUDY this ninth chapter it is well to note
how definitely it links with the promise given to
Ahaz in chapter seven, for here we read once
more of the One who is the fulfillment of all God's ways
with men, the Man of His counsel who came in grace to
reveal the Father, to bring in everlasting righteousness.

Nevertheless the dimness shall not be such as was in her vexation, when at the first he lightly afflicted the land of Zebulun and
the land of Naphtali, and afterward did more grievously afflict her
by the way of the sea, beyond Jordan, in Galilee of the nations.
The people that walked in darkness have seen a great light: they
that dwell in the land of the shadow of death, upon them hath the
light shined. Thou hast multiplied the nation, and not increased
the joy: they joy before thee according to the joy in harvest, and
as men rejoice when they divide the spoil. For thou hast broken
the yoke of his burden, and the staff of his shoulder, the rod of
his oppressor, as in the day of Midian. For every battle of the warrior is with confused noise, and garments rolled in blood; but this
shall be with burning and fuel of fire (verses 1-5).

The opening verses of the chapter form a continu-
ance of what has just gone before in chapter eight.
When darkness had spread over the land of Palestine
and men were groping for the light, Christ came in
infinite grace, the Light of the World, by the way of
the sea beyond Jordan in Galilee of the Gentiles. Prophetically, Isaiah seemed to behold Him moving about

among men declaring the counsel of God and manifesting His grace toward those that walked in darkness, so that they beheld a great light dwelling in the shadow of death; upon them the light shone.

It is as though Isaiah could look down through the ages and see the Lord Jesus full of grace and truth making known the wonders of God's redeeming love to those who heard Him gladly and found Him the Light of Life. This is the passage quoted by Matthew (4:15-16), the differences in rendering arising from the fact that in the New Testament the quotation is taken from the Septuagint instead of the Hebrew.

But for the moment the prophet passes over His rejection and the long years that followed during which the people of Israel, themselves, are rejected. In verse 3 he looks on to the day when once more the nation will be recognized by God as in covenant relation with Himself. Note that it is Israel that is in question in verse 3 and not the Gentiles. It seems evident that here the authorized rendering is faulty and that the word *not* should be omitted. Really, the prophet was saying, "Thou hast multiplied the nation, and increased the joy." The consensus of opinion among most spiritually-minded scholars is in agreement with this rendering, as the passage looks forward to the future blessing of the favored nation when they shall be restored to the Lord and to their land, and will have learned to know Jesus as their Messiah—the one whom their fathers rejected but in whom all blessing is to be found.

Verses 4 and 5 contemplate the conditions that were to prevail in the world through the long centuries of the dispersion of Israel. While they had a local application to the destruction of the Assyrian army besieging Jerusalem, there will be a complete fulfillment when

Christ returns to deliver the people from all their enemies. "Every battle of the warrior is with confused noise, and garments rolled in blood." Undoubtedly, the prophet describes the sad conditions destined to be the portion of the nations until Christ comes again to bring peace. This agrees with the words of our Lord Jesus as recorded in Matthew 24:6, 7, "Ye shall hear of wars and rumours of wars: see that ye be not troubled: for all these things must come to pass, but the end is not yet. For nation shall rise against nation, and kingdom against kingdom: and there shall be famines, and pestilences, and earthquakes, in divers places." Such are the conditions that have prevailed during all the centuries since Christ was rejected. He who was once offered to the world as the Prince of Peace was rejected by both Israel and the nations, and therefore, He said ere He left this scene, "Suppose ye that I am come to give peace on earth? I tell you, Nay; but rather division."

In the next two verses we have one of the most complete prophecies concerning our Lord that is to be found in the Old Testament.

For unto us a child is born, unto us a son is given: and the government shall be upon his shoulder: and his name shall be called Wonderful, Counsellor, The mighty God, The everlasting Father, The Prince of Peace. Of the increase of his government and peace there shall be no end, upon the throne of David, and upon his kingdom, to order it, and to establish it with judgment and with justice from henceforth even for ever. The zeal of the Lord of hosts will perform this (verses 6, 7).

"Unto us a Child is born, unto us a Son is given." In these two expressions we see the humanity and the deity of our Saviour. The child born refers to His humanity. As we have already seen, He was to come into the world as the virgin's Son. He was a true Man, spirit, soul, and body, as born of Mary, but without a human father. He was also the eternal Son of the Father who had come from the glory that He had with the Father from all the past eternity, given in grace for our redemption, who linked His deity with our humanity apart from its sin, and, thus was God and Man in one blessed adorable Person.

"The government shall be upon His shoulder." He is destined to exercise supreme rule over all the universe. It has often been noticed that when the Good Shepherd finds the lost sheep He puts it upon His shoulders, but here the government of the entire world is said to rest upon His shoulder. There is surely a beautiful suggestion in this plural in Luke 15 of the security of those who have put their trust in Him. "His name shall be called Wonderful." It may be that we should link together the two words *Wonderful* and *Counsellor*, but if we separate them we may see in this first word a suggestion of the mystery of His Sonship, which no man can apprehend, as He tells us in Matthew 11:27, and as we also learn from Revelation 19:12. Under this name *Wonderful* He appeared of old to the parents of Samson (Judges 13:18, R.V.). Only the Father understands this mystery of godliness (1 Timothy 3:16). It is beyond human comprehension. Nevertheless, as we read the divinely inspired records of His lowly birth, His sinless life, His vicarious death and His glorious resurrection, we find our hearts exclaiming again and again, Is He not wonderful! He stands supreme, above all the sons of men, the blessed, adorable Son of God, His heart touched with the feeling of our infirmities; His grace manifested in a thousand ways; His loving kindness reaching down to the utterly lost and depraved. His name is Wonderful because He Himself is wonderful and also because of the work which He accomplished. He is called Counsellor because He comes to us as the Revealer of the Father's will. That is what is implied in His divine title, "The Word." It is by the Word that God makes known His mind; and the Lord Jesus, who was with the Father from the beginning—that is, when everything that ever had beginning, began—came into this scene to make God known, and so in Him the Father has spoken out all that is in His heart. His words make known to us the path of life and show us the only safe way for a pilgrim people to travel through a world of sin. As the Eternal Word He is the Revealer of the mind and heart of God, come to earth not only to show us the way to the Father, but also to empower us that we may walk in a manner well pleasing to the One who has redeemed us.

Notice that also He is called the "mighty God." Some would seek to tone this down in order to make Him less than the words imply, but He is so called in Romans 9:5 and in 1 John 5:20. Even when here on earth He was just as truly God as He was Man, and as truly Man as He was God. He could not have made atonement for sin otherwise. He had to be who He was in order to do what He did.

"The everlasting Father." A better rendering would be the "Father of Eternity," or as some have suggested, "The Father of the Coming Age." The Son is not to be confounded with the Father, though He and the Father are one (John 10:30). But He is the One in whom all the ages meet (Heb. 1:2, *margin*), therefore, He is rightfully designated, "The Father of the Ages," or "The Father of Eternity."

"The Prince of Peace." As such He was presented to the world and heralded by angels (Luke 2:14) ; but because of His rejection there can be no lasting peace for Israel or the nations until He comes again. Then He will be manifested as the One who will speak peace to all peoples (Isaiah 32:1-18). Meantime, having made peace by the blood of His Cross, all who put their trust in Him have peace with God; and as we learn to commit all that would naturally trouble or distress to God in prayer, peace fills our hearts and controls our lives.

In verse 7 we are told that "Of the increase of His government and peace there shall be no end, upon the throne of David, and upon His kingdom, to order it, and to establish it with judgment and with justice from henceforth even for ever. The zeal of the Lord of hosts will perform this." God made a covenant with David that his Son should sit upon his throne and reign in righteousness forever. This has not yet been fulfilled. When the forerunner of our Lord was born, his father, Zacharias, declared that God had raised up an horn of salvation for us in the house of His servant David (Luke 1:69). These prophetic declarations make clear that David's throne was to be established forever, and that he should never be without a man to sit upon that throne. Our Lord, on His mother's side, was from the line of David, as we know, and because of her marriage to Joseph, who was heir to the throne, the throne-rights passed to Jesus. But He has never taken His seat upon the throne of David: this awaits His Second Coming. Even as He declared through His servant, John, "To him that overcometh will I grant to sit with Me in My throne, even as I also overcame, and am set down with My Father in His throne (Rev. 3 :21). He is sitting now at the right hand of the Majesty on high, on the throne of Deity. Soon He will return in glory and will take His own throne, which is really the throne of David, and will reign in righteousness over all the earth.

This seventh verse will have its fulfillment literally, for the zeal of the Lord of hosts will perform it.

The Lord sent a word into Jacob, and it hath lighted upon Israel. And all the people shall know, even Ephraim and the inhabitant of Samaria, that say in the pride and stoutness of heart, The bricks are fallen down, but we will build with hewn stones: the sycamores are cut down, but we will change them into cedars. Therefore the Lord shall set up the adversaries of Rezin against him, and join his enemies together; the Syrians before, and the Philistines behind; and they shall devour Israel with open mouth. For all this his anger is not turned away, but his hand is stretched out still (verses 8-12).

The prophet now turns back to local conditions. Those of the north kingdom were vaunting themselves. In spite of the calamities that were befalling them, they would rise above them and become once more a strong and secure people, but the Lord declared that He would raise up adversaries from among the Syrians who had been their allies, and the Philistines, the ancient enemies of His people who should devour Israel with open mouth; this because His anger was toward them only on account of their sins, and His hand stretched out in judgment. There had been no return to Him even when affliction came, as we see from the prophet's next words :

For the people turneth not unto him that smiteth them, neither do they seek the Lord of hosts. Therefore the Lord will cut off from

Israel head and tail, branch and rush, in one day. The ancient and honourable, he is the head; and the prophet that teacheth lies, he is the tail. For the leaders of this people cause them to err; and they that are led of them are destroyed. Therefore the Lord shall have no joy in their young men, neither shall have mercy on their fatherless and widows: for every one is an hypocrite and an evil-doer, and every mouth speaketh folly. For all this his anger is not turned away, but his hand is stretched out still (verses 13-17).

In the Epistle to the Hebrews we are told, "No chastening for the present seemeth to be joyous, but grievous: nevertheless afterward it yieldeth the peaceable fruit of righteousness unto them which are exercised thereby" (12:11,12). On Israel's part there had been no exercise because of the chastening hand of God upon them; rather, was there resentful pride. They dared to boast themselves even against God and against His servants who came to instruct them in His truth. The leaders of the sheep were terribly guilty in that they misled those who were subject to them, causing them to err, and so lead them to destruction because of their unrepentant condition. The Lord could not find His joy in them; nor were His compassions free to flow out toward them. Their continual waywardness called for further judgment. This is next emphasized:

For wickedness burneth as the fire: it shall devour the briers and thorns, and shall kindle in the thickets of the forest, and they shall mount up like the lifting up of smoke. Through the wrath of the Lord of hosts is the land darkened, and the people shall be as the fuel of the fire: no man shall spare his brother. And he shall snatch on the right hand, and be hungry; and he shall eat on the left hand, and they shall not be satisfied: they shall eat every man the flesh of his own arm: Manasseh, Ephraim; and Ephraim, Manasseh; and they together shall be against Judah. For all this his anger is not turned away, but his hand is stretched out still (verses 18-21).

"Wickedness burneth as the fire: it shall devour the briers and thorns." Men may think lightly of sin and pay little or no attention to the solemn warnings that God gives concerning its evil effects, but if they persist in rebellion against God they will find that wickedness does indeed burn as a fire and that those who refuse to turn to God in repentance will have to endure the judgment that they have brought upon themselves. God's holy nature will not permit Him to condone iniquity. So, "Through the wrath of the Lord of hosts is the land darkened, and the people shall be as the fuel of the fire." Famine and pestilence added to their wretchedness and misery. Yet, instead of turning to Him and confessing their sin and seeking forgiveness, they blamed one another for the troubles that had come upon them. Manasseh turned upon Ephraim and Ephraim upon Manasseh, and both together turned upon Judah. All this was the sad result of forsaking the way of the Lord.

The chapter closes with the solemn refrain repeated for the third time: "For all this His anger is not turned away, but His hand is stretched out still."

CHAPTER TEN

THE ASSYRIAN AND HIS DOOM

I T IS a well-known principle of Scripture interpretation to recognize a double application or fulfillment of many prophecies. Conditions through which Israel and the nations have passed already often depict circumstances that will yet have to be faced in the future, in the days of the great tribulation, the time of Jacob's trouble, when divine wrath will be poured out upon guilty and apostate Christendom and Judaism alike. We see this set forth in the present chapter which deals primarily with Judah and Assyria in the days of King Hezekiah, but which also looks forward to the time when the last great Assyrian, the haughty enemy of the Jews in the time of the end, will be destroyed in Immanuel's land ere he can wreak his vengeance upon the remnant nation who will be gathered back to God and to their land at that time. Only as we keep these two applications of the prophetic word before us can we understand aright what is here set forth.

In the opening verses we see Judah's sad internal condition calling for judgment on the part of the God they professed to serve but whom they had so grievously dishonored.

Woe unto them that decree unrighteous decrees, and that write grievousness which they have prescribed; To turn aside the needy from judgment, and to take away the right from the poor of my

people, that widows may be their prey, and that they may rob
the fatherless! And what will ye do in the day of visitation, and in
the desolation which shall come from far? To whom will ye flee for
help? and where will ye leave your glory? Without me they shall
bow down under the prisoners, and they shall fall under the slain.
For all this his anger is not turned away, but his hand is stretched
out still (verses 1-4).

Another solemn woe is pronounced upon those who
in their pride and selfishness issued unrighteous decrees in order to legalize their oppression of the poor
and then enriched themselves at the expense of the
fatherless. Monopolies are not a recent expression of
the selfishness of the human heart. In Judah, as in our
civilized lands today, there were those who counted it
good business to take advantage of others in adverse
circumstances and to profit by the ruin of their less
fortunate fellows. All this is hateful to Him who is a
God of judgment and by whom actions are weighed.

Any economic system that is built up on the disre-
gard of the rights of the poor will inevitably be destroyed at last. Then what of the men who have ignored
the Word of the Lord and gloried in their success while
trampling on their competitors and forcing them to
yield to their demands or go down in ruin? "What,"
asks the prophet, "will ye do in the day of visitation,
and in the desolation which shall come from far? To
whom will ye flee for help? and where will ye leave
your glory?" God has decreed that them that honor
Him, He will honor, and they who despise Him shall be
lightly esteemed. He permits men and nations to go
just so far in their own wilful way; then He deals with
them in His indignation, sweeping away their ill-gotten
wealth and causing them to bewail the luxuries which
they can no longer retain. What can men say to this?

Where can they turn to save themselves from even greater disaster?

In Judah's case the overrunning of the land by the armies of Sennacherib was the cause of much of their suffering, but was permitted by God as chastening for their sins. Without His deliverance they were helpless to defend themselves, and so would be taken as prisoners or slain by the cruel foe.

God addressed the Assyrians directly in the next section and that in a way that shows He had far more than the invasion of Sennacherib in view. The passage looks on to the final enemy in the last days.

O Assyrian, the rod of mine anger, and the staff in their hand is mine indignation. I will send him against an hypocritical nation, and against the people of my wrath will I give him a charge, to take the spoil, and to take the prey, and to tread them down like the mire of the streets. Howbeit he meaneth not so, neither doth his heart think so; but it is in his heart to destroy and cut off nations not a few. For he saith, Are not my princes altogether kings? Is not Calno as Carchemish? is not Hamath as Arpad? is not Samaria as Damascus? As my hand hath found the kingdoms of the idols, and whose graven images did excel them of Jerusalem and of Samaria; shall I not, as I have done unto Samaria and her idols, so do to Jerusalem and her idols? Wherefore it shall come to pass, that when the Lord hath performed his whole work upon mount Zion and on Jerusalem, I will punish the fruit of the stout heart of the king of Assyria, and the glory of his high looks (verses 5-12).

Notice that it is when the Lord has performed His whole work on Mount Zion and Jerusalem that the Assyrian is to be punished. This needs to be kept in mind as the passage is read and studied. When King Ahaz was threatened with utter ruin by the kings of Israel and Syria, he sent to the king of Assyria for help—only to find later that this covetous ruler aspired to complete ascendancy over all the lands to the west, including Judah. Later Sennacherib descended on the land like a mighty torrent, his army driving all before it until it was destroyed by pestilence in one night as it besieged Jerusalem in the days of Hezekiah. This terrible ruthless enemy became the type of the godless foe which, in the last days, will attempt to bring Palestine under its control, only to be destroyed by omnipotent power on the mountains of Israel.

As the rod of Jehovah's anger, Assyria was used, as other nations had been used, before and since, to chasten the people of God because of their turning away from Himself; but in the day of their repentance He would destroy the enemy that had brought disaster upon Judah.

On the part of the haughty destroyer there was no realization of the fact that he was just a rod in the hand of Jehovah, the God whose name he despised, but he was to learn at last by bitter experience that after he had been used to punish "an hypocritical nation" he, himself, was doomed to utter destruction. To him Jerusalem was but another city to be overthrown as he had destroyed so many others, but he was to learn that the God whose temple was in that city was supreme above all that men called gods and which had been powerless to deliver these pagan cities out of his hands.

Jehovah's whole work upon Mount Zion and on Jerusalem will mean the return of His people to Himself. Then in the days that He takes them up again as a nation He will deal with the Assyrian and with all who have afflicted them.

For he saith, By the strength of my hand I have done it, and by my wisdom; for I am prudent: and I have removed the bounds of the people, and have robbed their treasures, and I have put down the inhabitants like a valiant man: and my hand hath found

as a nest the riches of the people: and as one gathereth eggs that
are left, have I gathered all the earth; and there was none that
moved the wing, or opened the mouth, or peeped. Shall the axe
boast itself against him that heweth therewith? or shall the saw
magnify itself against him that shaketh it? as if the rod should
shake itself against them that lift it up, or as if the staff should
lift up itself, as if it were no wood. Therefore shall the Lord, the
Lord of hosts, send among his fat ones leanness; and under his
glory he shall kindle a burning like the burning of a fire. And the
light of Israel shall be for a fire, and his Holy One for a flame: and
it shall burn and devour his thorns and his briers in one day; and
shall consume the glory of his forest, and of his fruitful field,
both soul and body: and they shall be as when a standardbearer
fainteth. And the rest of the trees of his forest shall be few, that
a child may write them (verses 13-19).

Not understanding the use that God was making of
him, the Assyrian vaunted himself as though he accomplished everything and won all his victories because of his own wisdom and prudence. So he had
robbed and oppressed the nations, including Israel and
Judah, ruthlessly and heartlessly. To him all other
people were but as the eggs in the nests of birds that
were open to be despoiled and their armies were as
helpless as the mother birds when their nests were
rifled.

Knowing not that he was but as an axe in the hand
of him who hewed down the trees of the forest, he
boasted as though the power and might were all his
own, and so he magnified himself against the One who
designed to use him to chasten the nations because of
their wickedness and corruption.

Therefore in the reckoning day that was coming,
God would deal as sternly with him as he had dealt with
others, and as he had sown hatred and cruelty so he
should reap indignation and wretchedness. In that day
of Jehovah's triumph He will vindicate the remnant in

Israel who have put their trust in Him, and they will be as a flame to devour the nations that have sought their destruction. As in the days of Ahasuerus and Mordecai the Jews will execute judgment on those who had plotted to destroy them and root them out of the earth. The Word of God will be fulfilled concerning His promise that while He would punish His people in measure for their sins He would never break His covenant with them—a covenant made first to Abraham and confirmed to David. Although a full end will be made of many of the nations that have afflicted Israel He will not make a full end of them, as we see in the verses that follow.

And it shall come to pass in that day, that the remnant of Israel, and such as are escaped of the house of Jacob, shall no more again stay upon him that smote them; but shall stay upon the Lord, the Holy One of Israel, in truth. The remnant shall return, even the remnant of Jacob, unto the mighty God. For though thy people Israel be as the sand of the sea, yet a remnant of them shall return: the consumption decreed shall overflow with righteousness. For the Lord God of hosts shall make a consumption, even determined, in the midst of all the land (verses 20-23).

When the judgments of God are being poured out upon the earth in the dark days of the great tribulation, a remnant of the Jews will turn to the Lord in deep repentance and in living faith. These will prove the greatness of His mercy and the unfailing character of His promises. No longer relying for their help on the powers that persecuted and failed them in the hour of their need, as when Ahaz turned first to Assyria and then to Egypt in his desperate plight, they will find their resource and protection in God Himself.

The prophetic Word is clear and free of all obscurity.

Only unbelief can deny its definite application to a literal remnant of the sons of Jacob when they turn to the Lord in the time of their greatest trouble. Then He will awake and will come to their help, and He will save the nation in the remnant. We need to remember that they are not all Israel which are of Israel. The great majority "as the sand of the sea" will go into utter apostasy and be destroyed in their sins, but a remnant shall return and be acknowledged by God as His people. And so, as we learn in Romans 11, "All Israel shall be saved," for this remnant will be the true Israel in that day of Jehovah's power.

In view of this declaration of the divine purpose, God calls upon His people to trust His Word and not to fear the Assyrian, proud and powerful though he may be.

Therefore thus saith the Lord God of hosts, O my people that dwellest in Zion, be not afraid of the Assyrian: he shall smite thee with a rod, and shall lift up his staff against thee, after the manner of Egypt. For yet a very little while, and the indignation shall cease, and mine anger in their destruction. And the Lord of hosts shall stir up a scourge for him according to the slaughter of Midian at the rock of Oreb: and as his rod was upon the sea, so shall he lift it up after the manner of Egypt. And it shall come to pass in that day, that his burden shall be taken away from off thy shoulder, and his yoke from off thy neck, and the yoke shall be destroyed because of the anointing (verses 24-27).

In clear and definite terms, the prophet predicts the overthrow of the enemy who was hammering, as it were, at the gate of Jerusalem. God would prevent the carrying out of his purpose even though it might seem for a time that Judah's case was hopeless. Literally, all was fulfilled in due time so far as the prophecy had to do with the Assyrian of the past. When in the last days another mighty power comes against Palestine from the same region as that occupied by the Assyrians of old, his doom will be just as certain as was that of the enemy in the past.

The progress of the Assyrian army marching down through the land is depicted graphically in the verses that close this chapter.

He is come to Aiath, he is passed to Migron; at Michmash he hath laid up his carriages: they are gone over the passage: they have taken up their lodging at Geba; Ramah is afraid; Gibeah of Saul is fled. Lift up thy voice, O daughter of Gallim: cause it to be heard unto Laish. O poor Anathoth! Madmenah is removed; the inhabitants of Gebim gather themselves to flee. As yet shall he remain at Nob that day: he shall shake his hand against the mount of the daughter of Zion, the hill of Jerusalem. Behold, the Lord, the Lord of hosts, shall lop the bough with terror: and the high ones of stature shall be hewn down, and the haughty shall be humbled. And he shall cut down the thickets of the forest with iron, and Lebanon shall fall by a mighty one (verses 28-34).

Prophecy is history written beforehand, and here Isaiah foretold the path that the Assyrian would take as he marched through Palestine, wreaking his vengeance upon city after city; but the closing verses tell of his defeat at last when the Lord of hosts intervened in His mighty power for the deliverance of those who cried to Him in the hour of their distress. No military strategy, no weapons of war would avail to save the haughty invader when the hand of God was stretched out against him.

What a lesson for faith we have here! These things, while applying directly to Judah and her foes, have precious lessons for us today. It is *not* true that God is on the side of the greatest armies, as some have said.

He stands ready to uphold all who put their confidence in Him and who rely, not upon an arm of flesh but upon His omnipotence and unchanging love for His own.

WHEN GOD'S ANOINTED
TAKES OVER

THERE is a very close connection with that which now comes before us and that which we have seen in the last chapter. After the Assyrian is destroyed and Israel will have been delivered from all her enemies, we have the peaceful reign of Him who is the Rod out of Jesse's stem, the Branch of the Lord who is to bring all things into subjection to God and rule with the iron rod of inflexible righteousness. Of Him we read:

And there shall come forth a rod out of the stem of Jesse, and a Branch shall grow out of his roots: and the spirit of the Lord shall rest upon him, the spirit of wisdom and understanding, the spirit of counsel and might, the spirit of knowledge and of the fear of the Lord; and shall make him of quick understanding in the fear of the Lord: and he shall not judge after the sight of his eyes, neither reprove after the hearing of his ears: but with righteousness shall he judge the poor, and reprove with equity for the meek of the earth: and he shall smite the earth with the rod of his mouth, and with the breath of his lips shall he slay the wicked. And righteousness shall be the girdle of his loins, and faithfulness the girdle of his reins (verses 1-5).

Here we have the One who is presented in the Apocalypse as having the seven spirits of God: that is, the Holy Spirit in the sevenfold plenitude of His power. Coming by virgin birth through David's line He is the

Branch out of the root of Jesse, the father of David. Upon Him rests "the Spirit of Jehovah," one; the Spirit of wisdom, two; and of understanding, three; the Spirit of counsel, four; and of might, five; the Spirit of knowledge, six; and of the fear of Jehovah, seven. The fear of Jehovah is the spirit of reverence. We are told in John that the Father giveth not the Spirit by measure to His beloved Son (3:34). From the moment of His birth the Lord Jesus was under the controlling power of the Holy Spirit, for as Man on earth, He chose not to act in His own omnipotence but as the Servant of the Godhead. After His baptism in the Jordan, the Spirit was seen descending upon Him as a dove. This was the anointing of which the Apostle Peter spoke, in preparation for His gracious public ministry. Never for one moment was He out of harmony with the Spirit. It was this that made it possible for Him to grow in wisdom as He grew in stature, and in favor with God and man. Confessedly, this mystery is great: that the Eternal Wisdom should have so limited Himself as Man in all perfection that He grew in wisdom and knowledge from childhood to physical maturity as under the tutelage of the Father, who by the Spirit revealed His will to Jesus from day to day, so that He could say, "I speak not Mine own words but the words of Him that sent Me." And as to the works He wrought, He attributed them all to the Spirit of God who dwelt in Him in all His fullness.

Scripture guards carefully the truth of the perfect Manhood of our Lord, as also that of His true Deity. We see Him here as the Servant of Jehovah speaking and acting according to the Father's will. So His judgment was inerrant and His understanding perfect.

When in God's due time He takes over the reins of

the government of this world, all will be equally right
and just at last. David's prophetic words will be
fulfilled when there shall be "a righteous ruler over
men, a Ruler in the fear of God" (2 Samuel 23:3, *literal
rendering*). Earth's long centuries of selfish misrule
will have come to an end, and Israel and the nations
will enjoy the blessings of Messiah's gracious and
faithful sway; then all wickedness will be dealt with in
unsparing judgment and the meek of the earth will be
protected and enter into undisturbed blessedness.

In that day the curse will be lifted from the lower
creation and the very nature of the beasts of the earth
will be changed.

The wolf also shall dwell with the lamb, and the leopard shall
lie down with the kid; and the calf and the young lion and the
fatling together; and a little child shall lead them. And the cow
and the bear shall feed; their young ones shall lie down together:
and the lion shall eat straw like the ox. And the sucking child shall
play on the hole of the asp, and the weaned child shall put his hand
on the cockatrice' den. They shall not hurt nor destroy in all my
holy mountain: for the earth shall be full of the knowledge of the
Lord, as the waters cover the sea (verses 6-9).

Those who attempt to spiritualize all these expressions must needs take the beasts here to represent
violent and savage men whose hearts will be changed
by regeneration. But the prophet gives no hint of such
an application of his words. He very definitely speaks
of that which God will do for the animal kingdom in
the day when the curse will be lifted. There is no hint
that the prophet was speaking allegorically or that
his language is to be interpreted other than in strict
literality. It seems evident that when the Second Man,
the Last Adam, is set over this lower universe, that

ideal conditions will prevail on earth, such as characterized the world before sin came in to mar God's fair creation with its sad entail of violence and rapine on the part of the beasts of the earth and the evil effects upon the bodies of men and women, resulting in sickness and death. All this will be undone in the day when Christ shall come as the Restorer of all things spoken by the prophets, and "the earth shall be filled with the knowledge of the Lord as the waters cover the sea." While the millennium is not to be confounded with the new heavens and the new earth, it will nevertheless be a period of wonderful blessing for all who shall dwell in the world when in the administration of the fullness of the seasons, God shall head up all things in Christ.

And in that day there shall be a root of Jesse, which shall stand for an ensign of the people; to it shall the Gentiles seek: and his rest shall be glorious. And it shall come to pass in that day, that the Lord shall set his hand again the second time to recover the remnant of his people, which shall be left, from Assyria, and from Egypt, and from Pathros, and from Cush, and from Elam, and from Shinar, and from Hamath, and from the islands of the sea. And he shall set up an ensign for the nations, and shall assemble the outcasts of Israel, and gather together the dispersed of Judah from the four corners of the earth. The envy also of Ephraim shall depart, and the adversaries of Judah shall be cut off: Ephraim shall not envy Judah, and Judah shall not vex Ephraim (verses 10-13).

It is when Jesus returns in glory and as the Root of Jesse fulfills the promises made to David that all these things shall come to pass. Then Jacob's prophecy, as given in Genesis 49:10, will have its glorious fulfillment, "Unto Him shall the gathering of the peoples be" (*literal rendering*).

In that day we are told God will not only magnify

Him in the eyes of Israel, but also unto Him shall the Gentiles seek.

His own earthly people, scattered for so long among the nations, will be gathered back to their own land. Many have thought that the promises of their restoration were fulfilled long ago when a remnant returned in the days of Zerubbabel, Ezra, and Nehemiah. But here we are informed definitely, "The Lord shall set His hand again the *second time* to recover the remnant of His people"; and we learn that they will return—not simply from Babylon as before—but from all the lands where they have been dispersed throughout the long centuries of their sorrow and suffering. Israel and Judah, no longer divided, will be drawn to the Lord Himself—the Ensign to be set up in that day—and shall flow together to the land of their fathers, no longer as rival nations but as one people in glad subjection to their King and their God.

The closing verses of the chapter give further details as to the manner of their return, assisted by the nations that were once their enemies.

But they shall fly upon the shoulders of the Philistines toward the west; they shall spoil them of the east together: they shall lay their hand upon Edom and Moab; and the children of Ammon shall obey them. And the Lord shall utterly destroy the tongue of the Egyptian sea; and with his mighty wind shall he shake his hand over the river, and shall smite it in the seven streams, and make men go over dryshod. And there shall be an highway for the remnant of his people, which shall be left, from Assyria; like as it was to Israel in the day that he came up out of the land of Egypt (verses 14-16).

Certain geographical and geological changes are indicated here which no doubt will be effected at the time when the feet of our Lord shall stand again upon the Mount of Olives, and there shall be a great earthquake with far-reaching results, as foretold in Zechariah 14.

The twelfth chapter gives us the song of joy and triumph which will rise exultantly from the hearts of the redeemed of the Lord as in the days when the people sang of old on the shore of the Red Sea after all their enemies had been destroyed.

> And in that day thou shalt say, O Lord, I will praise thee: though thou wast angry with me, thine anger is turned away, and thou comfortedst me. Behold, God is my salvation; I will trust, and not be afraid: for the Lord JEHOVAH is my strength and my song; he also is become my salvation. Therefore with joy shall ye draw water out of the wells of salvation. And in that day shall ye say, Praise the Lord, call upon his name, declare his doings among the people, make mention that his name is exalted. Sing unto the Lord; for he hath done excellent things: this is known in all the earth. Cry out and shout, thou inhabitant of Zion: for great is the Holy One of Israel in the midst of thee (verses 1-6).

It is a blessed and precious experience when the heart is fixed upon the Lord Himself and when the soul realizes the gladness of reconciliation to the One against whom it had sinned, so as to be able to say, "Though Thou wast angry with me, Thine anger is turned away, and Thou comfortedst me."

It means much to know God as the One through whom deliverance has been wrought and who is Himself "salvation." This is the end of all worry and anxiety. And so we hear the remnant saying, "I will trust, and not be afraid." Faith is the antidote to fear. As we learn to look to God in confidence all anxiety disappears, for we know that He who saved us will stand between us and every foe. He does not leave His people to fight their battles in their own power, but He is the Strength of all who rest upon His Word.

From the wells of salvation, so long spurned by the self-righteous Jew, seeking to save himself by his own efforts, the returned remnant draw the water of life as they call upon His name and bear witness before all the world to the salvation He has wrought.

The psalm, for it is a psalm, ends with a call to praise and adore the God of Israel, who will dwell in the midst of His redeemed people in that day of His manifested glory. Even now those who come to Him in faith can make this song their own as they know the reality of His saving grace.

THE BURDEN OF BABYLON

W E NOW COME to a distinct section of Isaiah's prophecy, dealing particularly with the nations with whom Israel had to do in the past centuries and some of whom it will have to meet in the coming Day of the Lord. In chapters thirteen through twenty-three we have "burdens," that is, prophetic messages, relating particularly to Babylon (13, 14), Moab (15, 16), Damascus, the capital of Syria (17), some unnamed maritime power west of Ethiopia (18), Egypt (19), Egypt and Ethiopia (20), Edom and Arabia, (21) and of Tyre (23). Two messages also refer definitely to Palestine itself in connection with the attacks of their enemies, namely, part of chapter twenty-one and chapter twenty-two. The nations mentioned in these chapters were those from whom Israel suffered in the past and some of them will appear on the scene in the last days, still manifesting their old enmity toward the chosen race.

In chapters thirteen and fourteen Isaiah looks on into the future, predicting the destruction that he foresaw would come upon Babylon as a result of the Medo-Persian invasion of Chaldea. It may seem strange that Babylon should occupy the place it does in these prophetic visions inasmuch as it was but an insignificant power in Isaiah's day, completely overshadowed by Assyria, but the spirit of prophecy enabled Isaiah to look on to the time when these two would be combined in one great dominion of which the city of Babylon would be the capital. This was the power destined to carry out the judgments of God against Judah because of its rebellion and idolatry. As we read these chapters it is easy to see that back of the literal rulers of Babylon there was a sinister spirit-personality denominated as Lucifer, the son of the morning. That this evil angel is identical with Satan himself seems to be perfectly clear. We note, then, the first part of the prophecy, which will have a double fulfillment: first, Babylon's destruction by the armies of Cyrus and Cyaxares (who is probably the same as the Darius of Daniel 5), and then the final destruction of the Assyrian in the last days. In eloquent and dramatic language Isaiah pictures the downfall of the future oppressor of the people of God.

The burden of Babylon, which Isaiah the son of Amoz did see. Lift ye up a banner upon the high mountain, exalt the voice unto them, shake the hand, that they may go into the gates of the nobles. I have commanded my sanctified ones, I have also called my mighty ones for mine anger, even them that rejoice in my highness. The noise of a multitude in the mountains, like as of a great people; a tumultuous noise of the kingdoms of nations gathered together: the Lord of hosts mustereth the host of the battle. They come from a far country, from the end of heaven, even the Lord, and the weapons of his indignation, to destroy the whole land. Howl ye; for the day of the Lord is at hand; it shall come as a destruction from the Almighty. Therefore shall all hands be faint, and every man's heart shall melt: and they shall be afraid: pangs and sorrows shall take hold of them; they shall be in pain as a woman that travaileth: they shall be amazed one at another; their faces shall be as flames. Behold, the day of the Lord cometh, cruel both with wrath and fierce anger, to lay the land desolate: and he shall destroy the sinners thereof out of it. For the stars of heaven and the constellations thereof shall not give their light: the sun shall be darkened in his going forth, and the moon shall not cause her light to shine.

And I will punish the world for their evil, and the wicked for their iniquity; and I will cause the arrogancy of the proud to cease, and will lay low the haughtiness of the terrible (verses 1-11).

The picture presented goes far beyond that of the literal destruction of Babylon on the Euphrates in the days of the Medo-Persian conquest. It vividly presents the conditions that will prevail not only among the nations of central and western Asia, but of all Gentile powers in the day of the Lord's indignation. In other words, the doom that fell upon Babylon of old was an illustration of the terrible fate that awaits the godless Gentile powers who will be taken in red-handed rebellion against the Lord and His Anointed in the last days. It will be noted that many of the expressions used in these verses are practically identical with those of other prophecies concerning the Day of the Lord and with the events to follow the breaking of the sixth seal in the book of Revelation.

I will make a man more precious than fine gold; even a man than the golden wedge of Ophir. Therefore I will shake the heavens, and the earth shall remove out of her place, in the wrath of the Lord of hosts, and in the day of his fierce anger. And it shall be as the chased roe, and as a sheep that no man taketh up: they shall every man turn to his own people, and flee every one into his own land. Every one that is found shall be thrust through; and every one that is joined unto them shall fall by the sword. Their children also shall be dashed to pieces before their eyes; their houses shall be spoiled, and their wives ravished (verses 12-16).

As we compare this passage with Haggai 2:6, 7; Hebrews 12:25-29; Zechariah 14:4, 5, and other passages relating to the Day of the Lord, we learn that not only will the kingdoms of the world be broken to pieces but there will be tremendous natural convulsions that will shake the earth and cause disorder even among the heavenly bodies, so that the people of the world will be in abject terror because of the judgments of the Lord. So large a portion of the human race will be destroyed in the conflicts and natural catastrophes of those days that a man will be more precious than gold, and fear and terror will take hold upon all of the inhabitants of the earth who do not know and wait for the Lord in that day of His power.

Behold, I will stir up the Medes against them, which shall not regard silver; and as for gold, they shall not delight in it. Their bows also shall dash the young men to pieces; and they shall have no pity on the fruit of the womb; their eye shall not spare children. And Babylon, the glory of kingdoms, the beauty of the Chaldees' excellency, shall be as when God overthrew Sodom and Gomorrah. It shall never be inhabited, neither shall it be dwelt in from generation to generation: neither shall the Arabian pitch tents there; neither shall the shepherds make their fold there. But wild beasts of the desert shall lie there; and their houses shall be full of doleful creatures; and owls shall dwell there, and satyrs shall dance there. And the wild beasts of the islands shall cry in their desolate houses, and dragons in their pleasant palaces: and her time is near to come, and her days shall not be prolonged (verses 17-22).

Here the prophet reverts to the literal destruction of Babylon which began with its siege and overthrow by the Medes and Persians, but was not consummated fully until some centuries later when at last that one-time proud city was leveled to the dust, its palaces destroyed, its hanging gardens ruined, and its destruction made so complete that in all the centuries since it has never been able to rise again. It is true that from time to time small villages have been built near the site of the ancient city, but the ruins of Babylon recently uncovered by archeologists show how completely the prophet's words have been fulfilled. Even to this day the Arabian refuses to pitch his tent there, thinking that demons prowl by night among the ruins of the city, where owls and lizards (dragons) and other creatures of the night abound. God has decreed that Babylon shall never rise again. The Babylon of the Apocalypse is a symbolic picture of the great religious-commercial organization of the last days which will become fully developed after the true Church has been caught up to be with the Lord. Its doom, like that of the ancient city, will soon be consummated and it too will fall, never to lift itself up again against God and His people.

In chapter fourteen, we see that God links Israel's future restoration with Babylon's doom. Though centuries were to elapse between the two events yet, inasmuch as through the decree of Cyrus a remnant was permitted to return to Jerusalem, thus fulfilling a part of the divine predictions concerning the recovery of Judah, so their final restoration is linked with the complete overthrow of Gentile power.

> For the Lord will have mercy on Jacob, and will yet choose Israel, and set them in their own land: and the strangers shall be joined with them, and they shall cleave to the house of Jacob. And the people shall take them, and bring them to their place: and the house of Israel shall possess them in the land of the Lord for servants and handmaids: and they shall take them captives, whose captives they were; and they shall rule over their oppressors (verses 1, 2).

Note the expression, "They shall take them captives, whose captives they were." This seems to give the true explanation of that much-controverted passage in Ephesians 4:8, "He led captivity captive." These words are quoted from Psalm 68:18. The same Hebraism is found in Judges 5:12 where the meaning is perfectly clear: Barak was to lead captive those who had held Israel captive. So Christ, by His triumphant resurrection, has overthrown the powers of hell and led captive Satan and his hosts who held humanity captive for so long. Satan was utterly defeated at that time (Heb. 2:14) and those who had once been his victims are now delivered from his power. In Colossians 2:15 we are told that Christ, in rising from the dead, spoiled, or made a prey of, principalities and powers, that is, the hosts of evil; therefore Satan is now a defeated foe. His judgment has not yet been carried out but is as certain as that God's Word is true. It is for the believer to resist the devil, steadfast in the faith, knowing that he can have no power against those who cleave to the Word of God.

In the section that follows, Israel is seen exulting over the destruction of her great enemy.

And it shall come to pass in the day that the Lord shall give thee rest from thy sorrow, and from thy fear, and from the hard bondage wherein thou wast made to serve, that thou shalt take up this proverb against the king of Babylon, and say, How hath the oppressor ceased! the golden city ceased! The Lord hath broken the staff of the wicked, and the sceptre of the rulers. He who smote the people in wrath with a continual stroke, he that ruled the nations in anger, is persecuted, and none hindereth. The whole earth is at rest, and is quiet: they break forth into singing. Yea, the fir trees rejoice at thee, and the cedars of Lebanon, saying, Since thou art laid down, no feller is come up against us (verses 3-8).

The "king of Babylon" seems to be used here as a synonym for all Gentile powers that throughout the centuries have taken part in the persecution of God's ancient people. When the last great enemy shall be de-

stroyed they will be able to rejoice in the manifestation
of Jehovah's power, and just as Israel sang on the
shores of the Red Sea as they viewed the destruction of
Pharaoh and his host, so in that coming day will they
be able to raise the Song of Moses and the Lamb as they
see all their enemies brought to naught.

We come to something now that enables us to understand how sin began in the heavens, and also to comprehend something of the unseen powers that throughout the centuries have dominated the minds of
evil-disposed men, seeking to thwart the purpose of
God. The fall of Lucifer portrays the fall of Satan.
The passage links very closely with Ezekiel 28, which
should be carefully considered in the effort to understand this fully.

Hell from beneath is moved for thee to meet thee at thy coming: it stirreth up the dead for thee, even all the chief ones of the
earth; it hath raised up from their thrones all the kings of the
nations. All they shall speak and say unto thee, Art thou also become weak as we? art thou become like unto us? Thy pomp is
brought down to the grave, and the noise of thy viols: the worm
is spread under thee, and the worms cover thee. How art thou fallen
from heaven, O Lucifer, son of the morning! how art thou cut down
to the ground, which didst weaken the nations! For thou hast said
in thine heart, I will ascend into heaven, I will exalt my throne
above the stars of God: I will sit also upon the mount of the congre-
gation, in the sides of the north: I will ascend above the heights of
the clouds; I will be like the most High. Yet thou shalt be brought
down to hell, to the sides of the pit (verses 9-15).

These words cannot apply to any mere mortal man.
Lucifer (the light-bearer) is a created angel of the
very highest order, identical with the covering cherub
of Ezekiel 28. He was, apparently, the greatest of all
the angel host and was perfect before God until he fell
through pride. It was his ambition to take the throne of

Deity for himself and become the supreme ruler of the universe. Note his five "I wills." It was the assertion of the creature's will in opposition to the will of the Creator that brought about his downfall, and so an archangel became the devil! Cast down from the place of power and favor which he had enjoyed, he became the untiring enemy of God and man, and down through the millennia since has exerted every conceivable device to ruin mankind and rob God of the glory due to His name. It is of him our Lord speaks in John 8:44. The Lord there shows that Satan is an apostate, having fallen from a position once enjoyed, and we know from other Scriptures how he ever goes about as a roaring lion, seeking whom he may devour. The Cross was the precursor of Satan's doom, but he is determined to wreak his vengeance upon mankind so far as he can before his own final judgment takes place, because his heart is filled with hatred against God and against those whom God loves. We know from other passages that Lucifer was not alone in his rebellion (2 Pet. 2:4), and our Lord speaks of "the devil and his angels" (Matt. 25:41), and this is confirmed in Revelation 12:7, where we read of the coming war in heaven between Michael and his angels, and the dragon and his. These evil angels are the world-rulers of this darkness (Eph. 6:12, *literal rendering*). They seek to dominate the hearts and minds of the rulers of the nations, stirring them up to act in opposition to the will of God. Therefore we need not be surprised to find in the next verses of our chapter that the king of Babylon seems to be, as it were, confounded with Lucifer. The actual meaning, of course, is that he was controlled or dominated by him.

His downfall is described:

They that see thee shall narrowly look upon thee, and consider thee, saying, Is this the man that made the earth to tremble, that did shake kingdoms; that made the world as a wilderness, and destroyed the cities thereof; that opened not the house of his prisoners? All the kings of the nations, even all of them, lie in glory, every one in his own house. But thou art cast out of thy grave like an abominable branch, and as the raiment of those that are slain, thrust through with a sword, that go down to the stones of the pit; as a carcase trodden under feet. Thou shalt not be joined with them in burial, because thou hast destroyed thy land, and slain thy people: the seed of evildoers shall never be renowned. Prepare slaughter for his children for the iniquity of their fathers; that they do not rise, nor possess the land, nor fill the face of the world with cities. For I will rise up against them, saith the Lord of hosts, and cut off from Babylon the name, and remnant, and son, and nephew, saith the Lord. I will also make it a possession for the bittern, and pools of water: and I will sweep it with the besom of destruction, saith the Lord of hosts (verses 16-23).

This passage is highly poetical, but describes in no uncertain terms the utter destruction of the last great enemy of Israel in the Day of the Lord. See also Ezekiel 31:16-18. All the glory of the warrior and the pride of world conquest end in utter destruction. None who has dared to rise up in pride and arrogance to defy the living God has ever been able to escape the inevitable result of his folly.

In the Assyrian of the last days, we see as it were the incarnation of all the persecuting powers who have distressed Israel since their dispersion among the Gentiles.

The Lord of hosts hath sworn, saying, Surely as I have thought, so shall it come to pass; and as I have purposed, so shall it stand: that I will break the Assyrian in my land, and upon my mountains tread him under foot: then shall his yoke depart from off them, and his burden depart from off their shoulders. This is the purpose that is purposed upon the whole earth: and this is the hand that is stretched out upon all the nations. For the Lord of hosts hath purposed, and who shall disannul it? and his hand is stretched out, and who shall turn it back? (verses 24-27).

When the nations are gathered together for the Armageddon conflict, the Lord Himself will destroy the Assyrian with every other enemy of Christ and His truth. Israel will be completely delivered and God glorified in the kingdom to be set up in righteousness.

In the last five verses of the chapter we have a separate prophecy, given in the last year of King Ahaz, relating to Palestine and its people.

In the year that king Ahaz died was this burden. Rejoice not thou, whole Palestina, because the rod of him that smote thee is broken: for out of the serpent's root shall come forth a cockatrice, and his fruit shall be a fiery flying serpent. And the firstborn of the poor shall feed, and the needy shall lie down in safety: and I will kill thy root with famine, and he shall slay thy remnant. Howl, O gate; cry, O city; thou, whole Palestina, art dissolved: for there shall come from the north a smoke, and none shall be alone in his appointed times. What shall one then answer the messengers of the nation? That the Lord hath founded Zion, and the poor of his people shall trust in it (verses 28-32).

For the time being God had turned back the armies of Syria and of Assyria, but greater conflicts were in the future. These we know came to pass in the days of Hezekiah, and finally, at the close of the short reign of Zedekiah. First, the land was overrun by the Assyrians who, however, were turned back without accomplishing their purpose, but because of Judah's lack of repentance and self-judgment, eventually the armies of Nebuchadnezzar destroyed Jerusalem, slew thousands of the people, and carried many more into captivity. Nor was this to be the last distress that would come upon that doomed land. Throughout the long years since their dispersion, Palestine has been a veritable battle-ground and Israel's sufferings have beggered all description, but the day of their deliverance is yet to come through the very One whom the nation rejected when He came in lowly grace as the promised Saviour and Messiah.

THE BURDEN OF MOAB

IN THE short fifteenth chapter the prophet predicts the eventual destruction of Moab. The country bearing this name lay to the north of the land of Edom and was bounded on the west by the Dead Sea and on the east by the Arabian desert. The north boundary ordinarily was the River Arnon though, owing to frequent strife with the Ammonites, the border changed from time to time so that occasionally it extended some miles north of this river. The Moabites were descended from the illegitimate son of Lot and his eldest daughter by incestuous relationship. Moab, therefore, might picture for us those who make a profession of being children of God while actually with no legitimate claim to that name. In other words, Moab may represent to us the easy-going religious profession with which many are contented who fail to recognize the importance of the new birth. Generally speaking, Moab was somewhat friendly toward Israel but when the nation was first passing through their borders on the way to their inheritance in the Promised Land, Balak was fearful of being destroyed by them and so hired Balaam, the son of Beor, to curse them, but as we know, God turned the curse into a blessing.

The book of Ruth tells us of the visit of Elimelech and his family to Moab in the time of famine and the unhappy results of that period of sojourn. When David was pursued by Saul he took his parents to the country of Moab and put them under the protection of its king, but as the years went on Moab, like Edom, became an enemy of Israel, for no matter how friendly religious professors may seem to be at times to the true children of God, the day always comes when they resent what seems to them to be the assumed superiority of those who really know the Lord. So from time to time we find Moab allied with the enemies of Israel and Judah.

Isaiah here depicts most graphically the day of their destruction.

The burden of Moab. Because in the night Ar of Moab is laid waste, and brought to silence; because in the night Kir of Moab is laid waste, and brought to silence; he is gone up to Bajith, and to Dibon, the high places, to weep: Moab shall howl over Nebo, and over Medeba: on all their heads shall be baldness, and every beard cut off. In their streets they shall gird themselves with sackcloth: on the tops of their houses, and in their streets, every one shall howl, weeping abundantly. And Heshbon shall cry, and Elealeh: their voice shall be heard even unto Jahaz: therefore the armed soldiers of Moab shall cry out; his life shall be grievous unto him. My heart shall cry out for Moab; his fugitives shall flee unto Zoar, an heifer of three years old: for by the mounting up of Luhith with weeping shall they go it up; for in the way of Horonaim they shall raise up a cry of destruction. For the waters of Nimrim shall be desolate: for the hay is withered away, the grass faileth, there is no green thing. Therefore the abundance they have gotten, and that which they have laid up, shall they carry away to the brook of the willows. For the cry is gone round about the borders of Moab; the howling thereof unto Eglaim, and the howling thereof unto Beerelim. For the waters of Dimon shall be full of blood: for I will bring more upon Dimon, lions upon him that escapeth of Moab, and upon the remnant of the land (chapter 15).

When or how all these predictions had their initial fulfillment in the past we may not be familiar enough with history to know, but the day came when Moab

was utterly destroyed as a nation and for centuries
their land has been inhabited by the Arabians of the
desert. Their destruction evidently came about to a
great extent through the armies of Assyria and, later,
of Babylonia. Their doom may be looked upon as a
solemn warning of the judgment that will fall at last
upon those who have a name to live but are dead
toward God and are content to go on with an empty
profession instead of turning to God in repentance and
finding new life in Christ.

The following chapter continues the subject, bringing before us first of all an earnest entreaty on the
part of the Lord Himself for Moab to turn from its
enmity against His people and meet their ambassadors
in a spirit of friendliness.

> Send ye the lamb to the ruler of the land from Sela to the
> wilderness, unto the mount of the daughter of Zion. For it shall be,
> that, as a wandering bird cast out of the nest, so the daughters of
> Moab shall be at the fords of Arnon. Take counsel, execute judg-
> ment; make thy shadow as the night in the midst of the noonday;
> hide the outcasts; bewray not him that wandereth. Let mine out-
> casts dwell with thee, Moab; be thou a covert to them from the
> face of the spoiler: for the extortioner is at an end, the spoiler
> ceaseth, the oppressors are consumed out of the land (16:1-4).

Moab was devoted largely to the raising of sheep and
cattle, and during the reigns of David and Solomon and
even later, paid tribute to Israel and Judah by sending
annually a specified number of their flocks and herds.
In Isaiah's day they had revolted and refused to continue to pay this tribute. The prophet, speaking by
divine inspiration, pleads with them to send the lamb
again to the ruler of the land, that is, the land of Israel,
and to cease acting vindictively toward those who
fled across the Jordan for refuge when in terror of

invading armies. By thus manifesting friendliness to Jehovah's people Moab might, at least for the time being, avert her judgment. To what extent the prophet's words influenced this nation at that time, we do not have any way of knowing. The prophecy goes on to emphasize the authority given to the prince who sat upon David's throne, but looks on to the coming of the Messiah, God's anointed King, who was to sit upon this throne and rule the nations in righteousness.

And in mercy shall the throne be established: and he shall sit upon it in truth in the tabernacle of David, judging, and seeking judgment, and hasting righteousness (verse 5).

It would seem, however, that there was no response to the plea made above. Instead, the Moabites met the pleadings of the prophet with coldness and arrogance, therefore judgment must take its course.

We have heard of the pride of Moab; he is very proud: even of his haughtiness, and his pride, and his wrath: but his lies shall not be so. Therefore shall Moab howl for Moab, every one shall howl: for the foundations of Kir-hareseth shall ye mourn; surely they are stricken. For the fields of Heshbon languish, and the vine of Sibmah: the lords of the heathen have broken down the principal plants thereof, they are come even unto Jazer, they wandered through the wilderness: her branches are stretched out, they are gone over the sea. Therefore I will bewail with the weeping of Jazer the vine of Sibmah: I will water thee with my tears, O Heshbon, and Elealeh: for the shouting for thy summer fruits and for thy harvest is fallen. And gladness is taken away, and joy out of the plentiful field; and in the vineyards there shall be no singing, neither shall there be shouting: the treaders shall tread out no wine in their presses; I have made their vintage shouting to cease. Wherefore my bowels shall sound like an harp for Moab, and mine inward parts for Kir-haresh. And it shall come to pass, when it is seen that Moab is weary on the high place, that he shall come to his sanctuary to pray; but he shall not prevail (verses 6-12).

Like many another people with whom God has pleaded earnestly through His prophets, beseeching them to turn from their evil ways and submit to His authority, the leaders of Moab met the prophet's entreaties with defiance and refused to give heed to the call to be subject to the God of Israel. Therefore there was no hope of recovery but they were to be exposed to the ravages of the armies of Assyria; first of all under Sennacherib and then under other leaders, till their national existence was brought to an end. The language used by the prophet is stirring indeed and indicates how deeply he, himself, yearned for the deliverance of Moab and longed to see them yield to the commands of Jehovah.

A preliminary judgment is predicted in the last two verses of the chapter.

This is the word that the Lord hath spoken concerning Moab since that time. But now the Lord hath spoken, saying, Within three years, as the years of an hireling, and the glory of Moab shall be contemned, with all that great multitude; and the remnant shall be very small and feeble (verses 13, 14).

Just when or how these words were fulfilled we may not know because of lack of familiarity with the ancient records—records which have, to a great extent, now been destroyed—but we may be certain that the prophecy was fulfilled as predicted and Moab's destruction began in Isaiah's day.

CHAPTER SEVENTEEN

DAMASCUS AND EPHRAIM

NOW WE COME to consider the burden of Damascus. Closely linked with Damascus we have the nation of Israel, generally known as Ephraim after the break with Judah. Because of the fact that they had formed an alliance with Syria, the kingdom of which Damascus was the capital, they must share in the judgment that was about to fall on that proud city and the Syrian dominion. Damascus is sometimes said to be the oldest city in the world. This may or may not be so, but it certainly has existed through several millennia and has passed through many wars and other distressing experiences, yet it stands today as a great commercial center in the midst of a beautiful district—so strikingly beautiful that we are told that when Mohammed and his army drew near the city and looked down upon it from a hilltop, the Arabian false prophet turned to his followers and said, "It is given to men to enter but one Paradise. We will not go into Damascus," and so he and his cohorts turned away.

At the time when Isaiah prophesied, Sennacherib's hosts were rapidly moving toward Israel and Syria and it is of this onslaught that the first verses speak.

The burden of Damascus. Behold, Damascus is taken away from being a city, and it shall be a ruinous heap. The cities of Aroer are forsaken: they shall be for flocks, which shall lie down, and none shall make them afraid. The fortress also shall cease from Ephraim, and the kingdom from Damascus, and the remnant of Syria: they shall be as the glory of the children of Israel, saith the Lord of hosts. And in that day it shall come to pass, that the glory of Jacob shall be made thin, and the fatness of his flesh shall wax lean. And it shall be as when the harvestman gathereth the corn, and reapeth the ears with his arm; and it shall be as he that gathereth ears in the valley of Rephaim (verses 1-5).

There were two cities or districts known as Aroer. One, east of the Dead Sea in the land of Moab, the other near to Damascus. It is evidently this latter that is here in view. As a result of the Assyrian attack, Damascus and all the surrounding towns and villages were to fall a prey to this great eastern power. Israel, too, was to suffer at the hand of the Assyrian. All of this has had its fulfillment, and yet we may look upon the entire passage as prophetic of that which will take place again in the last days when God will deal once more both with Israel and the nations. In that time, as of old, a remnant of Jacob will be preserved who will seek the face of the Lord.

Yet gleaning grapes shall be left in it, as the shaking of an olive tree, two or three berries in the top of the uppermost bough, four or five in the outmost fruitful branches thereof, saith the Lord God of Israel. At that day shall a man look to his Maker, and his eyes shall have respect to the Holy One of Israel. And he shall not look to the altars, the work of his hands, neither shall respect that which his fingers have made, either the groves, or the images (verses 6-8).

This remnant is distinguished in many of the books of the prophets and comes before us clearly again in the New Testament. It is this godly company who will turn to the Lord in the last days and in whom "all Israel shall be saved" (Rom. 11:26). Many have thought that this implied that the entire nation would be delivered in the time of Jacob's trouble, but we need to remember that "they are not all Israel, which are of Israel," and that it is the remnant in whom God recognizes the true seed of Jacob. These will be preserved in the last time of trouble as they were in the past, and through them the land will again be inhabited. Abhorring idolatry, they will find their resource in the God of their fathers and as they look to Him for protection He will undertake for them.

> In that day shall his strong cities be as a forsaken bough, and an uppermost branch, which they left because of the children of Israel: and there shall be desolation. Because thou hast forgotten the God of thy salvation, and hast not been mindful of the rock of thy strength, therefore shalt thou plant pleasant plants, and shalt set it with strange slips: In the day shalt thou make thy plant to grow, and in the morning shalt thou make thy seed to flourish: but the harvest shall be a heap in the day of grief and of desperate sorrow (verses 9-11).

Are we to take these words literally or figuratively? Possibly both, for they surely picture the folly of Israel in days gone by when although they had turned away from the Lord God of hosts, they still encouraged themselves to believe that they should prosper in their sinful condition, and so they planted lovely gardens and built great cities only to be visited at last by divine judgment. But may we not see in these verses something that perhaps has had its literal fulfillment on more than one occasion in the past, and at the present time is being fulfilled again? It is a well-known fact that during the long years of Turkish misrule, the land of Palestine was almost denuded of trees. The forests of Lebanon had long since been cut down and the wood used for many different purposes. The trees that once grew upon the Mount of Olives and Mt. Scopus were, we are told by Josephus, all cut down by Titus and used during the siege of Jerusalem. During the last century of Turkish dominion the Ottoman Government put a tax on all trees, which was so exorbitant that the inhabitants of Palestine rebelled against it, and rather than pay it cut down nearly every tree on their estates. But when, after the First World War, the mandate of Palestine was entrusted to Great Britain, one of the first things the British Government set in motion was the reforestation of the mountains of Lebanon, thousands upon thousands of young trees being planted upon those heights, while thousands of eucalyptus, or blue gum trees, were imported from Australia and planted in the swampier parts of the country in order to assist in draining the land. Following this, the returning Jews immediately began planting oliveyards and orchards of orange and other citrus fruits so that, literally, the entire country was planted with strange slips, and it certainly began to look as though Palestine had a wonderfully prosperous era before it. But all has not been according to the hope of the Jews. Troubles and disasters have fallen upon the land. Forest fires have again destroyed many of the trees on Lebanon, and what the future has in store we dare not attempt to say except that Scripture depicts great and terrible trials such as Jacob has never known in the past. Surely the harvest will be a day of grief and desperate sorrow. How this should move our hearts to cry to God for the salvation of Israel and to pray for the peace of Jerusalem.

Woe to the multitude of many people, which make a noise like the noise of the seas; and to the rushing of nations, that make a rushing like the rushing of mighty waters! The nations shall rush like the rushing of many waters: but God shall rebuke them, and they shall flee far off, and shall be chased as the chaff of the mountains before the wind, and like a rolling thing before the whirlwind. And behold at eveningtide trouble; and before the morning he is not. This is the portion of them that spoil us, and the lot of them that rob us (verses 12-14).

While these words also have had a primary fulfillment in the destruction of Israel's foes in the past, notably the Assyrian of Isaiah's day and the Chaldeans later on, yet they also coincide with what our Lord Himself has prophesied concerning the great tribulation, preceded by the time when nation shall rise against nation and kingdom against kingdom; when the sea and the waves shall roar and there shall be earthquakes in divers places and men's hearts shall fail them for fear of looking after the things that are coming upon the earth. As the closing hour of tribulation strikes, the nations shall be gathered together against Jerusalem. The hosts of the Gentiles will come from the east, the north, and the west to engage in bloody conflict, seeking to obtain possession of Immanuel's land, but the appearance of the Lord Jesus Christ in glory will bring the last great war to an end, when the Beast and the False Prophet and their adherents will perish by the breath of the Lord, and the hosts of Gog and Magog and the kings of the sun-rising will be destroyed by the omnipotent power of God acting for the deliverance of His people, Israel.

Chapter Eighteen

THE LAND SHADOWING
WITH WINGS

W E ARE now to consider a chapter which has given ground for many differences of opinion among Christian scholars, and particularly prophetic interpreters. Many have taken it for granted that the land shadowing with wings is Egypt, because of the winged solar disk which appears upon so many of its monuments and was really a symbol of its power and greatness. But it could hardly be said of Egypt that it lay beyond the rivers of Ethiopia when the Nile descended from Ethiopia, passed through the midst of Egypt, and emptied itself into the Mediterranean Sea in the north. Since the revival of interest in prophetic study during the last century and a half, some have thought that the symbol refers to the United States, because of the fact that on our Great Seal an eagle is represented with outstretched wings. Other nations have used the eagle upon their ensigns and coats-of-arms, but not with overshadowing wings, as it is officially used in America. Many others have assumed that, inasmuch as the reference is undoubtedly to some great maritime power, it was a prophecy of Great Britain who of old gloried in ruling the waves, but it does not seem possible to identify it as referring either to Britain or America with certainty. Perhaps, indeed, it might include both, and with them other nations linked together in the last great confederacy.

F. C. Jennings, in his monumental work on Isaiah, points out that there were two districts known as Cush, the Hebrew word translated "Ethiopia" in this passage; one on the banks of the Euphrates, and the other in what we have known as Abyssinia until recently its ancient name has been restored to it. The great stretch of country between these two lands was included in that promised to Abraham, and was ruled by both David and Solomon for a time. It seems evident from many prophetic scriptures that Israel will possess all of this land in the millennial day. According to this view, the powers referred to here would be outside and beyond these two rivers and therefore might well include western European lands and others of the western hemisphere unknown to the prophets of old. We know that ten kingdoms, rising out of the ancient Roman Empire, are to come to the front in the last days, bound together by an offensive and defensive alliance over which that sinister character designated "the Beast" in Revelation 13 will bear rule. This last confederation of the Gentile nations of the west will for a time act as the friend and ally of Israel, as a nation, restored to their own land. It is, therefore, reasonable to conclude that it is these that are referred to in the opening part of this chapter.

Woe to the land shadowing with wings, which is beyond the rivers of Ethiopia: that sendeth ambassadors by the sea, even in vessels of bulrushes upon the waters, saying, Go, ye swift messengers, to a nation scattered and peeled, to a people terrible from their beginning hitherto; a nation meted out and trodden down, whose land the rivers have spoiled! (verses 1, 2).

The word here translated "woe" is the same as that rendered "Ho" in Isaiah 55:1. It is a call to attention. Jehovah is summoning this great power lying beyond the rivers of Ethiopia to come to the aid of His people. Undoubtedly it is the people of Israel who are in view for they, indeed, have been through the centuries, "a nation scattered and peeled." What other people have suffered as they have done and yet maintained their unity and national existence in spite of every effort made to destroy them. They have been "terrible," or "dreadful," from their very beginning, for when they went forth as directed by the Lord, the fear of them fell upon all nations that confronted them and their power seemed unlimited, but when they became disobedient, then disaster followed.

All ye inhabitants of the world, and dwellers on the earth, see ye, when he lifteth up an ensign on the mountains; and when he bloweth a trumpet, hear ye. For so the Lord said unto me, I will take my rest, and I will consider in my dwelling place like a clear heat upon herbs, and like a cloud of dew in the heat of harvest. For afore the harvest, when the bud is perfect, and the sour grape is ripening in the flower, he shall both cut off the sprigs with pruning hooks, and take away and cut down the branches. They shall be left together unto the fowls of the mountains, and to the beasts of the earth; and the fowls shall summer upon them, and all the beasts of the earth shall winter upon them (verses 3-6).

The return depicted here is evidently not that which is spoken of elsewhere in the prophets and is based upon the repentance of the nation and their recognition of Jesus as the Messiah. The ships of the Gentiles will bring them back to the land while Jehovah, as it were, looks on but does not interfere in any special sense. An ensign lifted up in the land will be the signal for the returning to Palestine of those who through the centuries have wandered among the Gentiles. We may see this being fulfilled already. They are now in the land and recognized by other nations as an independent republic. One could well hope that their sufferings were over, did we not know that even greater distress awaits them in the future when the horrors of the great tribulation will burst upon them in all their fury. Then a remnant will be distinguished from the mass and with this remnant Jehovah will be identified.

In that time shall the present be brought unto the Lord of hosts of a people scattered and peeled, and from a people terrible from their beginning hitherto; a nation meted out and trodden under foot, whose land the rivers have spoiled, to the place of the name of the Lord of hosts, the mount Zion (verse 7).

This coincides with the actual return of the Lord when He will arise to deal in judgment with the enemies of Israel and will recognize the remnant as His people. The great trumpet will be blown, and the outcasts of Israel summoned to return from every land of earth to their ancient patrimony. Surely we may see in all that is going on at the present time in connection with Palestine and the new nation Israel now established there, how readily all these things will have their complete fulfillment as soon as the Church of God has been taken out of this scene and caught up to be with the Lord.

God's heart is ever towards Israel and while He has permitted them to pass through such terrible sufferings throughout the long centuries of their dispersion because they knew not the time of their visitation, the day will surely come when, their transgressions forgiven and their hearts renewed, they will be restored to Himself and planted again in their own land—that land which so often the rivers have spoiled! This refers to a well-known symbol in the prophetic Scriptures. Invading armies are often pictured as overflowing, destructive rivers. Such "rivers" have passed and re-passed over the land of Palestine throughout the nearly two millennia since the rejection of Christ and the destruction of Jerusalem and the temple which followed some forty years later. In all these stresses, Palestine has been an almost continual battleground. Assyria, Babylonia, Persia, Greece, Egypt, Rome, and later the Turks and other powers have fought over this land, and whoever has won, the Jew has always been the loser until when, in God's due time, General (later Lord) Allenby entered Jerusalem without firing a shot and the Turkish army fled beyond the borders of the land. God has been working providentially toward the fulfillment of His purpose for Israel. Their reliance has been, however, upon their own wisdom and might, as-sisted at times by the Gentiles, rather than upon God Himself, and so there have been many disappointments, and there will be more in the future before the prom-ises of God have their complete fulfillment.

THE BURDEN OF EGYPT

A S WE STUDY these chapters, however little we understand all the details referred to, we cannot fail to recognize the hand of God dealing with this one-time proud, haughty kingdom in retaliatory judgments because of its independent spirit and proud attitude toward the people of the Lord, who, in centuries gone by, had been subjected to cruel bondage and often since had suffered through Egyptian violence. Even though, at the time Isaiah prophesied, Egypt was outwardly in alliance with Judah, she proved utterly undependable when it came to helping Ahaz and, later, Hezekiah to stand against the onrush of the Assyrian armies.

The philosophy of history might be summed up in the words of Galatians 6:7 by substituting "nation" for "man" and "it" for "he": Whatsoever a nation soweth, that shall it also reap. All down through the centuries the blessing of God has rested upon nations that followed after righteousness, even in measure, and His judgments have fallen when corruption and violence took the place of subjection to His hand. There is not enough agreement among historians and archaeologists to enable us to speak positively as to just when the predictions contained in the first part of this chapter were fulfilled, but we may be absolutely certain that whether as yet we have monumental confirmation of them they all came to pass as divinely foretold. We do know that about the time of Isaiah's prophecy, Egypt was for some years in a state of internal strife, Pharaoh himself having proven unable to control the populace or even the Egyptian armies. As a result, his dynasty was overthrown and a number of independent states were set up, until eventually a king arose who was able to unite them again into one empire. It should be remembered that Egyptian records go back to the very dawn of history. In the beginning the religion of Egypt was a pure monotheism. That which the Apostle Paul in Romans 1 says of the heathen generally was manifested in that country to a marked degree. When they knew God they turned away from Him and worshiped and served the creature rather than the Creator, setting up images, first of all made like to corruptible men, whom they recognized as gods of the various forces of nature. Later they deified birds like the sacred Ibis, and beasts like the sacred Bull and the Cat of Bubastes, and then degenerated even to the worship of reptiles such as the sacred Crocodile and the Asp, and last of all, even deified certain forms of insect life, of which the sacred Scarab is the one with which we are most familiar. No man's life nor the life of a nation is any better than that of the gods that are worshiped, and so Egypt became debased politically, morally, and spiritually, until at last that once-proud empire was destroyed and became a base kingdom, not to be reckoned among the major dominions.

In the opening verses of chapter nineteen, God is pictured as riding upon the divine chariot, coming down from heaven to deal with this guilty nation.

The burden of Egypt. Behold, the Lord rideth upon a swift cloud, and shall come into Egypt: and the idols of Egypt shall be

moved at his presence, and the heart of Egypt shall melt in the
midst of it. And I will set the Egyptians against the Egyptians:
and they shall fight every one against his brother, and every one
against his neighbour; city against city, and kingdom against
kingdom. And the spirit of Egypt shall fail in the midst thereof;
and I will destroy the counsel thereof; and they shall seek to the
idols, and to the charmers, and to them that have familiar spirits,
and to the wizards (verses 1-3).

God's patience with Egypt had at last come to an
end. He Himself would deal with their false gods, dem-
onstrating their inability to deliver, and manifesting
His own omnipotence. Terrified by the sufferings to
which they were exposed, the worshipers of these idols
would seek in vain for help from their false deities.
The heart of the people would fail and in their desperation they would turn to those who professed to deal
with departed spirits, the necromancers and other
charlatans, who already abounded in great numbers
in that land of superstition. No longer respecting the
king who ruled over them, city after city would revolt
and independent rival states be set up. This new system, however, would not result in peace and security
because of the jealousies of the various nomes, or coun-
ties, as we might call them.

And the Egyptians will I give over into the hand of a cruel
lord; and a fierce king shall rule over them, saith the Lord, the
Lord of hosts. And the waters shall fail from the sea, and the river
shall be wasted and dried up. And they shall turn the rivers far
away; and the brooks of defence shall be emptied and dried up:
the reeds and flags shall wither. The paper reeds by the brooks, by
the mouth of the brooks, and every thing sown by the brooks, shall
wither, be driven away, and be no more. The fishers also shall
mourn, and all they that cast angle into the brooks shall lament, and
they that spread nets upon the waters shall languish. Moreover
they that work in fine flax, and they that weave networks, shall

be confounded. And they shall be broken in the purposes thereof,
all that make sluices and ponds for fish (verses 4-10).

After some years of almost constant civil war and
internal strife, history records the rise of a cruel and
tyrannical leader known as Psammetichus who founded
a new dynasty and succeeded in bringing about at least
an outward semblance of unity. He is generally considered to be the "cruel lord" referred to in verse 4. On
the other hand, a question may be raised as to whether
all that we have here was to follow in immediate se-
quence. Some have thought that the prophecy looked
on to the day when Egypt would be so weakened that
she would be powerless to resist the onslaught of the
Arabs and, later, the Ottoman Turks, and that the cruel
lord referred not to any one individual but to the succession of Ottoman rulers who subjected Egypt to the
very hardest servitude and taxed the people so as to
reduce them to the most desperate poverty. The verses
that follow tell of the destruction of all of the great
commercial enterprises in which Egypt once excelled,
and the centuries since bear witness to the literal fulfillment of these prophecies. In some way the great
fishing industry of Egypt was brought to an end and
the Nile that once abounded with fish ceased to be pro-
ductive. Egypt, at one time the center of the papyrus
industry which in olden times took the place of the
paper to which we are now accustomed, ceased to produce this material because the papyrus plant no longer
grew in quantities on the banks of the Nile. It is a well-
known fact that Egyptian linens were exported into all
civilized lands and this industry was a source of enormous income to the merchants of that land, but singu-
larly enough and in exact accord with this prophecy, the
production of flax came almost to an end, and that

which had been an Egyptian monopoly was taken up by other nations and Egypt never since has been a linen-producing country to any serious extent. So literally have these prophetic words been fulfilled.

Surely the princes of Zoan are fools, the counsel of the wise counsellors of Pharaoh is become brutish: how say ye unto Pharaoh, I am the son of the wise, the son of ancient kings? Where are they? where are thy wise men? and let them tell thee now, and let them know what the Lord of hosts hath purposed upon Egypt. The princes of Zoan are become fools, the princes of Noph are deceived; they have also seduced Egypt, even they that are the stay of the tribes thereof. The Lord hath mingled a perverse spirit in the midst thereof: and they have caused Egypt to err in every work thereof, as a drunken man staggereth in his vomit. Neither shall there be any work for Egypt, which the head or tail, branch or rush, may do (verses 11-15).

The prophecy definitely depicts a time of great business depression and political perplexity when Pharaoh's counselors proved themselves unable to handle the situation aright. Their advice offered no real solution of the problems that the nation was facing. The princes of Zoan (the Egyptian Tanis), and of Noph (known to us as Memphis), sought in vain for a way out of the conditions that confronted them. The reason for their failure comes out clearly in the closing verses of this section. They refused to turn to the only One who could have helped them, that is the God of Israel, whom they had despised. Therefore, they were like drunken men, unable to control themselves or their country, a spirit of perversity having taken hold upon them. In all that we have seen thus far, we are again reminded of that which comes out so plainly in other parts of Scripture, that Egypt is a type of this present evil world—that godless system which once held the people of God in bondage when they were made to serve with rigor under the lashing of the lusts of the flesh. This world has grown no better throughout all the centuries during which the gospel has been preached and the Lord has been taking out a people for His name. Rather has it become hardened in its attitude toward God and His Word; "Evil men and seducers," we are told, "shall wax worse and worse, deceiving, and being deceived" (2 Tim. 3:13). Nor will this state of things be changed until the now-rejected Christ returns from heaven in flaming fire, taking vengeance on those who know not God. Then will His kingdom of righteousness supersede all the kingdoms that man has set up and "the Lord alone shall be exalted in that day."

Starting with verse 16, we have five distinct sections each beginning with the words "In that day," all therefore looking forward to the Day of the Lord, the day of Jehovah's triumph.

In that day shall Egypt be like unto women: and it shall be afraid and fear because of the shaking of the hand of the Lord of hosts, which he shaketh over it. And the land of Judah shall be a terror unto Egypt, every one that maketh mention thereof shall be afraid in himself, because of the counsel of the Lord of hosts, which he hath determined against it (verses 16, 17).

There is a very definite sense in which these words are even now in course of fulfillment. We have seen Israel returning in unbelief to her own land and one of her chief adversaries has been the nation of Egypt, which appears to dread the growing power of the nation once enslaved by the Pharaohs. But according to these verses the acknowledged weakness of Egypt and the recognition of God's manifested power in permitting the resettlement of His people in their own land, will prove to be the precursor of blessing, and Egyptian enmity will come to an end in the day that Israel shall turn to God in repentance and receive the Messiah they once rejected. But if we take the prophecy as having to do with the times shortly following Isaiah's day, we see only the fear of Egypt, as of old, lest the Israelites should multiply and become stronger than they. However, Judah was carried away by Babylon and for the time being Jehovah's testimony ceased to exist in the land of Palestine.

In that day shall five cities in the land of Egypt speak the language of Canaan, and swear to the Lord of hosts; one shall be called, The city of destruction (verse 18).

Commentators generally refer this prophecy to the migration of many of the Jews to the land of Egypt following the destruction of the first temple. We know from history that the day came when many thousands of Israelites dwelt in the cities of Egypt and synagogues were erected there and the law of Moses read and taught. It may be that it is to this the verse refers, but there is also the possibility that it is looking on to a future day when the relations of the Egyptians and the Jews shall become very close indeed, as both together shall acknowledge the one true and living God. The City of Destruction mentioned here is generally considered to be Heliopolis, "The City of the Sun." Its Hebrew name was Ir-ha-cheres, which by the change of one letter became Ir-ha-heres, "The City of Destruction." John Bunyan was wisely guided when he selected this as the name for the original home of his Pilgrim, who declared that he was born in the City of Destruction, and had the name, Graceless.

In that day shall there be an altar to the Lord in the midst of the land of Egypt, and a pillar at the border thereof to the Lord. And it shall be for a sign and for a witness unto the Lord of hosts in the land of Egypt: for they shall cry unto the Lord because of the oppressors, and he shall send them a saviour, and a great one, and he shall deliver them. And the Lord shall be known to Egypt, and the Egyptians shall know the Lord in that day, and shall do sacrifice and oblation; yea, they shall vow a vow unto the Lord, and perform it. And the Lord shall smite Egypt: he shall smite and heal it: and they shall return even to the Lord, and he shall be intreated of them, and shall heal them (verses 19-22).

Many have been the conjectures as to the real meaning of this passage. Most of us are familiar with the views of the Anglo-Israelites and others, even including the founder of the Russellite Movement, now known as "Jehovah's Witnesses," who maintain that the altar and pillar here spoken of refer to the Great Pyramid. This pyramid is supposed to have been erected by divine instruction and the length of its passages, etc., to indicate the exact period of the Times of the Gentiles, and many theories have been founded upon it as to the time when this age would end by the coming of the Lord Jesus. But all the dates once suggested have expired and still the word remains true that of that day and hour knoweth no man. The Great Pyramid is not an altar nor is it a pillar. It is simply a gigantic tomb.

It seems evident that in the last days when Egypt shall turn to the Lord, this altar and pillar in the form of a memorial of some kind where worship is offered to Jehovah, will be set up in the border of Egypt, but it is useless to speculate where God has withheld further information. Surely, however, the Saviour yet to be sent to Egypt can be none other than our blessed

Lord Jesus who, after Egypt has learned its lesson because of the judgments that have been poured upon it, will heal it and bring it into lasting blessing.

In that day shall there be a highway out of Egypt to Assyria, and the Assyrian shall come into Egypt, and the Egyptian into Assyria, and the Egyptians shall serve with the Assyrians (verse 23).

This surely refers to millennial days when these two great Gentile powers, or perhaps more accurately, the people who shall dwell in their lands in that day, will have friendly commercial relations with one another and, with Israel, will be recognized as the people of the Lord. See also Isaiah 35:8-10. Then these one-time warring powers will be brought into fullness of blessing as we read in the next two verses.

In that day shall Israel be the third with Egypt and with Assyria, even a blessing in the midst of the land: whom the Lord of hosts shall bless, saying, Blessed be Egypt my people, and Assyria the work of my hands, and Israel mine inheritance (verses 24, 25).

Thus we see Jew and Gentile enjoying together the blessings of the promised kingdom when the Lord Himself takes over the government of the universe.

The twentieth chapter still refers to God's dealing with Egypt, but now a definite date is given.

In the year that Tartan came unto Ashdod, (when Sargon the king of Assyria sent him,) and fought against Ashdod, and took it; at the same time spake the Lord by Isaiah the son of Amoz, saying, Go and loose the sackcloth from off thy loins, and put off thy shoe from thy foot. And he did so, walking naked and barefoot. And the Lord said, Like as my servant Isaiah hath walked naked and barefoot three years for a sign and wonder upon Egypt and upon Ethiopia; so shall the king of Assyria lead away the Egyptians prisoners, and the Ethiopians captives, young and old, naked and barefoot, even with their buttocks uncovered, to the shame of Egypt. And they shall be afraid and ashamed of Ethiopia their expectation, and of Egypt their glory. And the inhabitant of this isle shall say in that day, Behold, such is our expectation, whither we flee for help to be delivered from the king of Assyria: and how shall we escape? (chapter 20).

Sargon, the king of Assyria, was unknown to history until his name was, in our times, found upon monuments, and thus Isaiah's record confirmed. Scripture does not need to be vindicated by the often conflicting histories of ancient times nor by archaeological inscriptions, for we may be sure of this, the Bible is God's inerrant Word and therefore always right, even though some of the ancient records might be in conflict with it; but again and again it has pleased God through the spade of the archaeologist to give full confirmation of the truth of His Word concerning doubts and questions that unbelievers have been only too glad to raise.

Sargon exercised tremendous power though but for a short time. Isaiah was commanded by God to become a sign to the Egyptians of the hardships that would be brought upon them by the Assyrian armies. He was commanded to lay aside his outer garments and put off his sandals and walk "naked and barefoot" before the people as an indication of the circumstances the Egyptians would have to face. Observe, it was not nudity but nakedness that was commanded. To an Oriental, the laying aside of his long robe gave him the appearance of nakedness, and it was in this way that Isaiah became a sign. Others have pointed out that we are not here told that the prophet had to go about in this manner for the three years of Egyptian punishment, but that in all likelihood, three days on his part answered to the three years in which they were to suffer. As to the rest of this chapter, in their desperation the Egyptians would recognize their helplessness and cry out for a deliverer. That Deliverer was yet to be revealed, as we have seen, in the coming Day of the Lord.

CHAPTER TWENTY-ONE

BABYLON, DUMAH, AND ARABIA

THREE burdens, or oracles, are grouped together in this chapter, all having a common interest to us because each country mentioned in its turn became prominent as an oppressor or enemy of Israel and Judah. Verses 1-10 relate to Babylon, and here the prophet is looking far on into the future, for in his lifetime Babylon could scarcely have been recognized as even a potential enemy to the people of God. After Hezekiah's healing, as recorded later on in this book, messengers came from the apparently friendly king of Babylon to bring their felicitations to the Jewish king and to inquire as to the wonder done in the land; that is, the going back of the shadow on the sundial of Ahaz. Hezekiah received this embassage without hesitation or suspicion, but Isaiah later informed him that the day would come when all that they had seen would be carried away to their distant land. God had already made it clear to His servant that Babylon was preeminently the enemy they had to fear. In this vision, however, he foreshows the doom of this great enemy, and that in a most graphic manner that fits perfectly with what actually took place in the day of its overthrow.

The burden of the desert of the sea. As whirlwinds in the south pass through; so it cometh from the desert, from a terrible land.

119

A grievous vision is declared unto me; the treacherous dealer dealeth treacherously, and the spoiler spoileth. Go up, O Elam: besiege, O Media; all the sighing thereof have I made to cease. Therefore are my loins filled with pain: pangs have taken hold upon me, as the pangs of a woman that travaileth: I was bowed down at the hearing of it; I was dismayed at the seeing of it. My heart panted, fearfulness affrighted me: the night of my pleasure hath he turned into fear unto me (verses 1-4).

It might seem strange to describe the great and prosperous city of Babylon as "the desert of the sea," but God speaks of the things which are not as though they are, and Isaiah was looking forward prophetically to the hour when that great political, religious, and commercial center would be utterly destroyed and become but a part of the waste desert lands through which the Euphrates flowed. In the Old Testament the literal city of Babylon was the original home of idolatry, and under its later kings was to become the great commercial center of the ancient world. Because of its opposition to God, it was at last entirely destroyed, as already depicted in chapter 13 of this book; as also in Jeremiah, chapters 50, 51. Literal Babylon is to remain a waste forever; it is never to be rebuilt. But that city was a type of a great religious, political, and commercial system which has been slowly rising for many centuries and is to come to the fullness of its power after the true Church has been caught up to be with the Lord. Of this Babylon we read in Revelation 17, 18, and it is a significant fact that when the angel called upon John to behold a vision of this mystical Babylon he took him out into a wilderness, for wherever Babylonish principles prevail, all true spirituality disappears and parched, arid wastes abound. So we need not be surprised at the designation of the vision here as "the burden of the desert of the sea." Isaiah foresaw in Babylon the treacherous enemy of everything divine, and yet it was the unconscious instrument in the hands of God for the chastisement of His rebellious people— the flail with which they were to be threshed in order to separate the chaff from the wheat. When God's purpose had thus been accomplished, Babylon itself was to to be judged, and so terrible was that judgment that the prophet's whole being was stirred with deepest concern as the Spirit of God revealed to him the fearfulness of the overwhelming disaster which was to bring that pretentious city to an inglorious end. God even declared the names of the countries whose mighty armies would be used to this end. Elam is Persia, and Media was to be confederate with it. Together they took the chief cities of Chaldea, Ecbatana and Borsippa, and finally Babylon itself, as told in Daniel 5.

Prepare the table, watch in the watchtower, eat, drink: arise, ye princes, and anoint the shield. For thus hath the Lord said unto me, Go, set a watchman, let him declare what he seeth. And he saw a chariot with a couple of horsemen, a chariot of asses, and a chariot of camels; and he hearkened diligently with much heed: and he cried, A lion: My lord, I stand continually upon the watchtower in the daytime, and I am set in my ward whole nights: and, behold, here cometh a chariot of men, with a couple of horsemen. And he answered and said, Babylon is fallen, is fallen; and all the graven images of her gods he hath broken unto the ground. O my threshing, and the corn of my floor: that which I have heard of the Lord of hosts, the God of Israel, have I declared unto you (verses 5-10).

It gave Isaiah no pleasure to be able to predict the awful suffering to which Israel's enemies were to be exposed. His tender heart grieved deeply over the desolation and destruction that their idolatry and corruption were to bring down upon them. He speaks almost as an eye-witness of the scene of revelry which took place on Belshazzar's last night. In few but lucid words, he pictures the scene of terror that followed the influx of the troops of the allies who entered Babylon through the dry bed of the Euphrates, according to Herodotus, after Cyrus had turned away the water of that river some miles above the city. It is true that some modern historians reject this story, but whether Herodotus was right or not, in some way the Medes and the Persians overcame every obstacle to the taking of the city and thronged its streets, slaying old and young, while the princes of Babylon, utterly unprepared for such an unexpected assault, tried in terror to rally the defenders of the city. But it was too late: "In that night was Belshazzar . . . slain. And Darius the Median took the kingdom" (Daniel 5:30, 31).

Isaiah, himself, takes the place of a watchman and beholds with prophetic eye the chariots of the triumphant conquerors and hears the cry, so similar to that which we have in the New Testament, "Babylon is fallen, is fallen; and all the graven images of her gods hath he broken unto the ground." And so at last this great fountainhead of idolatry was to be destroyed. That the vision was given by God, the prophet asserts solemnly even while he cries out as he realizes that Babylon's destruction means the deliverance of Israel, whom he designates "the corn of my floor."

The burden of Dumah, given in the next two verses, is worthy of our most careful attention. It has a message which applies to any time ere the final judgments of God fall upon the earth.

> The burden of Dumah. He calleth to me out of Seir, Watchman, what of the night? Watchman, what of the night? The watchman said, The morning cometh, and also the night: if ye will enquire, enquire ye: return, come (verses 11, 12).

Dumah means "silence" and the Hebrew word is almost exactly the same as our English word "dumb." It stands here as a synonym for the land of Edom, called also Seir. This was Esau's inheritance, a rugged mountainous region inhabited by a nation of the Esau type—virile men of the open air, delighting in war and the chase. Esau himself, their progenitor, was revered as a great hunter and a fearless fighter. So closely related to Israel, they might have been expected to be their allies, but the opposite was the case. The picture that we seem to have before us here is that of two watchmen on opposite sides of a great chasm. On the one side we may think of a city of the Judean wilderness, on the other an Edomite stronghold. As the watchmen pace back and forth upon the walls of these cities they are near enough to each other for their voices to be heard. Many have been the predictions uttered by Jewish prophets of Edom's coming doom, but these predictions were completely ignored by the Edomites. Now the voice from Dumah calls out in skeptical tones, "Watchman, how much off the night?" That is, "How much of the night has gone?" He seems to mean, "How near is it to the time when Israel's glory will be revealed as their prophets had been predicting?" The answer comes back, "The morning cometh." It is the declaration of a faith that takes God at His word and dares to believe that Israel shall then be brought into fullness of blessing, but the watchman adds, "And also the night." The day of Israel's glory will be the night of Edom's doom. And then comes the serious entreaty, "If ye will enquire, enquire ye: return, come." It is the voice of God speaking through His servant, calling upon Edom, as representing the insensate men of a godless world, and pleading with them to make diligent inquiry as to what the Lord has actually revealed and to return from their sin and rebellion to Him who still says "Come," and who waits to receive all who accept His invitation.

The burden of Arabia, though brief, contains much that we may not be able to explain clearly because of our limited knowledge of what actually took place in connection with the cities of the sons of Ishmael.

The burden upon Arabia. In the forest in Arabia shall ye lodge, O ye travelling companies of Dedanim. The inhabitants of the land of Tema brought water to him that was thirsty, they prevented with their bread him that fled. For they fled from the swords, from the drawn sword, and from the bent bow, and from the grievousness of war. For thus hath the Lord said unto me, Within a year, according to the years of an hireling, and all the glory of Kedar shall fail: and the residue of the number of archers, the mighty men of the children of Kedar, shall be diminished: for the Lord God of Israel hath spoken it (verses 13-17).

Whether or not we are able to follow each detail here recorded, it is evident that Arabia was to suffer at the hand of the Assyrians in a very definite manner. For the time at least, the pride of the Ishmaelite tribes was to be humbled and their cities spoiled, yet there is no hint of their eventual destruction, as in the case of the Edomites, for Arabia is still to be blessed in the coming day and throughout all the centuries God has preserved these descendants of Abraham's son, born after the flesh, whereas the sons of him who was born after the promise have been scattered throughout all the world because of their iniquities.

CHAPTER TWENTY-TWO

THE VALLEY OF VISION

T HE prophet now turns to deliver a message from the Lord to the people of Jerusalem at a time when it was in danger of being destroyed by the Assyrian armies of Sennacherib and his allies from Elam and Kir. Elam, as we know, is Persia and had been for centuries an enemy of Assyria, but at this very time it had become tributary thereto and sent an army to cooperate with Sennacherib in an attempt to conquer the land of Judah. In the opening verses, Isaiah exposes the true state of those who were professedly the people of God but had forgotten Him and turned aside from obedience to His Word.

The burden of the valley of vision. What aileth thee now, that thou art wholly gone up to the housetops? Thou that art full of stirs, a tumultuous city, a joyous city: thy slain men are not slain with the sword, nor dead in battle. All thy rulers are fled together, they are bound by the archers: all that are found in thee are bound together, which have fled from far. Therefore said I, Look away from me; I will weep bitterly, labour not to comfort me, because of the spoiling of the daughter of my people. For it is a day of trouble, and of treading down, and of perplexity by the Lord God of hosts in the valley of vision, breaking down the walls, and of crying to the mountains. And Elam bare the quiver with chariots of men and horsemen, and Kir uncovered the shield. And it shall come to pass, that thy choicest valleys shall be full of chariots, and the horsemen shall set themselves in array at the gate. And he discovered the covering of Judah, and thou didst look in that day to the armour of the house of the forest (verses 1-8).

While like many of the passages in this book these words evidently will have a second fulfillment in the last days when Palestine will be exposed to the great Eastern powers that will be seeking to dispossess the Jew and take over their land, they had their primary application to those in Hezekiah's day who, while they dreaded the approach of Sennacherib's armies, nevertheless tried to stifle their fears by mirth and frivolity rather than by turning in heart to the Lord and seeking that deliverance which He alone could give. The condition of His people caused the prophet intense anguish of heart, and as he looked down, as it were, upon the city which some two centuries later was to be destroyed by the Babylonians, he wept over it even as our blessed Lord at a later day looked down from the Mount of Olives upon the glorious temple that Herod had built, and bewailed the fact that Jerusalem knew not the time of her visitation and so must be devoted to destruction. In Isaiah's day that destruction was deferred because of the faithfulness of King Hezekiah, and later of Josiah, but nevertheless, the prophet recognized the fact that the Holy City was evidently to become the prey of the cruel and covetous Gentile nations.

In the following verses Isaiah speaks of the preparations that Hezekiah made to enable the city to resist the threatened siege.

Ye have seen also the breaches of the city of David, that they are many: and ye gathered together the waters of the lower pool. And ye have numbered the houses of Jerusalem, and the houses have ye broken down to fortify the wall. Ye made also a ditch between the two walls for the water of the old pool; but ye have not looked unto the maker thereof, neither had respect unto him that fashioned it long ago (verses 9-11).

We read elsewhere of these precautions which demonstrated Hezekiah's wisdom and foresight, but these alone would not have saved the city. It was divine intervention alone which destroyed the Assyrian army and delivered Jerusalem. While on Hezekiah's part there was, as we know, sincere turning to the Lord, it was otherwise with the mass of the people. Even the grave danger to which they were exposed failed to bring them consciously into the presence of God or to lead them to self-judgment that they might be in a position to seek His face and count upon His mercy.

And in that day did the Lord God of hosts call to weeping, and to mourning, and to baldness, and to girding with sackcloth: and behold joy and gladness, slaying oxen, and killing sheep, eating flesh, and drinking wine: let us eat and drink; for to morrow we shall die. And it was revealed in mine ears by the Lord of hosts, Surely this iniquity shall not be purged from you till ye die, saith the Lord God of hosts (verses 12-14).

There seemed to be no true realization either of their danger nor of their lamentably low spiritual condition. When they should have been humbled before the Lord, waiting upon Him with fasting and prayer and other evidences of repentance, they were feasting and rejoicing, living as though life was only intended for merriment and frivolity. Their motto seemed to be "let us eat and drink; for to morrow we die." It will be remembered that the Apostle Paul quotes these words when, in the fifteenth chapter of the First Epistle to the Corinthians, he demonstrates the folly of those who, while professing to be saved through faith in Christ, yet denied the Resurrection. This would leave Christians absolutely hopeless. For Christ's name's sake they gave up the pleasures of the world and yet they would have nothing to look forward to in eternity. Why not then take the ground of the Epicurean poets, Aratus and Cleanthes, who also expressed exactly the same sentiment as that of the careless, materialistic Jews of Isaiah's day?—for they too wrote, "Let us eat and drink; for to morrow we die." To every thoughtful person this is the height of folly. It is a tremendously serious thing to be alive in a world like this and to know that an eternity of either happiness or misery lies beyond. Surely then every sensible man would recognize the fact that life is not given to be frittered away in pleasure-seeking, but to be used sensibly and in the fear of God, "with eternity's values in view."

The last part of the chapter is of an altogether different character. Now our attention is directed to two men, both of whom held positions of trust in Hezekiah's government. We read of them again in chapters thirty-six and thirty-seven of this book. Shebna was what we might call Hezekiah's Premier and also Chancellor of the Exchequer, or, to use a term more common in our land, Secretary of the Treasury. But he was evidently a man of selfish character, greedy, crafty, and ambitious, using his office for personal enrichment and self-glorification. This comes out clearly:

> Thus saith the Lord God of hosts, Go, get thee unto this treasurer, even unto Shebna, which is over the house, and say, What hast thou here? and whom hast thou here, that thou hast hewed thee out a sepulchre here, as he that heweth him out a sepulchre on high, and that graveth an habitation for himself in a rock? (verses 15, 16).

Shebna had caused a grand mausoleum to be built, or cut out, for himself, in the limestone rock where the kings of Judah were buried. He desired in this way to

perpetuate his memory in years to come. But God, who
sees not as man sees, discerned the worthlessness of his
character and was about to deal with him in judgment.
He was to be removed from his office and carried into
captivity, to die in a distant land. Who then would
occupy the sepulcher he had prepared for himself?

Many think of this man as a type of the antichrist
of the last days and it may be that this interpretation
is correct. At any rate, the characters of the Man of
Sin and that of Shebna are akin one to the other, and
the judgment of the one, in each instance, gives place
for the recognition of another who will fulfill God's
purpose. The successor to Shebna was Eliakim, who is
manifestly a type of our Lord Jesus Christ who will
take over the reins of the government of this world
when antichrist has been destroyed.

Behold, the Lord will carry thee away with a mighty captivity,
and will surely cover thee. He will surely violently turn and toss
thee like a ball into a large country: there shalt thou die, and there
the chariots of thy glory shall be the shame of thy lord's house.
And I will drive thee from thy station, and from thy state shall
he pull thee down. And it shall come to pass in that day, that I
will call my servant Eliakim the son of Hilkiah: and I will clothe
him with thy robe, and strengthen him with thy girdle, and I will
commit thy government into his hand: and he shall be a father to
the inhabitants of Jerusalem, and to the house of Judah. And the
key of the house of David will I lay upon his shoulder; so he shall
open, and none shall shut; and he shall shut, and none shall open.
And I will fasten him as a nail in a sure place; and he shall be for
a glorious throne to his father's house. And they shall hang upon
him all the glory of his father's house, the offspring and the issue,
all vessels of small quantity, from the vessels of cups, even to all
the vessels of flagons (verses 17-24).

Eliakim was a trustworthy man, a true statesman,
and loyal servant of Hezekiah. He was a statesman, not

a mere politician. He was motivated by sincere love for his country and characterized by the fear of God. He was to take the office vacated by Shebna. To him was to be committed the key of David, that is, the key to the royal treasury, over which he was given authority to open and close as he saw fit. In this we see a very clear type of our blessed Lord, who uses the very expressions which we have here when He addresses the church in Philadelphia, Revelation 3:7: "These things saith He that is holy, He that is true, He that hath the key of David, He that openeth, and no man shutteth; and shutteth, and no man openeth." To those who look up to Him as their divinely-given Guide and Protector, He opens the treasure-house of divine truth, revealing to them the precious things which God has stored away in His Word. Eliakim was to be as a nail, fastened in a sure place. The reference is to the wooden peg, driven into the supporting post of a tent. Upon this peg were hung vessels used in camp-life and the garments of those dwelling in the tent. So upon Eliakim would depend the means of refreshment and comfort which God had provided for His people.

We may see in this figure an illustration of the security of those who have put their trust in Christ for salvation. He is, indeed, a nail fastened in a sure place, and upon Him may be hung the various vessels, from the little cups to the large flagons. Their safe-keeping consists not in their own ability to cling to the nail, but in the fact that they are hung upon that nail so that they remain in security so long as the nail itself abides in its place, and for our blessed Lord there will never be any failure. While the old creation fell in Adam, the new creation stands in Christ, upon whom all the glory of the house of God is suspended.

The last verse evidently reverts to Shebna. It could not by any possibility refer to Eliakim as it would be a direct contradiction of what has just been declared concerning him.

> In that day, saith the Lord of hosts, shall the nail that is fastened in the sure place be removed, and be cut down, and fall; and the burden that was upon it shall be cut off: for the Lord hath spoken it (verse 25).

The expression "In that day" refers definitely to the day spoken of above when Shebna would be set to one side and Eliakim would take his office. Thank God, the day is not far distant when all that is of Satan will be annulled and destroyed and only that which is of God will remain. Then our Lord Jesus will take over the authority conferred upon Him by the Father and all things will be subjected to His will and sustained by Him.

Chapter Twenty-three

THE BURDEN OF TYRE

W E NOW COME to the last of these special prophecies, or burdens, relating to nations and cities with whom Israel had to do. Three of these may be looked at as very definite types of this present evil world, to deliver us from which, Christ died. Egypt speaks of the world as we first knew it in our natural state; a scene of darkness, bondage, and death. Its Pharaohs were recognized by the mass of the people not only as kings but as gods, and divine honors were paid to them. Thus they may well speak to us of Satan, the prince and god of this world. From Egypt Israel was delivered by the blood of the passover lamb and the omnipotent power of God who led them triumphantly through the dried bed of the Red Sea where Pharaoh's hosts, who plunged in after them, were destroyed. On the farther shores of the Red Sea they sang praises to Him who had so wonderfully delivered them. We too, through grace, have known such deliverance and can say that henceforth just as Egypt was dead to Israel and Israel dead to it, so we have died to the world and the world to us by our identification with the crucified Saviour.

Babylon speaks rather of the religious world—a religion based not upon divine revelation but upon the vain imaginations of men, not subject to the will of God.

From this idolatrous city the worship of images was spread far and wide throughout the ancient world. It has its counterpart today in the sphere of worldly religion which has a form of godliness without the power. We see it in its completeness in the mystery of Babylon the Great in the book of Revelation; a vast religious-commercial system which will dominate the greater part of the world after the Church has been caught up to be with the Lord. But at last the rulers of earth's kingdoms themselves will tire of this incubus and will destroy it utterly.

Tyre speaks of the world as a great commercial system where men through material pursuits seek to enrich themselves and their families, revelling in every kind of luxury and in forgetfulness of God. This is the pervading aspect of the world as we know it today, when nation after nation is reaching out for commercial gain and people are living on a luxurious scale such as has never been known in previous centuries. But the day is soon coming when all these things upon which men have set their hearts shall be destroyed and the present world system pass away. We may see a prediction of this in the prophecy relating to the doom of Tyre.

The burden of Tyre. Howl, ye ships of Tarshish; for it is laid waste, so that there is no house, no entering in: from the land of Chittim it is revealed to them. Be still, ye inhabitants of the isle; thou whom the merchants of Zidon, that pass over the sea, have replenished. And by great waters the seed of Sihor, the harvest of the river, is her revenue; and she is a mart of nations. Be thou ashamed, O Zidon: for the sea hath spoken, even the strength of the sea, saying, I travail not, nor bring forth children, neither do I nourish up young men, nor bring up virgins. As at the report concerning Egypt, so shall they be sorely pained at the report of Tyre (verses 1-5).

The prophet foresaw the complete destruction of Tyre as a great metropolis whose ships reached every known port in the world of that day. Sidon was the mother city but it never attained to the greatness of its daughter, Tyre, settled by merchants who left Sidon to build a great city by the seaside, partly on the land and partly on a rocky island some distance from the shore, the two being connected by a stone causeway. The history of Tyre reads like a thrilling romance and will repay anyone who takes the time to acquaint himself with it. The Sidonians were Phoenicians, an active, progressive race from which sprang some of the more progressive peoples of modern times. They are credited with having invented the alphabet at a time when other nations still used pictographs in order to express themselves in writing. Our own alphabet in many respects is linked with these ancient Phoenician characters. It must have seemed incredible at the time of Isaiah's prophecy that Tyre should ever become little more than a memory, yet the predictions were fulfilled to the letter. The Tyre of today is but a squalid reminder of the great metropolis of olden days. The doom of the city would affect nations as near as Egypt and as far away as Tarshish because it was through the ships of Tyre that their merchandise was profitably disposed of.

Pass ye over to Tarshish; howl, ye inhabitants of the isle. Is this your joyous city, whose antiquity is of ancient days? her own feet shall carry her afar off to sojourn. Who hath taken this counsel against Tyre, the crowning city, whose merchants are princes, whose traffickers are the honourable of the earth? The Lord of hosts hath purposed it, to stain the pride of all glory, and to bring into contempt all the honourable of the earth (verses 6-9).

Tarshish seems to be a somewhat general term, certainly including Spain, possibly also Great Britain. We are told that the Tyrian merchants brought from Tarshish tin, lead, and other metals (Ezek. 27:12). These were found in the mines of Spain and Britain, the very word "Brittania," the ancient name of that island kingdom, meaning "the land of tin." On the other hand, in 1 Kings 10:22 we are told that Solomon's navy brought to Palestine from Tarshish, gold, silver, ivory, apes, and peacocks. The last came originally from India so that Tarshish would seem to refer not only to Western Europe but also to Eastern Asia. Solomon's navy made the round trip once every three years. This would suggest a lengthy sea voyage through the Mediterranean, out past the Pillars of Hercules into the broad Atlantic, southward past the shores of Africa, rounding the Cape of Good Hope, up through the Indian Ocean to Hindustan and back. It is noteworthy that these voyages were made in ships of Tyre, though belonging to King Solomon. We can well understand how the great merchant princes of Tyre were looked upon as the honorable of the earth, even as today men give honor to those who amass vast fortunes through commercial enterprises. Unhappily, men who thus become wealthy, seldom give the glory to the God who gave them the ability to earn such vast sums. Tyre did not take God into account at all and so He would bring against it other great powers in order to "stain the pride of all glory," for He has decreed that no flesh shall glory in His presence.

For us as Christians today it is the Cross of Christ that speaks of the shameful death of the One whom the great ones of earth rejected, but in whose death we may now see the end of all earthly glory. So with the Apostle Paul we may well exclaim, "God forbid that I should glory, save in the cross of our Lord Jesus Christ."

Pass through thy land as a river, O daughter of Tarshish; there is no more strength. He stretched out his hand over the sea, he shook the kingdoms: the Lord hath given a commandment against the merchant city, to destroy the strong holds thereof. And he said, Thou shalt no more rejoice, O thou oppressed virgin, daughter of Zidon: arise, pass over to Chittim; there also shalt thou have no rest (verses 10-12).

The destruction of Tyre would involve to a very large extent the loss of prestige of many of the great merchant cities which had been founded by or were in close alliance with Tyre. Tartessun in Spain was a daughter of Tyre because founded by Phoenicians. The same was true of Cartagena and also of Carthage in North Africa. Chittim, or Cyprus, owed its prosperity chiefly to the business done with Tyre. Hence, the howling of the merchants of all of these commercial centers when the great city to which they looked as the chief source of their prosperity fell beneath the judgment of God whom it had ignored.

Behold the land of the Chaldeans; this people was not, till the Assyrian founded it for them that dwell in the wilderness: they set up the towers thereof, they raised up the palaces thereof; and he brought it to ruin. Howl, ye ships of Tarshish: for your strength is laid waste. And it shall come to pass in that day, that Tyre shall be forgotten seventy years, according to the days of one king: after the end of seventy years shall Tyre sing as an harlot. Take an harp, go about the city, thou harlot that hast been forgotten; make sweet melody, sing many songs, that thou mayest be remembered. And it shall come to pass after the end of seventy years, that the Lord will visit Tyre, and she shall turn to her hire, and shall commit fornication with all the kingdoms of the world upon the face of the earth (verses 13-17).

The immediate agency for the accomplishment of this prophecy of the destruction of Tyre was Nebuchadnezzar and his Chaldean armies. Babylon, origi-

nally founded by Nimrod and known as Babel, had
existed for many centuries, but it never became a great
world power until it was enlarged and taken over by
the Assyrians long before Nebuchadnezzar's day. Separated from Assyria, it eventually became the domi-
nant power in the region west of the Euphrates. Nebuchadnezzar besieged Tyre and partially destroyed it,
carrying away many of its people into captivity. During that same seventy years in which Israel remained
in captivity, the Phoenician city was in a state of deg-
radation and collapse, but after the death of Nebuchadnezzar and, a few years later, the capture of Babylon
by the Medes and Persians, Tyre was largely rebuilt,
though it never again became the commercial city it
had been. But it sought to establish intimate relations
with various surrounding peoples in the effort to recoup
its misfortunes. During the Persian period of world
ascendancy Tyre flourished to some extent, but was at
last almost completely destroyed by the armies of Alex-
ander the Great when he overcame the Persians and
conquered most of Western Asia and Egypt. Tyre has
never come into prominence since and yet there is a
future of blessing predicted for it. It is evident that
the last verse of our chapter, like so many other prophetic scriptures, carries us beyond the present age to
the establishment of the Messianic kingdom of our
Lord Jesus Christ. In that day a new city will be raised
up on the ruins of Tyre and will be subject to Him
whose right it is to reign, and will bring her glory and
honor to His feet. This is predicted both here and in
Psalm 45:12 where we see Israel, once more recognized
as the wife of Jehovah, and the daughter of Tyre
among those who rejoice in her blessing and bring their
gifts to the king.

And her merchandise and her hire shall be holiness to the Lord: it shall not be treasured nor laid up; for her merchandise shall be for them that dwell before the Lord, to eat sufficiently, and for durable clothing (verse 18).

Chapter Twenty-four

COMING DESTRUCTION AND DESOLATION

THE chapter to which we now turn presents a scene of destruction and desolation unparalleled, and is closely linked with the similar passage in Jeremiah 4:23-31. Many different interpretations have been given to it, some supposing that it pictures the earth in its chaotic state as referred to in Genesis 1:2 after it had fallen from the glory of its original creation. Others again, as for instance Mrs. Ellen G. White of the Seventh-day Adventist cult, take it to refer to the millennial earth, for she denies the reality of Christ's kingdom during that period and makes the earth to be the bottomless pit into which Satan will be cast to wander about until his final judgment and destruction in the lake of fire. But a careful study of both passages would seem to make it clear that they refer primarily to the land of Palestine in the darkest period of the great tribulation yet to come, and not only to that land but to the prophetic earth as a whole, that is, the region once occupied by the Roman Empire. Throughout this chapter the Hebrew word *eretz* is translated "land," "world," and "earth." The scholars who produced the Authorized Version were very fond of using synonyms, and wherever a word occurred frequently either in the Greek or Hebrew originals, they used as many different terms as seemed right to them. But at least in the early part of the chapter, it is not the world as such that is in view but the land of Israel which the prophet sees as empty and desolate because of the terrible experiences through which the covenant people will pass in the last days.

> Behold, the Lord maketh the earth empty, and maketh it waste, and turneth it upside down, and scattereth abroad the inhabitants thereof. And it shall be, as with the people, so with the priest; as with the servant, so with his master; as with the maid, so with her mistress; as with the buyer, so with the seller; as with the lender, so with the borrower; as with the taker of usury, so with the giver of usury to him. The land shall be utterly emptied, and utterly spoiled: for the Lord hath spoken this word (verses 1-3).

Palestine is often described in Scripture as a land flowing with milk and honey, but here we see it as the very opposite, a land parched and dry, no longer able to sustain its inhabitants who flee in terror because of the judgments of the Lord. Note the expression, "the Lord . . . turneth it upside down." Everything that unbelieving Israel has trusted in will be broken to pieces. All the hopes in which they have indulged will prove to be but idle dreams because of the fact that Israel will have returned to their own land, even as they are doing now, in unbelief, counting on their own ability and prowess to enable them to build again a great nation in the home of their forefathers. But there are greater disasters ahead of them than they have ever known in the past. Not until they turn to the Lord and look upon Him whom they have pierced will their hopes be realized. Till then they are doomed to one terrible disappointment after another, a disappointment in which all classes of the people shall share.

The earth mourneth and fadeth away, the world languisheth and fadeth away, the haughty people of the earth do languish. The earth also is defiled under the inhabitants thereof; because they have transgressed the laws, changed the ordinance, broken the everlasting covenant. Therefore hath the curse devoured the earth, and they that dwell therein are desolate: therefore the inhabitants of the earth are burned, and few men left. The new wine mourneth, the vine languisheth, all the merry-hearted do sigh. The mirth of tabrets ceaseth, the noise of them that rejoice endeth, the joy of the harp ceaseth. They shall not drink wine with a song; strong drink shall be bitter to them that drink it. The city of confusion is broken down: every house is shut up, that no man may come in. There is a crying for wine in the streets; all joy is darkened, the mirth of the land is gone. In the city is left desolation, and the gate is smitten with destruction (verses 4-12).

The reason for the desolation here depicted is plainly declared. God's law has been transgressed, the everlasting covenant referred to in Genesis 9:16 wherein God pledged Himself to show His loving-kindness toward the world, which has been by Israel utterly disregarded. Instead of looking to Him for the mercies of each passing season, they think to avert disaster and procure happiness by their own efforts, thus failing to put their trust in Him who has manifested His unbounded mercy toward a fallen race. It is a mistake to suppose that the covenant here referred to is that of the law of the ten commandments, given at Sinai, for nowhere is that declared to be an everlasting covenant. It came in by the way, as we know from the Epistle to the Galatians, as a means of the full manifestation of man's sinfulness and need of a Saviour. Nor can these words refer to the covenant made with Abraham because it is impossible for man to break that covenant, inasmuch as God Himself is the only party to it, unless one might understand the rejection of the promised Seed as the breaking of the covenant so far as man is concerned. When Messiah came in accordance with the promises made to Abraham and confirmed to David, He was rejected and cut off, as Daniel 9:26 predicted. Certainly Israel then broke the everlasting covenant so far as it was in their power to do it. Later they will enter into covenant with the last head of Gentile power, thus repudiating their allegiance to their own Messiah. That covenant will be for the last week of the seventy and will be broken at the end of three-and-a-half years when the Man of Sin will declare himself to be the only object of worship.

The reference most probably, however, refers to the covenant made by God as the Creator and Sustainer of the universe to bless the labors of men's hands and give to them fruitful fields and bountiful harvest as they trusted in Him. Under Noah God set up human government, of which we read nothing in the chapters that deal with antediluvian days. This involves the subjection of the nations to God as their supreme ruler, but this is the very thing which not only Israel but the nations of the Gentiles have failed to acknowledge. The bow in the cloud which was intended to be a perpetual reminder of God's goodness and man's responsibility, has become meaningless because of unbelief and willful disobedience, therefore every effort of men to establish stable government on the earth and peace among the nations is doomed to failure. Our Lord's own words come to mind here. When discussing the horrors of the great tribulation, the rise of nation against nation in bloody warfare, He says, "Except those days should be shortened, there should no flesh be saved." Knowing as we do today the terribly destructive power of modern weapons of warfare whereby whole cities may be blotted out in a few moments of time, we need have no difficulty in accepting these words literally. Palestine will experience the ravages of warfare perhaps to a greater extent than any other country because she knew not the time of her visitation. But in the day when these judgments are falling upon that devoted land and the contiguous territory, a remnant will be separated from the mass of the people who will return to the Lord and yield glad subjection to His holy will, acknowledging their sins and trusting His word. To them the grace of God will be revealed, assisting and caring for them even as it were in a blazing world, and bringing them at last to their desired haven to dwell in peace in their own land.

When thus it shall be in the midst of the land among the people, there shall be as the shaking of an olive tree, and as the gleaning grapes when the vintage is done. They shall lift up their voice, they shall sing for the majesty of the Lord, they shall cry aloud from the sea. Wherefore glorify ye the Lord in the fires, even the name of the Lord God of Israel in the isles of the sea (verses 13-15).

While we like to think of the expression, "Glorify ye the Lord in the fires," as indicating the faithfulness of this remnant during the time when the judgments are falling on the earth, it would seem that the rendering of the Authorized Version is perhaps hardly correct. Others translate as follows, "Glorify the Lord in the east," or "in the land of light," thus suggesting that the dark days of the tribulation are after all the harbinger of the coming day of blessing when not only the remnant of Israel, but a great multitude saved out of the Gentile nations, will be brought to the place where they will wait expectantly for the Second Advent of the once-rejected Christ of God and so enter into fullness of blessing in the kingdom age.

As the prophet contemplates the sufferings of his people and the desolation of the land during that time of tribulation, he cries out in the anguish of his soul.

From the uttermost part of the earth have we heard songs, even glory to the righteous. But I said, My leanness, my leanness, woe unto me! the treacherous dealers have dealt treacherously; yea, the treacherous dealers have dealt very treacherously (verses 16).

Even though Isaiah, with prophetic vision, sees the glory following the desolations, his whole being is stirred within him as he realizes the sufferings his people must go through before they are brought back to God and to their land. An alternative rendering of the expression, "My leanness, my leanness," is, "My misery, my misery," as suggested by F. C. Jennings. At any rate, it is clear that the prophet is in the greatest mental anguish as he contemplates the results of departure from God and the breaking of His covenant.

In the verses that follow he reverts to the conditions with which this chapter began.

Fear, and the pit, and the snare, are upon thee, O inhabitant of the earth. And it shall come to pass, that he who fleeth from the noise of the fear shall fall into the pit; and he that cometh up out of the midst of the pit shall be taken in the snare: for the windows from on high are open, and the foundations of the earth do shake. The earth is utterly broken down, the earth is clean dissolved, the earth is moved exceedingly. The earth shall reel to and fro like a drunkard, and shall be removed like a cottage; and the transgression thereof shall be heavy upon it; and it shall fall, and not rise again (verses 17-20).

Graphically indeed are the woes of the last days here set forth. Everything that men have considered stable and lasting will be shaken to pieces so that the land will seem to reel to and fro like a drunken man. Indeed, there may be more than seeming in this for it may suggest the great earthquakes which will add to the terror of those days of grief and sorrow.

At that time, not only will the misguided rulers of Israel and the nations be dealt with in judgment, but God will deal with those unseen principalities and powers that have sought to dominate the hearts and minds of men in authority so that they are also described in Ephesians 6 as the "world rulers of this darkness" (*literal translation*).

And it shall come to pass in that day, that the Lord shall punish the host of the high ones that are on high, and the kings of the earth upon the earth. And they shall be gathered together, as prisoners are gathered in the pit, and shall be shut up in the prison, and after many days shall they be visited. Then the moon shall be confounded, and the sun ashamed, when the Lord of hosts shall reign in mount Zion, and in Jerusalem, and before his ancients gloriously (verses 21-23).

The "host of the high ones that are on high" evidently refers to those wicked spirits in the heavenlies who attempt to control the minds of men in such a way as to set them in opposition to God and in the vain endeavor to thwart His unchanging plans. They and their dupes, who have given them such willing service, will be shut up together in prison, awaiting the time when the Lord will deal with them in the final judgment.

When the Lord arises to shake terribly the earth, those signs in the heaven to which Christ referred will be followed by the appearing of the glorified Son of Man accompanied by His heavenly saints descending to take over the government of this world and to bring in the long-awaited age of righteousness.

CHAPTER TWENTY-FIVE

EXULTANT SONG OF THE REMNANT

IT IS with growing interest and increasing joy that we move on now to contemplate the exultation of the remnant of Israel who will become the nucleus of the new nation after the powers of evil which have sought their complete destruction shall have been dealt with by the Lord Himself at His Second Advent. For this remnant "the time of the singing" (Song of Sol. 2:12) will at last have come. Down through the centuries the cries of misery and lamentation have been loud and long because they knew not the time of their visitation, but when at last they look upon Him whom they have pierced and recognize in the once-despised Galilean their own promised Messiah their hearts will well up with praise and thanksgiving to Jehovah their God who henceforth will be their everlasting portion. Let us consider the song, verse by verse.

O Lord, thou art my God; I will exalt thee, I will praise thy name; for thou hast done wonderful things; thy counsels of old are faithfulness and truth (verse 1).

They who had been so grievously misled in the past will then come to realize that Jehovah's counsels of faithfulness and truth have remained unchanged in spite of the fact that when the Lord Jesus appeared to bring in the blessings so long awaited, they fulfilled their own Scriptures in rejecting Him and giving Him up to the death of the Cross. But God made that very cross the great altar upon which the true propitiatory sacrifice was offered for the sins of the world. Nor did He change His plan because they said, "We will not have this Man to reign over us." For the time being the One whom they refused to acknowledge as king was taken up to glory and seated, in fulfillment of Psalm 110:1, at God's right hand. During the long years of His personal absence from this earth, Israel has become the nation of the wandering foot, seeking rest and peace in vain because the Prince of Peace, who alone could give what their hearts yearned for, was to them a stranger. But in that coming day they will recognize and adore Him and so enter into fullness of joy.

For thou hast made of a city an heap; of a defenced city a ruin: a palace of strangers to be no city; it shall never be built. Therefore shall the strong people glorify thee, the city of the terrible nations shall fear thee (verses 2, 3).

These verses clearly indicate the destruction of all God-defying Gentile power in the time of the end. The leaders of the Jews declared of old, "We have no king but Caesar." Unspeakably terrible have been their sufferings under the Caesars ever since, but at the end of the great tribulation, the time of Jacob's trouble, all the powers that have oppressed them will be destroyed and they will be freed forever from Gentile tyranny and persecution.

For thou hast been a strength to the poor, a strength to the needy in his distress, a refuge from the storm, a shadow from the heat, when the blast of the terrible ones is as a storm against the wall (verse 4).

Doubtless this verse may be interpreted as applying to the entire period of Israel's scattering and distress for although the nation as such was rejected by God when they rejected His Son, nevertheless, during all this present age there has remained an election of grace; Jews who in their anguish and misery have turned to God and have found in the Holy Scriptures the revelation of His Son as their Messiah and Saviour. To these He has ever been a refuge and a comfort, even in the midst of trial and sorrow, enabling them to rejoice in His unfailing love.

Thou shalt bring down the noise of strangers, as the heat in a dry place; even the heat with the shadow of a cloud: the branch of the terrible ones shall be brought low. And in this mountain shall the Lord of hosts make unto all people a feast of fat things, a feast of wines on the lees, of fat things full of marrow, of wines on the lees well refined (verses 5, 6).

Coincident with the destruction of the Beast and the False Prophet, as we read in Revelation 19, will come the fulfillment of the prophetic Word in regard to the return of the Lord and the establishment of His throne upon Mount Zion. From thence shall the law go forth into all the world, and men everywhere among those who have been spared from the judgments of that awful day will be invited to revel in the riches of God's abundant grace. He will spread His table, not only for Israel but for the saved from among the Gentiles too, as indicated in Revelation 7. We certainly are not to take this sixth verse as referring to some literal feast, but to the spiritual refreshment which will be offered to all in that day.

And he will destroy in this mountain the face of the covering cast over all people, and the vail that is spread over all nations.

He will swallow up death in victory; and the Lord God will wipe away tears from off all faces; and the rebuke of his people shall he take away from off all the earth: for the Lord hath spoken it (verses 7, 8).

Ever since sin came into the world, men have been blinded to the eternal truths of God's Word. As we read in Ephesians 4, "having the understanding darkened, . . . through the ignorance that is in them." But when the Lord Himself appears in glory, this blindness will pass away, not only from the eyes of Israel who are now unable to understand their own Scriptures because of the veil that is upon their hearts, but from the eyes of the Gentiles as well. The apostle quotes from verse 8 in opening up the truth of resurrection in 1 Corinthians 15. He shows that this passage will have its partial fulfillment at what we know as the Rapture, when the dead shall be raised and the living changed, and this corruption shall put on incorruption, and this mortal put on immortality. Then, indeed, will come to pass that of which Isaiah here speaks. For all the children of God, living and dead, at that time, death will be swallowed up in victory. That there will be a further fulfillment at the end of the great tribulation is evident from Revelation 20:4-6, for the first resurrection will include not only the saints of this and past ages, but also those who will be put to death for refusing to worship the Beast and his image during the days of the great tribulation. Together these will constitute the heavenly company, while the spared of Israel and the nations will enter into the millennial kingdom here on the earth.

And it shall be said in that day, Lo, this is our God; we have waited for him, and he will save us: this is the Lord; we have waited for him, we will be glad and rejoice in his salvation (verse 9).

One can imagine something of the exultant joy of the remnant as they look upon the once-despised Jesus and see in Him the God of their fathers manifested in flesh. "Lo," they cry, "this is our God; we have waited for Him." Under His beneficent but righteous reign, their wanderings come to an end and they enter into possession of the land promised to Abraham and confirmed in the promise to David.

> For in this mountain shall the hand of the Lord rest, and Moab shall be trodden down under him, even as straw is trodden down for the dunghill. And he shall spread forth his hands in the midst of them, as he that swimmeth spreadeth forth his hands to swim: and he shall bring down their pride together with the spoils of their hands. And the fortress of the high fort of thy walls shall he bring down, lay low, and bring to the ground, even to the dust (verses 10-12).

Moab, which we have already seen speaks of the pride of a false religious profession, will no longer be a menace to the peace of God's people. He will utterly destroy everything that would mar the joy of that day of blessing. This will be brought about, not by human effort, not by man's ingenuity, but by the Lord Himself, who will spread forth His hands in judgment upon those who refuse to bow to His will, and in grace upon those that put their trust in Him.

CHAPTER TWENTY-SIX

ISRAEL'S DELIVERANCE

WE CONTINUE to enter into the joyous experiences of the remnant of Israel as they praise Jehovah because of the fulfillment of His promises, resulting in their deliverance from the power of the oppressor and their spiritual enrichment under Messiah's righteous rule. It should surely be a joy to us, who through grace belong to the heavenly company, as we reflect upon what God has in store for His earthly people when, in accordance with His promise to Abraham, they enter upon the full possession of the land which He declared should be theirs forever. Their deliverance is a twofold one. First, from the power of their enemies who, for so many centuries, have oppressed them, and secondly, from their sins, when they enter into the true meaning of the great day of atonement and see in Christ Jesus the true Sin Offering. In that day they will sing the Song of Moses and the Lamb, whether they be among those slain as martyrs during the reign of the Beast and the Antichrist, as seen in Revelation 15:2, 3, or whether they are saved alive out of the time of Jacob's trouble and so are prepared to enter into the kingdom when the Lord Himself appears. We, today, look forward to the time when we shall sing the new song as gathered round the throne in glory, but that has nothing to do

with the overthrow of earthly powers or our deliver
ance from them. But with Israel it will be otherwise. A
of old, when God delivered them out of Egypt, they
sang with Moses the song of triumph over their
enemies, so in the coming day will they rejoice when
every oppressor has been destroyed; but with this wil
be the Song of the Lamb, that of redemption through
His precious atoning blood. We, today, can enter into
everything spiritual that this song brings before u
for we have been blessed with all spiritual blessing
in heavenly places in Christ. While it is not the Chris
tian attitude to rejoice in the destruction of evil-doers
we can well sympathize with the earthly people as w
reflect on what the overthrow of their enemies is going
to mean to them. Let us look then at their song, vers
by verse.

In that day shall this song be sung in the land of Judah; W
have a strong city; salvation will God appoint for walls and bul
warks. Open ye the gates, that the righteous nation which keepet
the truth may enter in. Thou wilt keep him in perfect peace, whos
mind is stayed on thee: because he trusteth in thee (verses 1-3).

Surely in these opening words the remnant speak o
the city in a spiritual rather than a material sense
While they look forward to the establishment of Jeru
salem as a great center of blessing to the whole eartl
and a fortress never again to be destroyed by their foes
they sing in anticipation, recognizing in the Lord Him
self their strong city and rejoicing in the assuranc
that their foes will never again be able to overcom
them. But they are also contemplating the actual re
building of the literal Jerusalem as they cry, "Open y
the gates, that the righteous nation which keepeth th
truth may enter in." Of Israel in that day God has said

"They shall be all righteous." Their iniquities will be purged, their hearts cleansed by the washing of the water by the Word, according to the promise given in Ezekiel: "Then will I sprinkle clean water upon you, and ye shall be clean: from all your filthiness, and from all your idols, will I cleanse you. A new heart also will I give you, and a new spirit will I put within you: and I will take away the stony heart out of your flesh, and I will give you an heart of flesh" (Ezek. 36:25, 26). The veil taken away from their eyes, they will be delivered from unbelief and will find an all-sufficient Saviour in Jesus, their once-rejected Messiah.

The third verse may well apply, not only to the remnant in that coming day, but to every trustful believer in all dispensations. Perfect peace, rest of heart and mind, and freedom from worry and anxiety, are found only as we learn to commit all our ways to the Lord and trust Him implicitly to undertake for us. It is as we give heed to the admonition of Philippians 4:5, 6 that the peace of God which passes all understanding keeps our hearts as with a military garrison. Peace with God every believer has through the blood of the Cross, as we read in Romans 5:1, "Being justified by faith, we have peace with God through our Lord Jesus Christ." But the peace of God, this perfect peace of which Isaiah speaks, is something more. It is that quiet assurance that all is well, no matter what adverse circumstances the soul has to face, because we realize that our Father is ordering everything for blessing. What untold comfort has come to myriads through meditation upon and faith in such a verse as Romans 8:28, "All things work together for good to them that love God, to them who are the called according to His purpose."

Trust ye in the Lord for ever: for in the Lord JEHOVAH is everlasting strength: for he bringeth down them that dwell on high; the lofty city, he layeth it low; he layeth it low, even to the ground; he bringeth it even to the dust. The foot shall tread it down, even the feet of the poor, and the steps of the needy (verses 4-6).

Faith, trust, and confidence, are synonomous terms. He who confidently looks up to the Lord, committing everything to Him, is lifted above all that might otherwise cause distress or anxiety. We, today, know God as our Father and rejoice in the fact that "Like as a father pitieth his children, so the Lord pitieth them that fear Him" (Ps. 103:13). To Israel He is known by the covenant name Jehovah, a Hebrew compound meaning literally, "the ever-living," or as we have it in the New Testament, "He which is, and which was, and which is to come." Aptly, in the French translations, the word *L'Eternel* is used and well expresses the true meaning of Him who declared Himself of old to be Jehovah, the I Am. Here the name is, as it were, doubled. The Lord JEHOVAH is literally, JAH, JEHOVAH; the name JAH speaking again of His eternity of Being, while the full name tells of His covenant relations to His people. It is to Him they ascribe their complete deliverance, and so they will praise Him because of the way in which He shall have dealt with their proud and cruel persecutors, the great Gentile powers that have sought their destruction.

The way of the just is uprightness: thou, most upright, dost weigh the path of the just. Yea, in the way of thy judgments, O Lord, have we waited for thee; the desire of our soul is to thy name, and to the remembrance of thee. With my soul have I desired thee in the night; yea, with my spirit within me will I seek thee early: for when thy judgments are in the earth, the inhabitants of the world will learn righteousness. Let favour be shewed to the wicked, yet will he not learn righteousness: in the land of uprightness will he deal unjustly, and will not behold the majesty of the Lord. Lord, when thy hand is lifted up, they will not see: but they shall see, and be ashamed for their envy at the people; yea, the fire of thine enemies shall devour them (verses 7-11).

Throughout these verses we have the contrast between the just and the unjust. We learn from the prophet Habakkuk that the just shall live by faith, therefore the just who walk in the path of uprightness are those in Israel who have learned to put their trust in the Lord and so to endure as seeing Him who is invisible. The unjust who know no shame are those who turn away from the living God, acting in independence of Him and persecuting those who seek to do His will. Although He showers His favors upon them, making His sun to shine and His rain to fall on the just and unjust alike, yet these evil-doers fail to be moved by His goodness or drawn to Him by His grace. They only become hardened because of the favors bestowed upon them. At last they will have to learn the importance of righteousness in the hard way, when His judgments fall upon them, and all the nations are made to know His wrath because of their sin and rebellion. In that day of Jehovah's power, the inhabitants of the world who are spared after the judgments are fallen, will learn righteousness and will, with Israel, enter into the blessedness of Messiah's reign.

Lord, thou wilt ordain peace for us: for thou also hast wrought all our works in us. O Lord our God, other lords beside thee have had dominion over us: but by thee only will we make mention of thy name. They are dead, they shall not live; they are deceased, they shall not rise: therefore hast thou visited and destroyed them, and made all their memory to perish. Thou hast increased the nation, O Lord, thou hast increased the nation; thou art glorified: thou hadst removed it far unto all the ends of the earth. Lord, in trouble have they visited thee, they poured out a prayer when thy chastening was upon them. Like as a woman with child, that draweth near the time of her delivery, is in pain, and crieth out in her pangs; so have we been in thy sight, O Lord. We have been with child, we have been in pain, we have as it were brought forth wind; we have not wrought any deliverance in the earth; neither have the inhabitants of the world fallen (verses 12-18).

At long last the people of Israel will have learned the lesson that peace, not only from conflict, but peace in regard to the sin question, is found alone in Christ, He who made peace by the blood of His Cross. In vain had God called upon them to take hold of Him in faith and thus make their peace with Him. They had never responded until now; after centuries of unbelief they have learned that peace is found in a person and that Person, the Lord Jesus Christ—He who is our peace. We know the blessedness of this peace. They will know it in that coming day, following their grievous travail of soul as they pass through the anguish of the great tribulation. There had, indeed, been what looked like travail-pains, or birth-pangs, throughout the centuries of their dispersion and their suffering under Gentile domination, but all ended in disappointment. Christ was not yet born so far as their apprehension was concerned. But in that day they will be able to enter into the full meaning of the prophecy, "For unto us a Child is born, unto us a Son is given." Then, in their own consciousness, they will recognize in Jesus the Man-child who is to rule the nations with a rod of iron.

The next verse has occasioned much controversy among prophetic students, some taking it to refer to the literal resurrection of the body at the return of the

Lord and others to the national and spiritual resurrection of the remnant of Israel who, like men long dead, will come up out of their graves among the Gentiles to enter into the enjoyment of the coming kingdom.

Thy dead men shall live, together with my dead body shall they arise. Awake and sing, ye that dwell in dust: for thy dew is as the dew of herbs, and the earth shall cast out the dead (verse 19).

It seems clear that the reference here is not to physical resurrection, but is rather to be linked with the vision in Ezekiel, as recorded in his thirty-seventh chapter. There he saw a valley full of dry bones, which were declared to be the whole house of Israel. These bones were seen coming together, bone to his bone, then flesh came upon them, and eventually breath entered into them. The meaning is made clear as the Spirit of God Himself interprets it. They are the whole house of Israel, that is, the remnant of the last days, who will stand for all Israel—those referred to in Romans 11:26. Daniel 12:2 speaks, if I mistake not, of this same resurrection of the nation, but includes not only the righteous but the unrighteous. Even today we see Israel once more a nation in the land, but we know from other scriptures that the great separation between the righteous and the unrighteous is yet to take place.

The last two verses of the chapter need not be considered as part of the song. Rather we have here a special prophetic message, telling of the provision that Jehovah will make to preserve the remnant who are to be saved out of the time of trouble and who will thus be able to sing the song we have just been considering.

Come, my people, enter thou into thy chambers, and shut thy
doors about thee: hide thyself as it were for a little moment, until
the indignation be overpast. For, behold, the Lord cometh out of
his place to punish the inhabitants of the earth for their iniquity:
the earth also shall disclose her blood, and shall no more cover her
slain (verses 20, 21).

Some have thought that these words referred to
some special hiding-place where the remnant will find
shelter from the Beast and the Antichrist, as, perhaps,
in the ruined cities of Petra, but it seems rather that
Jehovah, Himself, is to be their Protector, hiding them
away in the "wilderness of the peoples" (Ezek. 20:35,
R.V.). I take it that this means that when the abomination of desolation is set up in the holy place, as predicted both by Daniel and our blessed Lord, that this
remnant will flee to the far-off heathen nations who
will not be fully under the actual domination of the
Beast and who will give shelter to these outcasts for
the truth's sake.

Blessed it is for all who even now realize the truth of
the word, "The name of the Lord is a strong tower: the
righteous runneth into it, and is safe (Prov. 18:10).
Abiding under the shadow of the Almighty, all His
people are protected from the power of the enemy.

Chapter Twenty-seven

JEHOVAH'S VINEYARD RESTORED

ONCE again we have a song of the vineyard, but it depicts entirely different conditions from those set forth in the previous song recorded in chapter five. We saw the Lord looking for grapes and finding only wild grapes, for Israel after the flesh bore no fruit for God. Now all is changed, and we see vines loaded with luscious grapes, thus giving satisfaction to the heart of the Owner. In this way the Spirit of God tells us of the joy which Jehovah will find in His people when Israel shall be restored to Himself and shall blossom and bud and fill the face of the world with fruit.

The first verse, however, has no connection with the song, as such. It might have been better had the chapter divisions occurred after this verse, rather than to separate it from those that have gone before. It tells of the judgment to be meted out to that old serpent which is the devil and Satan, who is to be bound and cast into the bottomless pit for a thousand years when the kingdom of God is established in power and glory over all this earth where for so long the adversary has exercised his control over the hearts and minds of men.

In that day the Lord with his sore and great and strong sword shall punish leviathan the piercing serpent, even leviathan that crooked serpent; and he shall slay the dragon that is in the sea (verse 1).

The great dragon having thus been dealt with, we now hear the voice of the Lord Himself, lifted up in song as He rejoices over His delivered people.

In that day sing ye unto her, A vineyard of red wine. I the Lord do keep it; I will water it every moment: lest any hurt it, I will keep it night and day (verses 2, 3).

Wine, in Scripture, is a symbol of joy. We read in Judges 9:13 of wine that cheereth God and man. In Psalm 104:15, we have a similar expression. Because of its exhilarating effect when used in moderation, it expresses that which cheers the spirit and gladdens the heart. Jehovah Himself will find occasion for rejoicing when Israel shall return to Him in penitence and self-judgment after the long years of rebellion and self-will. Then will their lives be fruitful with the graces of the Holy Spirit, and God will rejoice over them as a bridegroom rejoices over the bride (Isa. 62:5). No longer will Jehovah's vineyard be let out to unfaithful husbandmen, but He will watch over it Himself, protecting from everything that would tend to make it unfruitful or destroy it.

Fury is not in me: who would set the briers and thorns against me in battle? I would go through them, I would burn them together. Or let him take hold of my strength, that he may make peace with me; and he shall make peace with me. He shall cause them that come of Jacob to take root: Israel shall blossom and bud, and fill the face of the world with fruit (verses 4-6).

No more will the Lord manifest His indignation against the people who are called by His name, because of their waywardness. His Spirit will be quieted toward them, and on their part it would be folly indeed for any again to rise up against Him. To do so would be to meet such immediate destruction as a fire consuming thorns and briers. By returning to God in contrition and confession they make peace with Him whose wrath would otherwise have been poured out upon them. This is the only place in the Scriptures where we have a suggestion of man making peace with God, and it is well to note that it does not have to do with eternal things but with submission to the government of God in this world. When it comes to the settlement of the sin question there is no man who, by any effort of his own, can make his peace with God. The glorious truth of the gospel is that Christ has made peace by the blood of His Cross and that peace becomes ours the moment we put our trust in Him. "Therefore, being justified by faith, we have peace with God through our Lord Jesus Christ" (Rom. 5:1). He, Himself, is our peace. We are reconciled to God through the death of His Son. Where it is a question of the divine government, man is called upon to submit himself to the will of God, recognizing the folly of rebelling against divine law. To this Israel will be brought in the coming day. Then, instead of being a curse among the nations (Jer. 29:18) and the Name of the Lord being blasphemed by the Gentiles because of Israel's perversity, they will be a means of blessing to the whole earth as God has intended from the beginning— a nation of priests, through whom God will make known His salvation to the ends of the earth.

Hath he smitten him, as he smote those that smote him? or is he slain according to the slaughter of them that are slain by him? In measure, when it shooteth forth, thou wilt debate with it: he stayeth his rough wind in the day of the east wind. By this therefore shall the iniquity of Jacob be purged; and this is all the fruit to take away his sin: when he maketh all the stones of the altar as chalkstones that are beaten in sunder, the groves and images shall not stand up (verses 7-9).

Elsewhere, the Lord declared concerning Israel, "You only have I known of all the families of the earth: therefore I will punish you for all your iniquities" (Amos 3:2). Even as He permitted the Gentile powers to chastise Israel and then, in turn, destroyed the very nations that had been His rod for the correction of His people, so others will be dealt with in the day of the Lord, but Israel will be preserved and after their time of affliction has passed will be restored to the divine favor. Then they will abhor themselves because of the idolatries and abominations to which they have given themselves in times past, but every evidence of these follies will be destroyed utterly and the Lord's Name alone will be exalted in the day of their recovery and repentance.

> Yet the defenced city shall be desolate, and the habitation forsaken, and left like a wilderness: there shall the calf feed, and there shall he lie down, and consume the branches thereof. When the boughs thereof are withered, they shall be broken off: the women come, and set them on fire: for it is a people of no understanding: therefore he that made them will not have mercy on them, and he that formed them will shew them no favour (verses 10, 11).

These words may refer not only to the cities of the nations, but to the apostate part of Israel. When God arises in His wrath to deal with man's defiance of His authority He will not cease to exercise His vengeance until all who continue to resist Him shall be blotted out.

Sin, of whatever character, is an insanity. It is a manifestation of a disordered mind. In the parable of the prodigal, in Luke 15, our Lord tells us that it was when the young man came to himself that he said, "I will arise and go to my father." Men may think of themselves as too wise or learned to accept the Word of God at its face value, but they little realize that their very unbelief and arrogance only make manifest the fact that they are a people of no understanding. It was thus with Israel when they turned away from God. It is thus with all men everywhere who refuse submission to His holy will.

And it shall come to pass in that day, that the Lord shall beat off from the channel of the river unto the stream of Egypt, and ye shall be gathered one by one, O ye children of Israel. And it shall come to pass in that day, that the great trumpet shall be blown, and they shall come which were ready to perish in the land of Assyria, and the outcasts in the land of Egypt, and shall worship the Lord in the holy mount at Jerusalem (verses 12, 13).

At the second advent of the Lord Jesus, when He comes as the Son of Man to set up the kingdom of God on earth, the great trumpet will be blown (Joel 2:15, 16) in order to summon the outcasts of Israel to return to Zion and be gathered unto their long-looked-for Messiah and to rejoice in His favor. Compare these two verses with Matthew 24:31. It is vain to say that this prophecy of Isaiah's concerning the regathering of Israel had its fulfillment in the days of Ezra and Nehemiah when a remnant returned to Palestine to rebuild the city and temple at Jerusalem. The Lord has declared, as we have already seen (chapter 11:11), that He will gather them a second time, and it is to this future gathering that these verses refer.

Chapter Twenty-eight

JUDGMENTS PAST AND FUTURE

T HIS chapter introduces a new series of prophetic messages embracing chapters 28-33. This section is characterized by six woes, reminding us of those of chapter five. These, however, all have to do particularly with Israel and the surrounding nations in the last days, although the first one has already had a partial fulfillment in the judgment that fell upon Samaria when Shalmanezer, King of Assyria, overthrew the northern kingdom in the year 721 B.C. But that judgment was a precursor of a greater disaster yet to fall upon the land to which Israel has now returned and has been recognized by the Gentile powers as an independent nation.

Verses 1-4 are complete in themselves and give us the reason for God's dealing with Ephraim, or Samaria, when He allowed the Assyrian to overrun the land, destroy the cities, and carry a vast number of the Israelites into captivity.

Woe to the crown of pride, to the drunkards of Ephraim, whose glorious beauty is a fading flower, which are on the head of the fat valleys of them that are overcome with wine! Behold, the Lord hath a mighty and strong one, which as a tempest of hail and a destroying storm, as a flood of mighty waters overflowing, shall cast down to the earth with the hand. The crown of pride, the drunkards of Ephraim, shall be trodden under feet: and the glorious beauty, which is on the head of the fat valley, shall be a fading flower, and as the hasty fruit before the summer; which when

he that looketh upon it seeth, while it is yet in his hand he eateth
it up (verses 1-4).

This gives a very vivid description of the luxurious
conditions prevailing in Samaria before the captivity.
Under Jeroboam II and the later kings of Israel, the
city of Samaria had become a grand and glorious
metropolis; built upon a high hill the sides of which
were terraced and planted with delightful gardens and
groves, it was perhaps the loveliest city in all Palestine.
The valley below, reaching to the great plain of Esdrae-
lon, or Jezreel, abounded in orchards, vineyards, and
fruitful fields. So richly had God Himself lavished His
benefits upon the people of the entire region that in
their enjoyment of His gifts they utterly forgot the
Giver and turned to idolatry of the vilest kind; idolatry
copied from the nations round about them. With the
worship of false gods they turned also to the ways of
the heathen so that, revelling in luxury, they gave
themselves to drunkenness and licentiousness until as
a people they became so corrupt that God Himself could
no longer tolerate them. Therefore, He caused the heart
of the king of Assyria to look covetously upon this
beautiful land and he came against it with a great
army. Israel, however, buoyed up by self-confidence
and a groundless optimism, scorned the power of the
invader, feeling secure in their own might. But when
the test came, their armies were utterly defeated and
the Assyrians everywhere were triumphant. Thus,
Samaria becomes for us a warning concerning the folly
of trusting in self rather than in the omnipotent power
of God. Had Israel been living for Him and worshiping Him they could have counted on Him to defend
them against every foe, but He had long since declared,

"Them that honour Me I will honour, and they that despise Me shall be lightly esteemed." So it was at that time, and so it ever will be in days to come.

> In that day shall the Lord of hosts be for a crown of glory, and for a diadem of beauty, unto the residue of his people, and for a spirit of judgment to him that sitteth in judgment, and for strength to them that turn the battle to the gate. But they also have erred through wine, and through strong drink are out of the way; the priest and the prophet have erred through strong drink, they are swallowed up of wine, they are out of the way through strong drink; they err in vision, they stumble in judgment. For all tables are full of vomit and filthiness, so that there is no place clean. Whom shall he teach knowledge? and whom shall he make to understand doctrine? them that are weaned from the milk, and drawn from the breasts. For precept must be upon precept, precept upon precept; line upon line, line upon line; here a little, and there a little: for with stammering lips and another tongue will he speak to this people. To whom he said, This is the rest wherewith ye may cause the weary to rest; and this is the refreshing: yet they would not hear. But the word of the Lord was unto them precept upon precept, precept upon precept; line upon line, line upon line; here a little, and there a little; that they might go, and fall backward, and be broken, and snared, and taken (verses 5-13).

For a moment the Lord directs the attention of His people to the coming day of His power; for the expression, "In that day," as used in the prophetic Scriptures almost invariably refers to the time when He shall arise in judgment on His enemies and for the deliverance of the remnant who put their trust in Him. Immediately after this glimpse of the coming glory, the prophet goes back to call attention to the bewildered and confused state in which the people of Judah were found, and though they gloried in having the temple of the Lord and in the fact that they remained faithful to the House of David, nevertheless, they were as far from God practically as their brethren of the north. Drunkenness, in Scripture, is often used to illustrate or represent the effects of spiritual intoxication brought about by refusing obedience to the Word of the Lord and giving heed to false teaching. Although God had so patiently dealt with His people, sending those to them who could teach them the way of righteousness, endeavoring to instruct them as one deals with little children, giving them "precept upon precept, precept upon precept; line upon line, line upon line; here a little, and there a little," as they were able to bear it, yet they had not profited by such careful teaching but had turned away from the truth and like many today accepted in its place the traditions of men. Therefore, judgment long delayed must at last fall upon them. They will still be taught by precept upon precept, precept upon precept; line upon line, line upon line; but it will be in order to prepare them for the doom that awaits all those who forsake the living God and walk in their own self-chosen paths.

In the day of the great tribulation, the time of Jacob's trouble, the apostate part of the nation will know the reality of this to the full, but in that day the Lord will deliver the faithful remnant who refused to obey the behest of the Beast and the Antichrist, and chose instead the path of obedience to the Word of God.

Because Judah refused to hear this Word, God was about to teach them the folly of departure from Himself by sending against them the armies of their enemies; men who spoke languages with which the Hebrews were not familiar. In this way He would teach them by men of stammering lips and of other tongues. In the New Testament, however, the Apostle Peter quotes this verse but applies it to the miraculous gift

of tongues when, as on the day of Pentecost, the disciples proclaimed the gospel in so many different languages. Thus with men of other tongues did He deliver
the message of grace. We need not think for a moment
that there was any misapplication of this passage. In
its primary meaning it clearly refers to the men of the
nations who were to come against Judah and teach
them by disaster what they would not learn in times of
peace, but in this gospel dispensation the Spirit of
God Himself takes up this passage and applies it as
indicated. God, who delights in mercy, deigned to use
this method in order to give men the gospel in the
quickest possible way. People today talk of the gift of
tongues and many profess to possess it, and we are told
distinctly in Scripture that we are not to forbid speaking in tongues. But where are there any who can
preach the gospel in a language they have never
learned? Should such miraculous instances occur
surely no right-minded Christian would object; but
where it is just a matter of uttering unmeaning gib-
berish we may be confident that it is not the Spirit of
God who is operating in such instances.

Wherefore hear the word of the Lord, ye scornful men, that
rule this people which is in Jerusalem. Because ye have said, We
have made a covenant with death, and with hell are we at agreement; when the overflowing scourge shall pass through, it shall not
come unto us: for we have made lies our refuge, and under falsehood have we hid ourselves (verses 14, 15).

In their immediate application, these words referred
undoubtedly to the attempt of Judah to form an alliance with Assyria or with Egypt in order to protect
them against one or the other of these two powers.
Though they thought that they had made sure

covenants, first with the one and then with the other of these nations, and they attempted to rest content with the assurance that they would thus be preserved from destruction, they were soon to find that their optimism was ill founded. That the passage has an application to the future, surely no instructed student of prophecy can question, for in the last days a covenant will be made between the "willful king" in Jerusalem, the head of the Jewish State at that time, and the "Beast," the head of the ten-kingdomed empire pictured by the ten toes on the feet of the image in Daniel 2, and the ten horns on the last beast in Daniel 7, as also the ten horns on the Beast in Revelation 13, and again in chapter 17. This covenant will be made for seven years as we are told in Daniel 9:27, but in the midst of the week, that is, at the end of three and a half years, the covenant will be broken. It is this that is described as a covenant with death and with hell. It will be the effort of the nation of Israel, returned to the Land in unbelief, to ensure protection from their foes in the east and the north, who will be looking with covetous eyes upon Palestine and its increasing wealth. They will find however that by looking to man instead of to the Lord Himself, they will fail to maintain the peace and security which they hoped thus to safeguard. Only in the Messiah whom they once rejected can lasting blessing be found. Of this the following verses speak:

Therefore thus saith the Lord God, Behold, I lay in Zion for a foundation a stone, a tried stone, a precious corner stone, a sure foundation: he that believeth shall not make haste. Judgment also will I lay to the line, and righteousness to the plummet: and the hail shall sweep away the refuge of lies, and the waters shall overflow the hiding place (verses 16, 17).

We know from 1 Peter 2:6 that the Stone here referred to is our Lord Jesus Christ Himself. He had come to Israel in lowly grace only to be rejected, but as Psalm 118:22 tells us, "The stone which the builders refused is become the head stone of the corner." All blessing for Israel and Judah, as well as for the Gentile world, is bound up with Him. To refuse God's testimony regarding His Son is to deliberately choose everlasting judgment. To receive Him means everlasting life and blessing. Alas, that Israel has been blinded for, so long, and that because of their failure to receive their King when He came in grace they have had to endure such incredible sufferings throughout the long centuries of their wanderings, and even after they return to their land they still have greater sufferings in store for them until at last they look upon Him whom they have pierced and mourn for Him as one mourneth for his only son (Zech. 12:10). When that day of trouble comes, those who refuse allegiance to the Beast and the Antichrist will wait in faith for the manifestation of this Living Stone which is to fall upon the feet of the great image of Gentile supremacy, grinding it to powder. It will be their portion to wait quietly, realizing the truth that he that believeth shall not make haste. God's plan will be fulfilled in His own time. Then righteousness and judgment will prevail and the refuge of lies will be utterly swept away.

And your covenant with death shall be disannulled, and your agreement with hell shall not stand; when the overflowing scourge shall pass through, then ye shall be trodden down by it. From the time that it goeth forth it shall take you: for morning by morning shall it pass over, by day and by night: and it shall be a vexation only to understand the report (verses 18, 19).

The Lord's appearing will destroy the refuge of lies
and annul the covenant with death and the agreement
with hell. Condign judgment will be the portion of all
those who accept the mark of the Beast and the number
of his name, but those who put their trust in Jehovah
will be vindicated and given their place in the coming
glorious kingdom of God when set up on earth in
visible power. Until that day, those who turn away
from the Lord will trust in their own plans for deliverance and will find themselves like the uncomfortable
sleeper described in the next verse:

For the bed is shorter than that a man can stretch himself on
it: and the covering narrower than that he can wrap himself in it.
For the Lord shall rise up as in mount Perazim, he shall be wroth
as in the valley of Gibeon, that he may do his work, his strange
work; and bring to pass his act, his strange act. Now, therefore be
ye not mockers, lest your bands be made strong: for I have heard
from the Lord God of hosts a consumption, even determined upon
the whole earth (verses 20-22).

As of old when God led His people through the
wilderness to the land of promise, delivering them from
their enemies by the manifestation of His own power
and enabling them to overcome, though themselves
weak compared with their foes, so in the coming day
will He deliver the remnant of His people from all
those that shall rise up against Him and pour out His
judgment upon all those that despise His name. He has
no delight in this. His heart goes out to all men everywhere. He desires that all men should be saved and
come to the knowledge of the truth. He has no pleasure
in the death of the wicked, but rather that all should
turn unto Him and live, but if men refuse His mercy
and spurn His loving-kindness, then in righteousness

He must deal with them in judgment. Judgment is His strange work, His strange act. He would far rather show mercy and save than condemn and punish. He respects the sanctity of the human will and if men will not turn to Him to find life, then they themselves deliberately choose death whether they realize it or not.

Give ye ear, and hear my voice; hearken, and hear my speech. Doth the plowman plow all day to sow? doth he open and break the clods of his ground? When he hath made plain the face thereof, doth he not cast abroad the fitches, and scatter the cummin, and cast in the principal wheat and the appointed barley and the rie in their place? For his God doth instruct him to discretion, and doth teach him. For the fitches are not threshed with a threshing instrument, neither is a cart wheel turned about upon the cummin; but the fitches are beaten out with a staff, and the cummin with a rod. Bread corn is bruised; because he will not ever be threshing it, nor break it with the wheel of his cart, nor bruise it with his horsemen. This also cometh forth from the Lord of hosts, which is wonderful in counsel, and excellent in working (verses 23-29).

Precious and important lessons are here drawn from the cultivation of herbs and cereals. First, the ground must be well prepared by plowing and then the soil further broken up by harrowing; after that the seed is cast in; and then when the herbs or grains are ready for harvest each one is dealt with in accordance with its own nature. So God seeks to break up the hard soil of man's opposition to Himself by the plowshare of His truth, and by careful instruction as to the way of life. If, when the seed has been cast into the ground of a good and honest heart, it brings forth abundantly, He has different methods of dealing with those who have responded to His truth according as they are able to bear. He does not deal with all in the same way, even as the careful farmer does not thresh the softer herbs in the way that he deals with the harder grains. Those who go forth in the name of the Lord, sowing the seed, need to have these principles in mind in order that they may deal wisely with those whom they endeavor to help.

CHAPTER TWENTY-NINE

SECOND AND THIRD WOES

AS THIS CHAPTER begins, we listen, for the second time in this section, to a woe pronounced by God through His servant, the prophet, and farther down in the chapter we have a third woe. The first message is addressed directly to Ariel, a name we have not found previously in this book, and which may be translated in two different ways. It is the same as that which is rendered "lionlike" in 2 Samuel 23:20. The margin there gives the rendering, "lion of God," but in Ezekiel 43:16 the first part of the word is translated "altar," so that Ariel might either be rendered "lion of God" or "altar of God." The reference, undoubtedly, is to Jerusalem, David's city.

Woe to Ariel, to Ariel, the city where David dwelt! add ye year to year; let them kill sacrifices. Yet I will distress Ariel, and there shall be heaviness and sorrow: and it shall be unto me as Ariel. And I will camp against thee round about, and will lay siege against thee with a mount, and I will raise forts against thee. And thou shalt be brought down, and shalt speak out of the ground, and thy speech shall be low out of the dust, and thy voice shall be, as of one that hath a familiar spirit, out of the ground, and thy speech shall whisper out of the dust. Moreover the multitude of thy strangers shall be like small dust, and the multitude of the terrible ones shall be as chaff that passeth away; yea, it shall be at an instant suddenly. Thou shalt be visited of the Lord of hosts with thunder, and with earthquake, and great noise, with storm and tempest, and the flame of devouring fire (verses 1-6).

After having taken Jerusalem, David made it his capital and built his palace on Mount Zion. In the years that followed the glory of God was manifested there in a marvelous way. In Solomon's day the temple of Jehovah was erected on Mount Moriah, another section of the Holy City. And the service of God was carried on by His anointed priests officiating as representatives of Deity, standing between God and His people to offer up their sacrifices and offerings; but as the centuries went by, declension came in. Judah turned away from the fear of the Lord; formality took the place of true spiritual worship until God Himself could no longer tolerate the unfaithfulness and hypocrisy which so frequently characterized the people with whom He had entered into covenant relationship. They had failed completely to carry out their part of the covenant; therefore, Jerusalem which had been as the lion of God should become as a great altar-hearth where its own population would be sacrificed through the ruthless enmity of their bitter foes. The reference cannot possibly be to the threatened destruction by Sennacherib and his army, for at that time God intervened to deliver Jerusalem and to destroy the Assyrian host. We must look to the future for the fulfillment of that which is here predicted. In the last days, the time of Jacob's trouble, God will gather all nations against Jerusalem to battle, as we read in Zechariah 14, and then the judgments on Ariel will be consummated. So terrible will be the sufferings of the people that they will cry to God as out of the dust, and their voices will be like the whisperings of those who profess to communicate with the spirits of the dead. Nevertheless, eventually the Lord will appear for their deliverance and for the destruction of their enemies.

And the multitude of all the nations that fight against Ariel, even all that fight against her and her munition, and that distress her, shall be as a dream of a night vision. It shall even be as when an hungry man dreameth, and, behold, he eateth; but he awaketh, and his soul is empty: or as when a thirsty man dreameth, and, behold, he drinketh; but he awaketh, and, behold, he is faint, and his soul hath appetite: so shall the multitude of all the nations be, that fight against mount Zion (verses 7, 8).

At the very time when it will seem as though Satan's effort to destroy Jerusalem utterly and to blot out the nation of Israel from the face of the earth will surely succeed, the Lord will go forth and fight against those nations that besiege Ariel as when He fought in the day of battle, and they will find themselves deprived of their prey, and after their "dream" of world conquest they will awaken to realize that they have been fighting not only against Judah but against Jehovah, whose power will completely annul their efforts to blot out the people whom He has separated to Himself. As when a hungry man dreams that he has a rich repast before him of which he is just about to partake, and then awakens to realize his starving condition; or as when a thirsty man dreams that he has an abundance of that which will refresh his parched throat, and awakens to realize that his condition is worse than before, so will it be with all those nations who will be taken in red-handed opposition to God and His people.

Stay yourselves, and wonder; cry ye out, and cry: they are drunken, but not with wine; they stagger, but not with strong drink. For the Lord hath poured out upon you the spirit of deep sleep, and hath closed your eyes: the prophets and your rulers, the seers hath he covered. And the vision of all is become unto you as the words of a book that is sealed, which men deliver to one that is learned, saying, Read this, I pray thee: and he saith, I cannot; for it is sealed: and the book is delivered to him that is not learned, saying, Read this, I pray thee: and he saith, I am not learned (verses 9-12).

Again the prophet turns to depict the reasons why God will give Judah up to judgment until the time when they turn to Him in repentance. Despite all the revelations of His will made known to them through His Word and confirmed by His prophets, they have turned away to their own devices, walking in the imaginations of their own hearts; like men surfeited with wine, they have become inebriated by the traditions of men which have made void the Word of God, and so have failed to act upon or even to comprehend the messages sent to them by the Lord. His Word has become to them unintelligible, not because it lacked in clearness of expression or in simplicity of teaching, but because they themselves were so blinded by unbelief that they read as men with a veil upon their hearts, as we are told in the New Testament (2 Cor. 3). That Word, if handed to the wise of this world, brought forth the declaration that it was sealed and therefore to them incomprehensible. If presented to the illiterate, they turned from it, declaring that they were not educated. In the New Testament we have one great prophetic book—that of The Revelation. May we not see in Israel's attitude to their prophetic records an illustration of the attitude of many in Christendom today toward this solemn book, God's final word to man before the return of His Son from heaven? How many of our so-called Christian scholars and prominent pulpiteers declare that it is useless to attempt to study the book of Revelation as it is sealed, or else a mere collection of weird dreams without meaning or coherence, while others take the ground that it is only the learned who can understand it and therefore simple Christians could not expect to unravel its mysteries. Yet the Lord Himself has twice pronounced a blessing on those who read this book and those who keep its sayings (Rev. 1:3 and 22:7).

Wherefore the Lord said, Forasmuch as this people draw near me with their mouth, and with their lips do honour me, but have removed their heart far from me, and their fear toward me is taught by the precept of men: therefore, behold, I will proceed to do a marvellous work among this people, even a marvellous work and a wonder: for the wisdom of their wise men shall perish, and the understanding of their prudent men shall be hid (verses 13, 14).

Because of this willful blindness, God will send judicial blindness so that those who had no heart for His Word will be given over to strong delusion and believe the lie of the Antichrist, that they all might be judged who obeyed not the truth but had pleasure in unrighteousness. Outwardly they kept up the form of religion, and professed to worship and honor the God of their fathers, even when in works they denied Him. Because of this, judgment, long delayed, must be poured out; and this has been true throughout all the centuries since the hand of God first fell upon them because of their disobedience to His Word and their rejection of the Saviour that He provided. In the time of the end their unbelief will come to its full consummation, when instead of the Christ of God they accept the false Messiah, the Man of Sin, and thus fill up their cup of iniquity to the brim. Then God will deal with them in unsparing judgment, destroying the apostate part of the nation, but saving a remnant who will turn to Him in that hour of desperate sorrow and will become the nucleus of the new nation to be blessed under Messiah's rule when He appears in glory to set up the kingdom of God in visible manifestation here on the earth, returning to the very city where He was crucified and from which He ascended to heaven. His feet shall stand on that day on the Mount of Olives, and He will take over His great power and reign.

Woe unto them that seek deep to hide their counsel from the Lord, and their works are in the dark, and they say, Who seeth us? and who knoweth us? Surely your turning of things upside down shall be esteemed as the potter's clay: for shall the work say of him that made it, He made me not? or shall the thing framed say of him that framed it, He had no understanding? (verses 15, 16).

Now we have the third woe pronounced upon those who presume to be wiser than God. We are at once reminded of the way in which the Apostle Paul, guided by the Holy Spirit, uses the same figure of the potter and the clay in the ninth chapter of the Epistle to the Romans. It is the greatest folly for man to strive with his Maker, to attempt to find fault with God, or to put upon Him the blame for the misery and wretchedness which he has brought upon himself by his own unbelief and waywardness. God, we are told in the book of Job, "giveth not account of any of His matters" (Job 33:13). It is well for man if he humble himself before the all-wise Creator and bow in subjection to His holy will. This alone is the path of blessing for the creature. Because of Judah's failure and that of all the nations, God has to deal in retributive justice, pouring out His wrath upon those who have refused His grace. But He will never forget His covenant with Abraham nor the promise He has made to bring blessing to all the earth through the Seed that was to come, even our Lord Jesus Christ. So in the verses that follow, we read once more of blessing to come upon Ariel and the land of Palestine after the judgments have been meted out.

Is it not yet a very little while, and Lebanon shall be turned into a fruitful field, and the fruitful field shall be esteemed as a forest? And in that day shall the deaf hear the words of the book, and the eyes of the blind shall see out of obscurity, and out of darkness. The meek also shall increase their joy in the Lord, and the poor among men shall rejoice in the Holy One of Israel. For the terrible one is brought to nought, and the scorner is consumed, and all that watch for iniquity are cut off: that make a man an offender for a word, and lay a snare for him that reproveth in the gate, and turn aside the just for a thing of nought (verses 17-21).

It is a millennial picture upon which we are now called to gaze. When the blight that has rested upon Palestine for so many centuries is removed and that country, once the glory of all lands, again becomes fruitful and populous as the redeemed of the Lord are sought out and restored from all countries of earth and brought back to their ancient patrimony, there to rejoice and flourish under Messiah's beneficent reign; then, in that day, the blindness that has veiled the heart of Israel for so long will be taken away. The Word of God will become clear and luminous to them and they will rejoice in the revelation that He has made known. The Gentile powers under which they have suffered for so long will no more affright them. The "terrible one," perhaps a direct reference to the Beast, and the "scorner," possibly the Man of Sin himself, and all who have been associated with them in their oppression of the Jew will be consumed by God and His people delivered from their power.

Therefore thus saith the Lord, who redeemed Abraham, concerning the house of Jacob, Jacob shall not now be ashamed, neither shall his face now wax pale. But when he seeth his children, the work of mine hands, in the midst of him, they shall sanctify my name, and sanctify the Holy One of Jacob, and shall fear the God of Israel. They also that erred in spirit shall come to understanding, and they that murmured shall learn doctrine (verses 22-24).

Never, in times past, have these words had their fulfillment, but we may be assured that nothing that God has spoken will ever come to naught. These words tell of a time when the spared of Israel will be all righteous because taught of God, and instead of following after the vain imagination of their own hearts, as in the past, they will be brought to the place of perfect subjection to His holy will. This will be the time when none will need to say to another, "Know the Lord," for all shall know Him, from the least to the greatest (Jer. 31:34). At that time the fullness of blessing promised to Abraham and his seed will be manifested, not only toward the natural children of him who was called the Friend of God, but all nations will be blessed with them in accordance with the promise.

CHAPTER THIRTY

JUDAH'S FAILURE—GOD'S FAITHFULNESS

ONCE more the Spirit of prophecy directs our attention to the internal condition of Judah in Isaiah's day when, threatened by the Assyrian under Sennacherib, they appealed to Egypt, that land from which they had once been delivered, for help. This, in the eyes of God, was a grievous sin, indicating their lack of confidence in Himself and their hope of securing help from the very power which had once enslaved them and from whose bondage they had been redeemed; first by blood, the blood of the passover lamb, and then by the omnipotent power of God who brought them triumphantly through the Red Sea, scattering its waters on either side and thus gathered them to Himself in the wilderness and eventually settled them in the land of promise. To go down now to Egypt for help meant that they had forgotten God's dealings with them in the past and that they no longer dared to depend on Him for their present deliverance. In the opening verses we have the fourth woe of this series.

Woe to the rebellious children, saith the Lord, that take counsel, but not of me; and that cover with a covering, but not of my spirit, that they may add sin to sin: That walk to go down into Egypt, and have not asked at my mouth; to strengthen themselves in the strength of Pharaoh, and to trust in the shadow of Egypt! Therefore shall the strength of Pharaoh be your shame, and the trust in the shadow of Egypt your confusion. For his princes were at Zoan, and his ambassadors came to Hanes. They were all ashamed of a people that could not profit them, nor be an help nor profit, but a shame, and also a reproach (verses 1-5).

The invasion of the Assyrian was but one of the evidences of God's displeasure with His people because of their waywardness. Instead of turning to the One they had sinned against, confessing their iniquities and judging themselves for their idolatry and their unreality, even in connection with the temple worship, they turned to their old enemy, hoping for assistance against the invader. It seemed, doubtless, to the leaders among them the path of wisdom thus to make a friend of Egypt in order that they might be strengthened against Assyria, but it was a mere human expedient and therefore doomed to failure. They hoped by such an alliance to ward off the impending danger. How much wiser they would have been had they taken the place of repentance toward God and sought counsel, not of worldly-minded leaders, but of God Himself who was at this time speaking to them through Isaiah and other prophets. May we not see in their attitude a lesson for ourselves today? How apt we are in times of stress to depend upon some human expedient instead of relying on the living God. It is always an evidence of declension when Christians look to the world for help rather than turning to the Lord Himself, whose chastening hand may be upon them because of unjudged sin. He always stands ready to meet His people in grace, and we are told that if we confess our sins, He is faithful and just to forgive us our sins and to cleanse us from all unrighteousness (1 John 1:9). But we are ever prone to forget this and to try to find a way out of our difficulties by human means instead of reliance upon the omnipotent God. Just as Judah involved themselves in deeper trouble by their folly in turning to Egypt, so do we always make conditions worse when, instead of looking to God, we endeavor by fleshly means to extricate ourselves from the difficult circumstances into which our own failures have plunged us.

The burden of the beasts of the south: into the land of trouble and anguish, from whence come the young and old lion, the viper and fiery flying serpent, they will carry their riches upon the shoulders of young asses, and their treasures upon the bunches of camels, to a people that shall not profit them. For the Egyptians shall help in vain, and to no purpose: therefore have I cried concerning this, Their strength is to sit still (verses 6, 7).

Egypt is depicted here as a land of ravenous beasts such as are found in African jungles. Yet to this land, Judah sent their ambassadors, bearing rich treasure loaded upon camels and asses with which they hoped to procure the favor of the Egyptian ruler. To them it seemed the only way out, and they doubtless congratulated themselves on their astuteness and political strategy in attempting to make a close ally of a former enemy. But their course was obnoxious to God because it involved utter forgetfulness of Himself. Though they did not realize it, their strength would have been manifested by quietly waiting upon God, sitting still even though the Assyrian came closer and closer to them, assured that if they but relied on the Holy One of Israel, in His own due time He would grant complete deliverance.

It is always difficult to wait for God to intervene. We have instance after instance in Scripture of those who only brought trouble upon themselves by precipitate action, feeling that something must be done in order to stave off disaster, whereas had they but left the matter in the hands of God, He would have risen up in ample time to fulfill His own purposes of grace. We need to distinguish between waiting on God and waiting for God. It is one thing to go to Him in the hour of stress and implore His delivering power; it is another thing to rest quietly in a sense of His infinite love and wisdom until He sees that the hour has struck to act on our behalf.

Now go, write it before them in a table, and note it in a book, that it may be for the time to come for ever and ever: that this is a rebellious people, lying children, children that will not hear the law of the Lord: which say to the seers, See not; and to the prophets, Prophesy not unto us right things, speak unto us smooth things, prophesy deceits: get you out of the way, turn aside out of the path, cause the Holy One of Israel to cease from before us. Wherefore thus saith the Holy One of Israel, Because ye despise this word, and trust in oppression and perverseness, and stay thereon: therefore this iniquity shall be to you as a breach ready to fall, swelling out in a high wall, whose breaking cometh suddenly at an instant. And he shall break it as the breaking of the potters' vessel that is broken in pieces; he shall not spare: so that there shall not be found in the bursting of it a sherd to take fire from the hearth, or to take water withal out of the pit (verses 8-14).

It is clear from these words that God intended the record of Judah's failure to be a salutary lesson to His people in future generations. For this purpose He would have all written in a book that it might be handed down from generation to generation. He knew well that even as in Isaiah's time many in centuries yet to come would refuse to hear His voice and would seek to silence the messengers, turning away from the truth and going after false prophets, because like so many

in Christendom today they had itching ears and pre-
ferred that which was pleasant and agreeable to that
which called for self-judgment and repentance. We
need not suppose that the people of Judah said in so
many words what is here recorded, but their attitude
expressed what was in their hearts. Is not this just
as true of vast numbers today? Outwardly they profess
reverence for the Holy Scriptures and for the authority
of our Lord Jesus Christ, but their lives make it evident that they are without any real faith, nor have
they any love for God's truth when it runs contrary to
their own desires. Such a course, on the part of any
who profess the name of the Lord, can only bring down
judgment upon those who thus turn away from the
truth and follow after that which pleases the flesh and
seems to the natural or the carnal mind far more satisfactory than dependence upon the Word of God.
Though Judah realized it not, they were like people
standing beside a high wall whose foundations had
been undermined and which was already bulging and
about to fall upon them. Or, like a potter's vessel which
was soon to be broken into so many pieces that not one
sherd could be found large enough to take up water
or to be of any use whatever.

For thus saith the Lord God, the Holy One of Israel: In returning and rest shall ye be saved; in quietness and in confidence shall
be your strength: and ye would not. But ye said, No; for we will
flee upon horses; therefore shall ye flee; and, We will ride upon
the swift; therefore shall they that pursue you be swift. One thousand shall flee at the rebuke of one; at the rebuke of five shall ye
flee: till ye be left as a beacon upon the top of a mountain, and
as an ensign on an hill (verses 15-17).

Beautiful, indeed, are the words of verse 15—words
that are ever true for the people of God, no matter

what they are called upon to suffer or endure. It is as we learn to wait upon God, returning to Him in confession of past failure and resting upon His assurance of present forgiveness and cleansing, that we find not only peace of conscience but peace of heart; salvation from whatever it may be that has caused unrest and fear.

As we look to the living God in simple faith, ceasing from all self-effort, refusing to look to the world for that help which God alone can give, we find strength to lift us above the trial. But the people of Judah refused to receive this message. Willfully they turned away from the advice of the prophet, whom God had sent to call them back to Himself. They would not heed His Word, nor cease from man whose breath is in his nostrils. How often has the Lord had to say to those whose unbelief grieved His heart, "I would, but ye would not."

All preparations were made to flee upon horses at the approach of the enemy if help did not arrive in time, for they knew in their hearts that their dependence on Egypt might, after all, prove to be in vain. "Therefore," said God, "shall ye flee," and though they trusted in the swiftness of their steeds to enable them to evade capture, the enemy would be swifter than they and overtake and destroy them. When God brought them out of Egypt and led them through the wilderness, He told them that if they walked in obedience to His Word they need never fear their enemy for, in the day of battle, through the might of Jehovah, one should chase a thousand, and two should put ten thousand to flight (Lev. 26:8). Now, however, because of their unbelief and disobedience, conditions would be reversed, and a thousand of Judah would flee from one Assyrian, and all of them before five of their ruthless enemies. What folly for men to put their confidence in flesh, only to prove, as so many have done, that the flesh profiteth nothing.

But once again, after having sought to reach their consciences, God, in remembrance of His covenant, declares that when His people have been chastened because of their sins He will bring them into blessing eventually, and so we read:

> And therefore will the Lord wait, that he may be gracious unto you, and therefore will he be exalted, that he may have mercy upon you: for the Lord is a God of judgment: blessed are all they that wait for him. For the people shall dwell in Zion at Jerusalem: thou shalt weep no more: he will be very gracious unto thee at the voice of thy cry; when he shall hear it, he will answer thee. And though the Lord give you the bread of affliction, yet shall not thy teachers be removed into a corner any more, but thine eyes shall see thy teachers: and thine ears shall hear a word behind thee, saying, This is the way, walk ye in it, when ye turn to the right hand, and when ye turn to the left (verses 18-21).

Clearly the prophecy here speaks of millennial blessing when, after all the centuries of the sufferings of Israel and Judah, they shall return to the Lord and find in Him that forgiveness which He is always ready to bestow upon the contrite and penitent heart. In that day, the day of Jehovah's power, He will bring them into everlasting blessedness: the sufferings of the past will seem but as an evil dream from which they have awakened, as they look up into the face of the Messiah they once despised and rejected, and find in Him an all-sufficient Saviour. No longer will they be led astray by the wisdom of man or by false visions, but led by the Lord Himself they will be guided in paths of righteousness. Even when there might seem to be danger of turning away, either to the right hand or to the left, His own voice will direct them, saying, "This is the way, walk ye in it." All tears will then be wiped away and all their sufferings past forever.

Surely no one can think that these words have ever been fulfilled in the past. They point forward to that which will be Israel's glorious portion in the day when their lessons have been learned and they become subject to the instruction of Him whose mandates they once refused to obey.

Ye shall defile also the covering of thy graven images of silver, and the ornament of thy molten images of gold: thou shalt cast them away as a menstruous cloth; thou shalt say unto it, Get thee hence. Then shall he give the rain of thy seed, that thou shalt sow the ground withal; and bread of the increase of the earth, and it shall be fat and plenteous: in that day shall thy cattle feed in large pastures. The oxen likewise and the young asses that ear the ground shall eat clean provender, which hath been winnowed with the shovel and with the fan. And there shall be upon every high mountain, and upon every high hill, rivers and streams of waters in the day of the great slaughter, when the towers fall. Moreover the light of the moon shall be as the light of the sun, and the light of the sun shall be sevenfold, as the light of seven days, in the day that the Lord bindeth up the breach of his people, and healeth the stroke of their wound (verses 22-26).

Idolatry had often been their ruin in times past, but in that coming day they will abhor themselves as they remember the folly of which they have been guilty, in forsaking the one true and living God for the worship of senseless images which could neither see nor hear, and were unable to deliver them from the dangers that beset them. Casting their idols to one side, they will find their joy in the Lord and He will feed them with the living bread and refresh them with the water of life. No doubt verse 23 will have a literal fulfillment, for in Messiah's day He will satisfy the poor with bread, but we are surely warranted in seeing in it a promise of great spiritual blessing, for God's Word is as food to the heart of him who meditates upon it, strengthening him in the inner man that he may know the will of God and have the power to do it. The streams of living water, too, which flow down from the hills and the mountains may well speak to us of that river of the water of life, the Holy Ghost's testimony to the risen Christ, which will bring joy to the heart of the people of God, not only in the heavenly sphere, but also in the earthly side of the kingdom yet to be set up.

Behold, the name of the Lord cometh from far, burning with his anger, and the burden thereof is heavy: his lips are full of indignation, and his tongue as a devouring fire: and his breath, as an overflowing stream, shall reach to the midst of the neck, to sift the nations with the sieve of vanity: and there shall be a bridle in the jaws of the people, causing them to err. Ye shall have a song, as in the night when a holy solemnity is kept; and gladness of heart, as when one goeth with a pipe to come into the mountain of the Lord, to the mighty One of Israel. And the Lord shall cause his glorious voice to be heard, and shall shew the lighting down of his arm, with the indignation of his anger, and with the flame of a devouring fire, with scattering, and tempest, and hailstones. For through the voice of the Lord shall the Assyrian be beaten down, which smote with a rod. And in every place where the grounded staff shall pass, which the Lord shall lay upon him, it shall be with tabrets and harps: and in battles of shaking will he fight with it. For Tophet is ordained of old; yea, for the king it is prepared; he hath made it deep and large: the pile thereof is fire and much wood; the breath of the Lord, like a stream of brimstone, doth kindle it (verses 27-33).

These closing verses speak of mingled judgment and blessing. Judgment upon the nations who, throughout the centuries, have sorely afflicted Israel, and blessing upon the covenant people when they return to the Lord and all His promises of both temporal and spiritual prosperity are fulfilled toward them. Undoubtedly, the judgments spoken of refer, in the first instance, to those which fell upon Sennacherib and his armies; but they surely go far beyond that, reaching down to the last days when another great Gentile power, as we have seen, will rise up in its God-defying might and seek to destroy Judah and take possession of Immanuel's land. In His indignation the Lord will pour out the vials of His wrath upon the Assyrian of that coming day so that his destruction will be complete and eternal. With him, too, will fall judgment upon every other enemy who has threatened the peace of the covenant nation.

The last verse is of a somewhat cryptic character, but with the help of other scriptures we need not have difficulty in understanding it. We should remember that no prophecy of Scripture is of its own interpretation, as we are told in 2 Peter 1:20. "Private interpretation" there does not mean the effort of an individual to understand the Scriptures apart from the instruction of ecclesiastical authorities, as taught by the Roman Catholic Church, but the point is that all the prophecies of Scripture need to be considered as one whole, for they are all given by the same Spirit, and are intimately connected one with the other. So here we read that Tophet is ordained of old, "yea, for the king it is prepared," or a better rendering would be, "for the king also it is prepared." The Assyrian we know, but who is the king here referred to? If we turn to Daniel 11:36 we read of the willful "king" who will head up the apostate Jewish nation during the time of the great tribulation. He is clearly identical with the Man of Sin, the Lawless One of 2 Thessalonians 2, and also with the second beast who looks like a lamb but speaks like a dragon, of Revelation 13. Both this sinister one and the "Beast" will be cast alive into a lake of fire, as we know from Revelation 19:19, 20. Some would identify the Assyrian with the Beast, and this may, perhaps, be correct, though to the present writer the two seem to be very distinct personages, the Beast being the little horn of Daniel 7 and the Assyrian, or king of the north, the little horn of Daniel 8. The doom of all of these enemies of God and His people will be everlasting destruction from the presence of the Lord and from the glory of His power.

Tophet was of old the lowest part of the valley of the Son of Hinnom, that is, Gehenna, the place where the filth and refuse of the city of Jerusalem was consumed, together with the carcases of criminals and of beasts. In the days of Israel's worst idolatry, it was there that the image of Moloch was set up, and to this vile god human sacrifices were offered, little children and young maidens being cast alive into the red-hot arms of the monstrous image that was itself a burning furnace, heated red hot. As the priests of Moloch beat their drums and chanted their idolatrous songs to drown out the cries of the burning victims, God looked down with abhorrence upon the terrible iniquity thus manifested, and so Tophet became the synonym for the lowest hell; and into that place of outer darkness will be cast the last enemies of God as the Day of the Lord is ushered in and man's day comes to a close.

CHAPTER THIRTY-ONE

REMONSTRANCE WITH PROMISE OF FUTURE BLESSING

IT SEEMS evident that the message of the previous chapter made little or no impression upon the king and the nobles of Judah. Therefore, the Lord again sent His servant, Isaiah, to warn them against the folly of still looking to Egypt for help, and so we have the fifth woe, which is practically the same in character as the fourth, already considered.

> Woe to them that go down to Egypt for help; and stay on horses, and trust in chariots, because they are many; and in horsemen, because they are very strong; but they look not unto the Holy One of Israel, neither seek the Lord! Yet he also is wise, and will bring evil, and will not call back his words: but will arise against the house of the evildoers, and against the help of them that work iniquity (verses 1, 2).

With a stinging rebuke, Jehovah reproves those who in the time of national danger turn to Egypt for help instead of looking to Him who had of old brought them forth triumphantly out of Egypt and had given them His holy covenant, promising blessing and deliverance so long as they walked in obedience to His Word. This they failed to do, and so when emergencies arose, they sought help from that power which had formerly enslaved them, and which, as we know, speaks to us typically of the world from which Christ delivered us by

195

giving Himself for us on the Cross. For a Christian today to turn back to that world, rather than to depend on the living God, is to dishonor the name of Him who has thus redeemed us to Himself. He has promised never to fail the soul that trusts Him, but we all know how easy it is to forget this when difficulties arise which seem to put us in jeopardy, and so in our desperation we seek help where it is not to be found instead of turning directly to Him who has said, "I will never leave thee, nor forsake thee." Whether He speaks in grace or in judgment, He will never go back on His word, but this we are slow to believe, often fancying in our folly that He will be better than His word or fearing that He may not carry out His promises of blessing. His faithfulness abides whether we believe it or not.

Now the Egyptians are men, and not God; and their horses flesh, and not spirit. When the Lord shall stretch out his hand, both he that helpeth shall fall, and he that is holpen shall fall down, and they all shall fail together (verse 3).

We are told elsewhere, "It is the Spirit that quickeneth; the flesh profiteth nothing." To Israel, Egypt seemed to speak of great strength and power which if acting on their behalf would meet the opposition of the Assyrian and effectually prevent his taking possession of Jerusalem and the land of Judah. But their hopes were vain, for only in God was true power to be found and the Egyptians knew Him not nor did God recognize them as His direct agents at this time. For the people of Judah to put their dependence upon Egypt was to make the mistake of supposing that the arm of flesh could save. By so doing they ignored the arm of the Lord which was mighty in power. Egyptian cavalry might make a brave showing, but their horses were flesh and not spirit, therefore not to be depended on in the day of battle.

For thus hath the Lord spoken unto me, Like as the lion and the young lion roaring on his prey, when a multitude of shepherds is called forth against him, he will not be afraid of their voice, nor abase himself for the noise of them: so shall the Lord of hosts come down to fight for mount Zion, and for the hill thereof. As birds flying, so will the Lord of hosts defend Jerusalem; defending also he will deliver it; and passing over he will preserve it (verses 4, 5).

While the Assyrian armies seemed almost invulnerable and, therefore, the help of Egypt appeared to be necessary, the Lord Himself still had His people in mind and would soon demonstrate His omnipotence in the destruction of the mighty host that came up against Jerusalem. Undoubtedly the prophecy referred directly to that of which we read later on when the army of Sennacherib was destroyed in a night, and that not by weapons of war but by the breath of Jehovah. A greater fulfillment will take place in the future when God will arise to destroy all who come up against Jerusalem in the last days. The hosts of all nations will, as we know, be gathered together against that devoted city, but when it appears as though all hope is gone, the Lord will arise in His might and go forth to fight against them as when He fought in the day of battle. When He shall be revealed from heaven in flaming fire, taking vengeance on those who know not God, the enemies of Israel will melt away at His presence and their leaders be dealt with in summary judgment.

In view of this, the Lord again calls upon His people to turn to Him in repentance, acknowledging their sins and putting away all their graven images and turning from all idolatrous practices.

Turn ye unto him from whom the children of Israel have deeply revolted. For in that day every man shall cast away his idols of silver, and his idols of gold, which your own hands have made unto you for a sin. Then shall the Assyrian fall with the sword, not of a mighty man; and the sword, not of a mean man, shall devour him: but he shall flee from the sword, and his young men shall be discomfited. And he shall pass over to his strong hold for fear, and his princes shall be afraid of the ensign, saith the Lord, whose fire is in Zion, and his furnace in Jerusalem (verses 6-9).

When Judah shall thus turn to the Lord and do works meet for repentance by cleansing the land of all their evil practices, God Himself will act on their behalf, and the enemy whose power they dreaded will become subservient to them, recognizing them as the chosen of the Lord. Instead of hating or despising them and seeking their ruin, the Gentile powers will acknowledge them as the favored of Jehovah and will seek their favor, as many other scriptures testify.

CHAPTER THIRTY-TWO

PREPARATIONS FOR THE COMING KINGDOM

B EFORE uttering the sixth woe, which is a proclamation of judgment upon Assyria, we have
here a message of hope and comfort for the
afflicted people of God, setting before them the glorious
Messianic kingdom to be ushered in at the second advent of our Lord Jesus Christ. He Himself is brought
definitely before us in the opening verses:

> Behold, a king shall reign in righteousness, and princes shall
> rule in judgment. And a man shall be as an hiding place from the
> wind, and a covert from the tempest; as rivers of water in a dry
> place, as the shadow of a great rock in a weary land (verses 1, 2).

We have no difficulty in identifying the righteous
King here spoken of. He can be none other than God's
Anointed, who was rejected when He came to Israel
telling of the kingdom then at hand. Refused by those
He came to deliver, He has gone into the far country to
receive for Himself a kingdom from the Father's hand
and to return in due time (Luke 19:12). David foresaw
His glorious reign as he exclaimed, "A righteous ruler
over men; a ruler in the fear of God" (2 Sam. 23:3,
literal rendering). When He returns to take over the
reins of government He will associate with Himself as
princes and judges certain ones taken from among

those who have been faithful to Him in the time of His rejection.

He comes before us here, not only as a King but as a Saviour. Beautiful are the figures used by the prophet as he declares, "a man shall be as an hiding place from the wind, and a covert from the tempest." It is Christ Himself bearing the brunt of the storm of judgment in order to provide shelter for all who flee to Him for refuge. Elsewhere we have seen Him as the Rock of Ages, in whose cleft the troubled soul can find a hiding-place. He is pictured, too, as a rock in a desert land, giving shelter from the fierce heat of the sun; another lovely illustration of that salvation which He provides so freely for all who put their trust in Him.

And the eyes of them that see shall not be dim, and the ears of them that hear shall hearken. The heart also of the rash shall understand knowledge, and the tongue of the stammerers shall be ready to speak plainly (verses 3, 4).

Those who find in Christ an all-sufficient Saviour obtain their instruction through His Word whereby they grow in grace and knowledge and are kept from the path of the destroyer. No matter how simple or untaught one may be when he first comes to Christ, nor how unaccustomed he may have been to receiving instruction and help through another, he will find all needed knowledge and wisdom in Him who delights to open up the truth to those who seek to be subject to His Word.

The vile person shall be no more called liberal, nor the churl said to be bountiful. For the vile person will speak villany, and his heart will work iniquity, to practise hypocrisy, and to utter error against the Lord, to make empty the soul of the hungry, and he will cause the drink of the thirsty to fail. The instruments also of

the churl are evil: he deviseth wicked devices to destroy the poor
with lying words, even when the needy speaketh right. But the
liberal deviseth liberal things; and by liberal things shall he stand
(verses 5-8).

On the other hand, the churl, that is, the crafty one,
who plays fast and loose with divine truth, need not
expect to find spiritual illumination as he pursues his
self-chosen way. In the day of Jehovah's power, all
such persons will be dealt with in judgment and will no
longer be acknowledged as teachers or directors of
others. Their true character will be fully manifested
and they will be judged accordingly. These haughty
despisers will no longer be permitted to mislead,
whereas those who have learned of God the way of
righteousness and found delight in walking in it will be
honored of Him and find their place in His kingdom,
there to be rewarded in accordance with the manner in
which they have dispensed to others that which God
has bestowed upon them. Our Lord has said, "freely ye
have received, freely give."

Rise up, ye women that are at ease; hear my voice, ye careless
daughters; give ear unto my speech. Many days and years shall ye
be troubled, ye careless women: for the vintage shall fail, the gathering shall not come. Tremble, ye women that are at ease; be
troubled, ye careless ones: strip you, and make you bare, and gird
sackcloth upon your loins. They shall lament for the teats, for the
pleasant fields, for the fruitful vine (verses 9-12).

In the third chapter the Lord had sternly rebuked
the daughters of Zion who lived in vanity and frivolity,
despising the Lord and thinking only of self-gratifica-
tion. Now He speaks again to those whose consciences
should have been active and who ought, therefore, to
have guided others in the way of righteousness but who

failed to realize that the judgments of God were soon to fall upon them and who lived only for the present moment, surrounding themselves with every luxury, and delighting themselves in worldly follies of every description. The day was soon to come when poverty would rob them of all these things which had ministered to their selfish desires, and they would realize at last the folly of forgetting God and thinking only of carnal pleasure and self-indulgence. When the fields and vineyards should be destroyed by invading armies and other means of sustenance come to an end, they would realize too late how foolish they had been in forgetting their responsibility to glorify God.

Upon the land of my people shall come up thorns and briers; yea, upon all the houses of joy in the joyous city: because the palaces shall be forsaken; the multitude of the city shall be left; the forts and towers shall be for dens for ever, a joy of wild asses, a pasture of flocks (verses 13, 14).

Again we have a prophecy which was not fulfilled in Isaiah's day but looked beyond to the siege and fall of Jerusalem under Nebuchadnezzar, and even later yet, to the grievous woes of the great tribulation. Jerusalem means, "Founded in peace," but this city has suffered more from war and strife than perhaps any other single city in the history of the world, and still greater horrors are in store for it in the future, immediately before the return of the Lord to reign as King on Mount Zion. It will never know lasting peace until that day.

Until the spirit be poured upon us from on high, and the wilderness be a fruitful field, and the fruitful field be counted for a forest. Then judgment shall dwell in the wilderness, and righteousness remain in the fruitful field. And the work of righteousness shall be peace; and the effect of righteousness quietness and assurance for ever. And my people shall dwell in a peaceable habitation, and in sure dwellings, and in quiet resting places; when it shall hail, coming down on the forest; and the city shall be low in a low place (verses 15-19).

Scripture not only teaches a first and second coming of our Lord Jesus Christ; it also predicts a first and second coming of the Holy Spirit. His first coming, to baptize believers into one body and empower them to carry His gospel throughout the world, occurred at Pentecost. Peter applied the words of Joel 2 to what then took place, not as indicating that the prophecy was exhausted by that outpouring, but that it was of the same character as what was yet to come when Israel shall be brought back to God and the Spirit poured out upon them from on high and all the spared nations be blessed accordingly. It is of this the present passage speaks. What a time of blessing it will be for this poor world when war and strife have come to an end; sickness and sorrow flee away; poverty and distress disappear; and men will enjoy the loving favor of the Lord and find every need met in abundance. So fruitful will the earth be at that time that a garden of herbs will become as a forest and the wilderness, as we are told elsewhere, will blossom as the rose. It is a great mistake to try to spiritualize all this and deny a coming literal fulfillment. There will, indeed, be great spiritual blessings at that time, but linked with the spiritual will be the literal fulfillment of this and other prophecies. The peace of God, which passeth all understanding, will be the portion of those who enter the kingdom and enjoy the blessings of Messiah's reign, but we may be sure that the promise that they shall dwell in a peaceable habitation is to be taken in absolute literalness. There will be protection from every ill when Messiah takes over the reins of government.

Blessed are ye that sow beside all waters, that send forth thither the feet of the ox and the ass (verse 20).

Until these promises of future blessing are all fulfilled, it is the responsibility of those who look for such things in faith to continue patiently sowing the seed of the Word of God and looking to Him to give an abundant harvest. This last verse of the chapter may well be taken to heart by all of God's servants in the present dispensation, for the blessing is for us today as truly as for the remnant of Israel in the time of Jacob's trouble, as we go forth weeping, bearing precious seed, assured that we shall come again with rejoicing, bringing our sheaves with us.

CHAPTER THIRTY-THREE

THE SIXTH WOE AND PROMISES
OF BLESSING

WE NOW COME to the last of the series of six woes, and this one is pronounced upon the enemies of the people of God, primarily Assyria, but also including the other nations that have sought to destroy Israel and Judah.

Woe to thee that spoilest, and thou wast not spoiled; and dealest treacherously and they dealt not treacherously with thee! when thou shalt cease to spoil, thou shalt be spoiled; and when thou shalt make an end to deal treacherously, they shall deal treacherously with thee (verse 1).

In all God's ways with men the principle abides true that whatsoever a man soweth, that shall he also reap. This applies to nations as well as to individuals. The powers that have wreaked their vengeance upon Israel unprovoked must in turn be visited with judgment after God has used them for the chastening of His people. As we look back over the pages of history we can see how these words have been fulfilled many times in connection with the different nations under whom the Jews have suffered so terribly. One need only instance Assyria, Babylon, Egypt, and the Roman Empire of old, as well as more modern nations like Spain, Poland, Russia, and Germany. Those who in future days will rise up to oppress the covenant people will be permitted to go only as far as God in His infinite wisdom and justice deems well, then they in turn will be destroyed and Israel delivered.

O Lord, be gracious unto us; we have waited for thee: be thou their arm every morning, our salvation also in the time of trouble (verse 2).

This is the cry of the remnant both in the past and as it will be in the future in the days of the Beast and the Antichrist. They are devoted to destruction but find deliverance as they look up to the God of their fathers and turn to Him in repentance. Then He will intervene on their behalf, stretching forth His hand of power to save and comfort.

At the noise of the tumult the people fled; at the lifting up of thyself the nations were scattered. And your spoil shall be gathered like the gathering of the caterpiller: as the running to and fro of locusts shall he run upon them (verses 3, 4).

Faith counts on God, and looks at the things that are not as though they are. It is still the voice of the remnant, declaring the might of Jehovah and His interference on their behalf.

The Lord is exalted; for he dwelleth on high: he hath filled Zion with judgment and righteousness. And wisdom and knowledge shall be the stability of thy times, and strength of salvation: the fear of the Lord is his treasure (verses 5, 6).

The hearts of those who confide in Him are moved to worship and thanksgiving as they see by faith His kingdom established over all the earth. It is surely a grievous misapplication of the scope of the prophetic Scriptures to spiritualize all this and to make Zion mean the Church, the Body of Christ. Throughout all these chapters every sober expositor recognizes the fact that the judgments predicted have fallen or are yet to fall upon the Jews or their oppressors. Surely then, it is very inconsistent to apply the blessings to the Church of the present age. Certainly the same people who have suffered at the hands of the Gentiles because of their disobedience to the Word of God are identical, nationally, with those who will participate in the privileges of the kingdom of God when it is set up in this world and Mount Zion will be the center of blessing for the whole earth.

> Behold, their valiant ones shall cry without: the ambassadors of peace shall weep bitterly. The highways lie waste, the wayfaring man ceaseth: he hath broken the covenant, he hath despised the cities, he regardeth no man. The earth mourneth and languisheth: Lebanon is ashamed and hewn down: Sharon is like a wilderness; and Bashan and Carmel shake off their fruits (verses 7-9).

The covenant referred to here doubtless was that which the Jews attempted to make with Egypt in order, as we have seen, to strengthen themselves against the Assyrian; a covenant which was to prove absolutely valueless. But we may also see in these verses a picture of the desolation that shall come in the last days when the covenant made between the Beast and the head of the Jewish State for seven years, as foretold in Daniel 9, will be broken in the midst of the week, and almost incredible sufferings will fall upon the remnant who, in that day, will refuse to worship the abomination of desolation, as predicted by our Lord in Matthew 24. Other scriptures have shown us something of the desolation that will come upon the land because of the apostasy of the mass when the day of the Lord begins.

Now will I rise, saith the Lord; now will I be exalted; now
will I lift up myself. Ye shall conceive chaff, ye shall bring forth
stubble: your breath, as fire, shall devour you. And the people shall
be as the burnings of lime: as thorns cut up shall they be burned
in the fire (verses 10-12).

No machinations of the apostate mass, the enemies of
the Lord in the last days, will avail to turn away the
judgments of the Lord. When He arises to shake terribly the earth, His power will brook no attempted interference on the part of men who deny His name. On
those also who honor His name with their lips but in
works deny Him, His judgments will surely fall.

Hear, ye that are far off, what I have done; and, ye that are
near, acknowledge my might. The sinners in Zion are afraid; fearfulness hath surprised the hypocrites. Who among us shall dwell
with the devouring fire? who among us shall dwell with everlasting
burnings? (verses 13, 14).

The sinners in Zion are those referred to above who,
while professing reverence for the name of Jehovah,
manifest their unbelief by the godlessness of their lives.
When God arises to deal with them, their religious pretensions will fail them and they will learn at last that
the hypocrite's hope shall perish. Only that which is
real can abide the Day of Jehovah.

The questions of verse 14 have, I think, often been
misunderstood. The prophet is not speaking here of
that which Scripture clearly teaches elsewhere, namely,
the everlasting punishment of the finally impenitent.
The "everlasting burnings" are not the fires of hell
but the holiness of God, before which no unrighteous
man can stand, whatever his pretensions to piety may
be. The verses that follow give the answer to the passage. "Our God is a consuming fire" (Heb. 12:29).

They only can abide before Him who have judged themselves in His holy presence and are seeking now to walk before Him in truth and uprightness.

He that walketh righteously, and speaketh uprightly; he that despiseth the gain of oppressions, that shaketh his hands from holding of bribes, that stoppeth his ears from hearing of blood, and shutteth his eyes from seeing evil; He shall dwell on high: his place of defence shall be the munitions of rocks: bread shall be given him; his waters shall be sure. Thine eyes shall see the king in his beauty: they shall behold the land that is very far off (verses 15-17).

Here we have the only possible answer to the question of the verses above. This is in full accord with Psalm 15:1-3. While in every dispensation all who are saved will owe everything for eternity to the propitiatory work of our Lord Jesus Christ, yet the proof that one has really been born of God and justified before His face is seen in a righteous life and in humble submission to His holy will. To the remnant, who will be characterized by subjection to God and integrity in their dealings with their fellows, these promises will be made real. These shall behold the King in all His beauty and glory when He returns to fulfill prophetic scripture. They shall behold the land, that is, the land promised by God of old to Abraham's seed, far extended, rather than "far off," as our Authorized Version reads. From the River of Egypt to the Euphrates, all will be the inheritance of Israel when restored to God.

Thine heart shall meditate terror. Where is the scribe? where is the receiver? where is he that counted the towers? Thou shalt not see a fierce people, a people of a deeper speech than thou canst perceive; of a stammering tongue, that thou canst not understand (verses 18, 19).

It will be remembered that the Apostle Paul quotes part of these words when he is expressing the limitations of the human mind in regard to divine ministries (1 Cor. 1:20). Who, unaided by the Spirit of God, would ever have understood His purpose of blessing for that nation which refused His Son and called down upon their own heads the awful malediction, "His blood be on us, and on our children"? In spite of all their waywardness, His counsels shall stand and He will bring them at last into blessing, not only for the millennial age but throughout eternity. No matter what they may be called upon to suffer in the interim through the fierceness and hatred of the persecuting nations, they will emerge at last triumphant over all their foes and be brought into fullness of blessing when the Lord Jesus descends to vindicate every promise that God has given. No longer will those who revere His name be called upon to endure reproach and suffering because of their faithfulness to Himself.

Look upon Zion, the city of our solemnities: thine eyes shall see Jerusalem a quiet habitation, a tabernacle that shall not be taken down; not one of the stakes thereof shall ever be removed, neither shall any of the cords thereof be broken. But there the glorious Lord will be unto us a place of broad rivers and streams; wherein shall go no galley with oars, neither shall gallant ship pass thereby. For the Lord is our judge, the Lord is our lawgiver, the Lord is our king; he will save us. Thy tacklings are loosed; they could not well strengthen their mast, they could not spread the sail: then is the prey of a great spoil divided; the lame take the prey. And the inhabitant shall not say, I am sick: the people that dwell therein shall be forgiven their iniquity (verses 20-24).

Glorious is the prospect here presented. Jerusalem, so long a city of strife and warfare, will become a peaceful habitation, for the Prince of Peace will dwell there and His law go forth to all the world. Isolated as Jerusalem has been, with no close seaport, in that day the Lord Himself will be its defense and will be to the people of the Holy City as a broad river, but a river wherein no enemy ship shall ever sail but where God will be the protector of His people. Sorrow and sickness will flee away and the weakest of the children of God will be stronger than the most powerful foes of the past. It is those who recognize their own lameness and insufficiency who overcome, because of their reliance on almighty power. While we should be careful not to take such a passage as this out of its setting and give it direct application to the Church of the present age, nevertheless, it has spiritual lessons for us from which we may well profit. It tells us what Scripture elsewhere ever emphasizes, that vain is the help of man but that he who relies upon the living God need fear no foe, whether human or demonic. Faith is ever the victory that overcomes the world, the flesh, and the devil.

THE DAY OF JEHOVAH'S VENGEANCE

THIS chapter, and that which follows, link very closely with what we have already considered, the one setting forth the judgment that is to fall upon the enemies of God and His chosen people, Israel, and the other telling of the blessing which this long-despised people shall enjoy under Messiah's benevolent despotism. We cannot read chapter thirty-four without thinking of many other passages of Scripture which clearly tell us of the same stupendous events. First, we have the doom of all the nations that shall come against Judah and Jerusalem in the last days.

Come near, ye nations, to hear; and hearken, ye people: let the earth hear, and all that is therein; the world, and all things that come forth of it. For the indignation of the Lord is upon all nations, and his fury upon all their armies: he hath utterly destroyed them, he hath delivered them to the slaughter. Their slain also shall be cast out, and their stink shall come up out of their carcases, and the mountains shall be melted with their blood (verses 1-3).

This prophecy is in perfect harmony with Revelation 19:19-21. In fact, these words of Isaiah might be looked upon as a commentary on, and explanation of, the vision found in the Apocalypse. It coincides also very closely with the first part of the 14th chapter of the book of Zechariah. When all nations shall be gathered together against Jerusalem, Jehovah will go forth and fight against them, we are told, as when He fought in the day of battle. In that day, the feet of our blessed Lord will stand upon the Mount of Olives when He returns to deliver His earthly people and to vindicate the promises of God made to them by all the prophets of old.

And all the host of heaven shall be dissolved, and the heavens shall be rolled together as a scroll: and all their host shall fall down, as the leaf falleth off from the vine, and as a falling fig from the fig tree (verse 4).

This, in turn, links with the judgment under the sixth seal in the book of Revelation, and also carries our minds on to the end of time, as predicted in Psalm 102:26 and Hebrews 1:11. It would seem as though the first fulfillment must be taken in a poetic or symbolic sense, that is, we are to understand by the heavens, the sun, and the stars, not the literal heavenly bodies but rather the ruling Gentile civil and ecclesiastical powers of the last days. Whereas the other two passages would seem clearly to point to the passing away of present conditions entirely, in order to bring in the new heavens and the new earth wherein dwelleth righteousness. One need have no difficulty in regard to this double application, for we have the same thing elsewhere in Scripture and that in a number of places. God often uses symbolic language to describe certain events which may later have a literal fulfillment. For instance, our Lord tells us of great earthquakes which will prevail immediately before His second advent. In the book of Revelation we read of such great earthquakes, but there, in accordance with the symbolic character of the book, they have to do with the shaking and breaking down of existing institutions, the destruction of civilization as we now know it.

The following verses deal particularly with the judgment which is to fall upon Idumea, a judgment that has never yet taken place but we may be assured will be fulfilled literally in the end days.

> For my sword shall be bathed in heaven: behold, it shall come down upon Idumea, and upon the people of my curse, to judgment. The sword of the Lord is filled with blood, it is made fat with fatness, and with the blood of lambs and goats, with the fat of the kidneys of rams: for the Lord hath a sacrifice in Bozrah, and a great slaughter in the land of Idumea. And the unicorns shall come down with them, and the bullocks with the bulls; and their land shall be soaked with blood, and their dust made fat with fatness. For it is the day of the Lord's vengeance, and the year of recompences for the controversy of Zion (verses 5-8).

God declared that He would cut off the people of Edom (Obadiah 18) ; and in the last days there will be a people in the land of Idumea where once the Dukes of Edom reigned, whose envy of and hatred toward the sons of Jacob will be as great as that of the Edomites of old. Upon these, unsparing judgment will fall. The sword of the Lord will be drawn out from its sheath and will not be returned to the scabbard until all the enemies of Israel will be blotted out. This will be the day of the Lord's recompense for all the sufferings that have fallen upon Zion and the people represented by that city throughout the centuries that have gone since they were scattered among the Gentiles, because they knew not the time of their visitation.

Next are described the desolations of the land of Edom, which apparently will continue throughout the entire millennial age as a reminder of the judgment of God meted out to a rebellious people, and thus as a warning to any who, even in the day of Jehovah's power, might contemplate turning away in rebellion against the King reigning in Zion.

And the streams thereof shall be turned into pitch, and the dust thereof into brimstone, and the land thereof shall become burning pitch. It shall not be quenched night nor day; the smoke thereof shall go up for ever; from generation to generation it shall lie waste; none shall pass through it for ever and ever. But the cormorant and the bittern shall possess it; the owl also and the raven shall dwell in it; and he shall stretch out upon it the line of confusion, and the stones of emptiness. They shall call the nobles thereof to the kingdom, but none shall be there, and all her princes shall be nothing. And thorns shall come up in her palaces, nettles and brambles in the fortresses thereof: and it shall be an habitation of dragons, and a court for owls. The wild beasts of the desert shall also meet with the wild beasts of the island, and the satyr shall cry to his fellow; the screech owl also shall rest there, and find for herself a place of rest. There shall the great owl make her nest, and lay, and hatch, and gather under her shadow: there shall the vultures also be gathered, every one with her mate (verses 9-15).

It is difficult to identify with certainty all of the beasts, birds, and reptiles here mentioned. Scholars are not agreed as to the exact meaning of each of the Hebrew words employed, but even though we may not understand each term used, we can see the full meaning of the passage, namely, that the land of Edom, once a flourishing kingdom, will become utterly desolate and an habitation only for wild creatures of the wilderness.

Seek ye out of the book of the Lord, and read: no one of these shall fail, none shall want her mate: for my mouth it hath commanded, and his spirit it hath gathered them. And he hath cast the lot for them, and his hand hath divided it unto them by line: they shall possess it for ever, from generation to generation shall they dwell therein (verses 16, 17).

Jehovah's word is absolutely sure. No prophecy of the Scriptures will fail of final and complete fulfillment. Just as type and antitype agree in connection with the truth of our Lord's Person and redemptive work, so prophecy and fulfillment will be in perfect harmony. Nothing that God has spoken will prove to be unreliable. He will never go back on His word whether it have to do with judgment or with grace.

CHAPTER THIRTY-FIVE

MILLENNIAL BLESSING

THIS precious portion, which concludes the first
division of our book is a beautiful inspired poem,
setting before us the delightful conditions which
will prevail in this world after the binding of Satan as
depicted in Revelation 20:1, and the enthronement of
our Lord Jesus Christ as Sovereign of the universe.
Isaiah's own heart must have been thrilled as he looked
forward to this time of peace and righteousness following the long years of strife and wickedness which have
caused such grief and suffering throughout human
history. Even creation itself will share in the blessings of that day of Jehovah's power, and so we read:

The wilderness and the solitary place shall be glad for them;
and the desert shall rejoice, and blossom as the rose. It shall blossom abundantly and rejoice even with joy and singing: the glory
of Lebanon shall be given unto it, the excellency of Carmel and
Sharon, they shall see the glory of the Lord, and the excellency of
our God (verses 1, 2).

All that is lovely in the present condition of the
world, such as the grandeur of Lebanon, the beauties
of Carmel and Sharon's plains will be retained in
that new era, and to these will be added many addi-
tional testimonies to the Creator's joy in the world
which He brought into being by the word of His power,
but which has been so terribly marred as a result of

man's sin. Every fruitful field or orchard, every lovely garden, presents a foretaste of what in Messiah's day will be everywhere prevalent, when the parched deserts will give place to verdant meadows, and the thorns and thistles brought in by the curse will vanish, and trees and shrubs bearing fruits to appeal to the appetite and flowers to delight the eye, will spring up instead.

But the physical and spiritual blessings that will come to all mankind will transcend all of these material changes.

Strengthen ye the weak hands, and confirm the feeble knees. Say to them that are of a fearful heart, Be strong: fear not: behold, your God will come with vengeance, even God with a recompence; he will come and save you. Then the eyes of the blind shall be opened, and the ears of the deaf shall be unstopped. Then shall the lame man leap as an hart; and the tongue of the dumb sing: for in the wilderness shall waters break out, and streams in the desert (verses 3-6).

"Hope deferred maketh the heart sick" (Prov. 13: 12). For long centuries the people of earth have yearned for deliverance from the countless ills that affect humanity. So the prophet exhorts those whose faith is weak and whose hearts are fearful to lift up their eyes and look on to the time when God Himself shall come down to earth to end its travail and bring in new and happy conditions. When Jesus came the first time all the signs of the coming age were manifested as sickness of every form fled away at the sound of His voice or the touch of His hand; when blind eyes were opened, deaf ears made to hear and the tongues of the dumb to sing. To some extent these signs followed the preaching of His apostles who could say with authority to the lame and helpless, "In the name of

Jesus Christ rise up and walk," and whose very shadow at times had healing power. All of these wonders were but foretastes of what shall be everywhere prevalent in millennial days.

And the parched ground shall become a pool, and the thirsty land springs of water: in the habitation of dragons, where each lay, shall be grass with reeds and rushes (verse 7).

Venomous and baneful creatures such as the crocodile and the alligator will no longer molest mankind nor prove a menace to the safety of children. Only what will minister to man's comfort and security will remain.

And an highway shall be there, and a way, and it shall be called The way of holiness; the unclean shall not pass over it; but it shall be for those: the wayfaring men, though fools [or, simple] shall not err therein. No lion shall be there, nor any ravenous beast shall go up therein, it shall not be found there; but the redeemed shall walk there: And the ransomed of the Lord shall return, and come to Zion with songs and everlasting joy upon their heads: they shall obtain joy and gladness, and sorrow and sighing shall flee away (verses 8-10).

The way into God's presence is ever the way of holiness. So in that day when men's hearts shall be turned to the Lord, He will lead them to Himself along the highway of holiness, to Mount Zion where His throne will be established and from which His law will go forth into all the earth. Under His beneficent and righteous reign sorrow and sighing shall come to an end and joy and gladness take their place.

While we who belong to the Church, the Body of Christ, have our hearts fixed on the heavenly hope, as we look for the coming of our Lord Jesus and our gathering together unto Him, we cannot but rejoice to know that God has such blessing in store for Israel His earthly people and for the nations of the earth who have been the prey of such distressing circumstances throughout their history, circumstances which they are so powerless to change. It is most humbling to man's pride, to realize that all our boasted civilization is utterly unable to prevent war and oppression in spite of Peace Conferences, a now effete League of Nations and our present United Nations Council. Christ alone can put things right. His return is man's only hope for lasting peace.

THE HISTORIC INTERLUDE

W E NOW GLANCE at the next four chapters which relate certain important incidents in the life of Hezekiah, King of Judah. I say "glance at," because I do not intend to take these chapters up verse by verse, quoting and endeavoring to explain them, as in the case of the first prophetic division of the book.

These chapters are almost duplicates of 2 Kings 18:13—21:26 and the major events are also covered by 2 Chronicles 32, 33. In all probability it was Isaiah who wrote these records and who was guided by the Holy Spirit in transferring the lengthier one into its place in his great prophetic book.

There was a very special reason for giving us these four historical chapters. They all have to do with a son of David upon whom all Judah's hopes were centered, who came down to the very verge of death but was raised up again in order that the purpose of God might be fulfilled. That, of course, points forward to our Lord Jesus Christ, who went down into death actually and was raised up again to carry out God's counsels. They have to do with certain events in the life of King Hezekiah, who in some degree foreshadowed this in the experiences through which he was called to pass.

In the fourteenth year of his reign the invasion of

the Assyrians under the cruel and ruthless Sennacherib took place. After destroying or capturing various fenced cities, he sent a great army to besiege Jerusalem. This host was under the direct leadership of a general named Rabshakeh, a bold but vulgar and blustering officer who had a supreme contempt for the Jews and for their religion.

He took his stand at a prominent place outside the wall of Jerusalem, where his voice could be heard easily by the defenders of the city, and called upon the leaders to surrender before he undertook to destroy them completely.

Eliakim, Shebna and Joah, who were what we would call members of Hezekiah's cabinet or privy council, undertook to parley with the arrogant Assyrian. Speaking on behalf of his master, Rabshakeh inquired as to what confidence they trusted in, daring to refuse to yield to his commands. Insolently he declared that if they hoped for deliverance to come through the power of their God, their expectations were doomed to disappointment. Had not Sennacherib proved himself more than a match for all the gods of the surrounding nations? And had not Hezekiah himself destroyed the altars of Jehovah and thus forfeited all claims upon Him even if He did have the power to protect him? Not realizing that the destroyed altars were connected with idolatrous shrines, Rabshakeh supposed that they had been dedicated to the God of Judah (chap. 36:1-7).

Demanding unconditional surrender to be ratified by a large tribute, as pledge that the Jews would abide by the proposed terms, Rabshakeh even went so far as to insist that it was by direction of Jehovah that

Sennacherib had come against Judah. He may in some
way have become familiar with some of the prophecies
which we have been considering; he knew of Samaria's fall, and so may have learned that their own
God had declared that He would use Assyria as a
rod to punish Judah for their disobedience and waywardness (vss. 8-10).

Fearful that these words might have an ill effect
upon the morale of the defenders of the city, the Jewish
leaders asked that the Assyrian general speak to them
in his own language with which they were familiar,
and not in the Hebrew tongue. This request only roused
Rabshakeh to greater insolence. He used language that
was disgusting and revolting as he declared that he
had been sent not to parley with the representatives
of Hezekiah as such, but with all the people of Jerusalem, of whom he continued to demand instant obedience to the call for surrender and the promise of
allegiance to the king of Assyria. In that case their
lives would be spared and they themselves transported
as prisoners of war to other lands where they would
be permitted to live in peace and security.

Derisively he referred again to the folly of trusting
in their God and reminded them that the gods of Hamath, Arphad, Sepharvaim and Samaria had been unable
to cope with the might of Sennacherib. What reason
had they then to hope that the Lord should intervene
on their behalf and deliver Jerusalem from threatened
ruin?

To all these demands and taunts the people answered
"not a word," for the king had so commanded them.
Eliakim and his companions returned to Hezekiah with
their clothes rent in token of their grief at being unable

to come to terms with the Assyrian general whose arrogant and defiant words they reported to their king (vss. 12-22).

When Hezekiah heard it, he too rent his clothes and covered himself with sackcloth and "went into the house of the Lord" (chap. 37:1). There he could pour out his heart to the God of his fathers who had so often given deliverance to His people in times of great distress and adversity. Feeling the need of counsel and prayer he sent Eliakim, Shebna, and the elders to call upon Isaiah, to whom he said, "Thus saith Hezekiah, This day is a day of trouble and of rebuke and of blasphemy: for the children are come to the birth, and there is not strength to bring forth. It may be the Lord thy God will hear the words of Rabshakeh, whom the king of Assyria his master hath sent to reproach the living God, and will reprove the words which the Lord thy God hath heard: wherefore lift up thy prayer for the remnant that is left" (vss. 3, 4).

Such faith could not go unrewarded. God never fails those who commit everything to Him. He has said, "Call upon Me in the day of trouble: I will deliver thee, and thou shalt glorify Me" (Ps. 50:15). Hezekiah was soon to prove the truth of this promise, even though his faith must first be tested severely.

Isaiah's answer was most cheering and reassuring. He said, "Thus shall ye say unto your master, Thus saith the Lord, Be not afraid of the words that thou hast heard, wherewith the servants of the king of Assyria have blasphemed Me" (vs. 6). It was not a question between the two opposing forces, or between Rabshakeh and Hezekiah. The Assyrian had dared to challenge the power of Jehovah. He, Himself, would take up the challenge, and would manifest His power and might, thus showing that He was not a mere idol, nor an imaginary deity like the gods of the heathen whose inability to save their devotees from destruction had been so readily manifested. Sennacherib and his servants had dared to rush upon the thick bosses of the bucklers of the Almighty (Job 15:25, 26), and were soon to prove the folly of daring to fight against the omnipotent God who had created the heavens and the earth, and who declared through His prophet, "Behold, I will send a blast upon him, and he shall hear a rumour, and return to his own land; and I will cause him to fall by the sword in his own land" (vs. 7). The "rumour" was a report that Tirhakah, King of Ethiopia, was on his way to fight against Assyria, whose armies were divided; part besieging Jerusalem, and part warring against Libnah. Reluctantly, Rabshakeh was obliged to lift the siege and to withdraw to Assyria, but he sent a last defiant message to the king of Judah as his armies were withdrawing. "Let not thy God, in whom thou trustest, deceive thee, saying, Jerusalem shall not be given into the hand of the king of Assyria. Behold, thou hast heard what the kings of Assyria have done to all lands by destroying them utterly: and shalt thou be delivered?" (vss. 10, 11). Again he taunted Hezekiah concerning the folly of presuming that his God would prove any more powerful than the gods of other nations. This message was put in the form of a letter which Hezekiah received at the hands of certain messengers who brought it from the camp of the Assyrians. It was a letter of blasphemy, and Hezekiah did right in not attempting to answer it himself. Instead, he took it into the house of the Lord and spread it out before God. Bowing in His presence, he pleaded that Jehovah would intervene to save His people. He frankly acknowledged that the fake gods of the nations had no ability to save, but he confessed his confidence that the living God would undertake for those who put their trust in Him. The conclusion of his prayer is very beautiful and heart-moving: "Now therefore, O Lord our God, save us from his hand, that all the kingdoms of the earth may know that Thou art the Lord, even Thou only" (vs. 20). Such confidence could not go unrewarded, nor such a prayer unheard.

The answer came through another message from Isaiah, assuring him that God had heard and was about to answer his petition; and that in such a way, that "The virgin, the daughter of Zion," should despise the haughty foe whose army had at first seemed invincible. Rabshakeh had reproached the Lord. He had blasphemed the God of Judah. In his pride and folly he had lifted up himself against the Holy One of Israel. Trusting in the vastness of his army, the number of his chariots and horsemen, he had thought it would be but a small matter to conquer Jerusalem and to carry its inhabitants away as captives, but he was soon to learn the difference between the senseless idols of the heathen and the One in whom Hezekiah had put his trust (vss. 21-28). Therefore the word of the Lord came to him saying: "Because thy rage against Me, and thy tumult, is come up into Mine ears, therefore will I put My hook in thy nose, and My bridle in thy lips, and I will turn thee back by the way by which thou camest."

To Hezekiah the promise was given that the land which had been overrun by the enemy should bring forth of itself for two seasons and in the third year should be planted and would produce an abundant harvest, while the remnant of Judah, escaped out of the hand of the Assyrian, should once more begin to prosper and "again take root downward, and bear fruit upward: for out of Jerusalem shall go forth a remnant, and they that escape out of Mount Zion: the zeal of the Lord of hosts shall do this."

As for the king of Assyria, he should not be permitted to enter Jerusalem, nor even shoot an arrow into it, nor threaten it again in any way. He was to return by the way that he came, for the Lord had undertaken to defend Jerusalem for His own sake and for His servant David's sake. The judgment was not long deferred, for God sent a terrible plague upon the camp of the Assyrians, so severe in character that in one night one hundred and eighty-five thousand died, and the scattered remnants of the once-great army of Sennacherib departed for their own land, led by their defeated and crestfallen ruler.

Upon reaching his home city and worshiping in the house of his god he was set upon by two of his own sons, Adrammelech and Sharezer, who slew their dishonored father with the sword and escaped into Armenia. One of their brothers, Esarhaddon, became king in his father's stead.

Thus had God vindicated His holy name and freed His people from the impending doom that seemed about to fall upon them.

In chapter thirty-eight we read of Hezekiah's illness and recovery. It might have been supposed that after such a remarkable experience of God's intervention on behalf of His people, in answer to prayer, Hezekiah would have been drawn so close to the Lord that he would never have doubted His love and care again, but have lived constantly in the sunshine of the divine approval. But alas, with him, as so often with us all, it was far otherwise. When new tests came doubts and fears again prevailed and only the grace of God could bear with His poor failing servant.

The first test came through illness. Hezekiah was "sick unto death," we are told. The prophet Isaiah was sent to say to him, "Thus saith the Lord, Set thy house in order; for thou shalt die and not live."

To the stricken king these words were evil tidings indeed. He was still a comparatively young man, for he had come to the throne at the age of twenty-five, and his entire reign was but twenty-nine years, so that at this time he was but thirty-nine. Long life was one of the promises to the obedient Israelite. Therefore the announcement that he was to die ere he was forty seemed to Hezekiah like an evidence of the divine displeasure. He received the message of the prophet with real distress and pleaded for a reprieve from the sentence imposed upon him.

In reading his prayer we need to remember that Old Testament saints, however godly they might be, did not have the light on the after-life that has now been vouchsafed to the children of God. Our Lord Jesus Christ has brought life and immortality to light through the gospel (2 Tim. 1:10). He has revealed the truth as to that which God has prepared for those who love Him. Having gone down unto death and come up in triumph, He has annulled him that had the power of death, even the devil, and so delivers those who, through fear of death, were all their lifetime subject to bondage (Heb. 2:14, 15). We know now that for the believer death simply means to be absent from the body and present with the Lord (2 Cor. 5:8), and that this is far better than any possible earthly experience (Phil. 1:23). But all this was unknown in the days before the advent of our Lord Jesus Christ, who declared, "If a man keep My saying he shall never see death" (John 8:51).

Therefore when the word came to Hezekiah that he must die, his soul was filled with fear, and he cried to God in his wretchedness, pleading the integrity of his life as a reason why his days should be prolonged.

God who sometimes grants our requests but sends leanness into our souls (Ps. 106:15), heard his cry and sent the prophet to him once more; this time to tell him that his prayer was heard, and that God would add to his life another fifteen years and would also continue to defend Jerusalem from the evil machinations of the Assyrian king. To confirm the promise, a sign was given which involved a stupendous miracle, for God said, "I will bring again the shadow of the degrees, which is gone down in the sun-dial of Ahaz ten degrees backward." When this actually took place, Hezekiah knew, beyond all question, that the prophet had spoken by divine authority.

This is not the place to discuss the miracle itself. Whether it was caused by some amazing event in the planetary system, or whether it was a miracle of refraction, we need not try to decide; but the fact that the astronomers of Babylon had knowledge of it would indicate that it was something far-reaching and of grave import.

Upon his recovery, Hezekiah wrote of his exercises and described vividly the experiences he passed through when he felt that he was under sentence of death. Bitterly he complained that he was about to be deprived of the residue of his years. To leave the world seemed to him like being banished from the presence of the Lord. His days and nights were filled with grievous pain, not only of body, but of mind, as he awaited in fear the carrying out of the decree, when God, as he put it, would "make an end" of him. He mourned "as a dove"; his eyes failed from "looking upward." Yet he knew that he was in the hands of the Lord, and his heart cried out to Him for help.

It is evident that as his exercises continued, his soul entered more restfully into the truth that all must be well when one is in the care of a covenant-keeping God. "O Lord, by these things men live, and in all these things is the life of my spirit: so wilt Thou recover me, and make me to live. Behold, for peace I had great bitterness: but Thou hast in love to my soul delivered it from the pit of corruption: for Thou hast cast all my sins behind Thy back." These precious words express his realization of the goodness and the wisdom of God, after health returned, for he took this as an evidence that God had pardoned all his sins and cast them away forever. As an unenlightened Old Testament believer, he could only think of early death as, in some sense, an expression of divine disapproval. He could see nothing in the grave but darkness and forgetfulness. In life the Lord could be praised, not in Sheol. He wrote, of course, of conditions as he understood them; but he closed his writing with a note of praise and thanksgiving for renewed strength and added years of life.

The deliverance came in a very simple way. He had been suffering from a malignant boil, but a poultice of figs, prescribed by Isaiah, drew out the poison, and started the king on the way to recovery.

It is hardly necessary to point out that had Hezekiah died at the age of thirty-nine, Manasseh, who proved to be the most wicked king who ever sat on the throne of Judah, would never have been born, for he was but twelve years old when he began to reign (2 Chron. 33:1).

He tried to undo everything that his father had done. Hezekiah had destroyed the altars of idolatry, had swept the land clear of idols. Manasseh brought in more forms of idolatry than were ever known before and he went to spiritists, mediums, and filled the land with those who professed to be able to talk with the dead, practices which God had forbidden. And he brought down the indignation of God upon Judah, because of the corruption and sin committed.

Yet how wonderful is the mercy of God; at last an old man fifty years of age and almost facing eternity, God brought that godless king to repentance. Manasseh broke down, confessed the sins of a long, ungodly life, undertook again to cleanse the land of its idols and tried to bring about a reformation, but it was too late to recover the people. His son Amon went right on in the sins of his father.

But in the next generation, God came in in wondrous grace again and raised up another son of David, King Josiah, who honored the Lord in his very youth and was the means of bringing about the great revival in Judah.

The thirty-ninth chapter tells of another failure on the part of this king who was, in the main, so devoted to the will of God. We read in 2 Chronicles 32:31 concerning him, "Howbeit in the business of the ambassadors of the princes of Babylon, who sent unto him to enquire of the wonder that was done in the land, God left him, to try him, that He might know all that was in his heart." There are few of us indeed, who could stand such a test as this. To be left alone by God, in order that our own hearts might be manifested, our

inmost thoughts revealed, could only mean a moral or
spiritual breakdown. Such was the trial to which Hezekiah was now exposed, and in which he failed through
self-confidence. He acted upon his own judgment instead of turning to the Lord for guidance, and the
result could only bring harm instead of blessing. After
the Lord had so graciously granted his request and
raised him up from the very brink of the grave, we are
told that "Merodach-Baladan, the son of Baladan, king
of Babylon, sent letters and a present to Hezekiah: for
he had heard that he had been sick, and was recov-
ered." How would the King of Judah react to this
apparently friendly overture from the prince of the
great city which was the very fountain-head of idolatry? When Rabshakeh sent a letter of blasphemy,
Hezekiah went into the sanctuary and spread it out
before the Lord; but when there came a letter and a
present, he felt no need of bringing this before God,
or seeking instruction from Him. Do we not all know
something of this self-confidence when we have to do
with the world, not seen as in open opposition to that
which we cherish most, as of God, but rather when it
approaches us in an apparently friendly, patronizing
manner, extending the hand of friendship instead of
the mailed fist of enmity? Yet we are never in greater
danger of missing the mind of God than at such a time
as this. The letter that is accompanied with a present
may cover up a far greater danger than the letter of
blasphemy.

Evidently elated by the visit of the Babylonian en-
voys and their retinue, and pleased with the present,
Hezekiah felt no need to ask counsel of the Lord, but
without hesitation he received the embassage, "and
shewed them the house of his precious things, the

silver, and the gold, and the spices, and the precious ointment, and all the house of his armour, and all that was found in his treasures: there was nothing in his house, nor in all his dominion, that Hezekiah shewed them not." This was exactly what the Chaldeans desired. No doubt, as they looked with covetous eyes on all these things, they were pondering in their hearts how best they should proceed in order that, some day, they might conquer Judah and have all this vast treasure for themselves.

Scarcely had they gone from the presence of Hezekiah before Isaiah appeared upon the scene to confront the king with two questions: "What said these men? And from whence came they unto thee?" Ingenuously Hezekiah replied, "They are come from a far country unto me, even from Babylon." Surely he could not have been ignorant of the prophecies Isaiah had spoken as to this reserve power in the northeast that was yet to come against Judah, and be used by the God whom His people had neglected, as a rod to punish them for their willful disobedience.

Isaiah put another question: "What have they seen in thy house?" The king answered: "All that is in mine house have they seen: there is nothing among my treasures that I have not shewed them." He had no idea of the serious import of this, for he had not realized that the princes were actually spies, who had come to search out the land, and to report to the King of Babylon all that which they found.

It must have been a real shock therefore to the unsuspecting monarch, when Isaiah said, "Hear the word of the Lord of hosts: Behold, the days come, that all that is in thine house, and that which thy fathers have laid up in store until this day, shall be carried to Baby-

lon: nothing shall be left, saith the Lord. And of thy
sons that shall issue from thee, which thou shalt beget,
shall they take away: and they shall be eunuchs in the
palace of the king of Babylon."

All this was fulfilled years later, when Nebuchadnezzar conquered Judah, and carried away their chief
men as captives to Babylon, including a large number
who were of the blood royal, as well as those very
treasures (2 Chron. 36:18).

One can imagine Hezekiah's disappointment and his
deep chagrin, as he heard these words of the prophet;
but he could only bow his head and accept them as the
revelation of the judgment of God. So he replied, "Good
is the word of the Lord which thou hast spoken . . .
For there shall be peace and truth in my days."

The after-history of Judah shows how, in spite of
occasional revivals, things went from bad to worse, until at last "there was no remedy" (2 Chron. 36:16) for
their evil condition, and the prophesied judgment was
fulfilled in the days of Zedekiah.

One to whom so many owe so much in rightly dividing the Word of truth, J. N. Darby, aptly points out
that in this first part of the book, "We have had rather
the outward history of Israel, but now we have their
moral or inward history in their place of testimony
against idolatry, in their relationship with Christ and
the separation of a remnant."

That inward history was a complete failure as the
next part of Isaiah's great prophecy clearly shows.

CHAPTER FORTY

GOD THE COMFORTER

Comfort ye, comfort ye my people, saith your God. Speak ye comfortably to Jerusalem, and cry unto her, that her warfare is accomplished, that her iniquity is pardoned: for she hath received of the Lord's hand double for all her sins. The voice of him that crieth in the wilderness, Prepare ye the way of the Lord, make straight in the desert a highway for our God. Every valley shall be exalted, and every mountain and hill shall be made low: and the crooked shall be made straight, and the rough places plain: and the glory of the Lord shall be revealed, and all flesh shall see it together: for the mouth of the Lord hath spoken it. The voice said, Cry. And he said, What shall I cry? All flesh is grass, and all the goodliness thereof is as the flower of the field: the grass withereth, the flower fadeth: because the spirit of the Lord bloweth upon it: surely the people is grass. The grass withereth, the flower fadeth: but the word of our God shall stand for ever (verses 1-8).

THE latter part of Isaiah is actually in a sense, the third part, because, as we have already considered, the first part of the book was divided into two sections—one, the prophetic, and the other, historical and typical.

Beginning with chapter forty this part of Isaiah's great book is the portion which some attribute to "the great unknown," or, as they put it, "the second Isaiah," some unnamed prophet who wrote after the Babylonian captivity and whose work was supposedly incorporated into the book of Isaiah by a later editor. But the New Testament definitely negatives this and attributes this section to Isaiah himself (Matt. 8:17; Luke 4:17, 18); so we need not trouble ourselves about such unfounded critical theories. The matter is settled for us.

The chapter commences with the words, "Comfort ye, comfort ye My people, saith your God. Speak ye comfortably to Jerusalem and cry unto her that her warfare is accomplished, that her iniquity is pardoned: for she hath received of the Lord's hand double for all her sins." God means to comfort His people, but in doing so He has to bring before them very definitely their true condition in His sight, and then shows His remedy. The first part of this message may not sound very comforting and yet God must begin that way. God wounds that He may heal; He kills that He may make alive. We never know Him in the fullness of His power to sustain and comfort until we have come to the end of our own resources.

In His gracious ministry of comfort God always begins by showing us our need and our dependence upon His omnipotent power. In this chapter forty he says to the prophet, "Comfort ye My people," and then proceeds to instruct the servant as to the character of his message. "The voice said, Cry." Isaiah asked, "What shall I cry?" The answer was, "All flesh is grass, and all the goodliness thereof is as the flower of the field." This is ever the divine order. It is not until we realize our own utter nothingness and helplessness that we are in a position to avail ourselves of the comfort which the Lord waits to give.

In the New Testament we see each Person of the blessed Trinity engaged in this ministry of comfort. God the Father is called "the God of all comfort" (2 Cor. 1:3). God the Holy Spirit is spoken of four times in our Lord's last discourse to His disciples as "the

Comforter" (John 14:16, 26; 15:26; 16:7). One character of our Lord's work and ministry is "to comfort
all that mourn" (chapter 61:2). He is also called our
"Advocate with the Father" (1 John 2:1). The word
for "Advocate" is exactly the same in the Greek as that
for "Comforter" in John's Gospel. How blessed to be
in fellowship with the Father, the Son, and the Holy
Spirit, so that one can enter into and enjoy the comfort They delight to give!

What greater privilege can we have on earth than to
enjoy the abiding presence of the God of all comfort as
we face the perplexities and bitter disappointments
that we are called upon to endure?

If we never knew grief or pain we would never be
able to appreciate what God can be to His suffering
people. When we cry to the Lord in hours of distress,
He does not remove the cause of our trouble in every
case, but always gives the needed grace to bear whatever we are called upon to endure. When in heaven we
"read the meaning of our tears" and see just what God
was working out in our lives, we shall praise Him for
every trial and affliction, as we see in them all the evidences of a Father's love and His desire to conform us
to Himself.

If God gives the comfort of the knowledge of forgiveness of sins, and of the salvation of the soul, He
begins by stressing the utterly lost condition of men,
their helplessness, their sinfulness, thus leading them
to take their true place before Him in repentance, confession and acknowledgment of their iniquities.

He looks forward here to the time, however, when
Israel's iniquities will all be put away. He says, Speak
to the heart of Jerusalem and tell her that her warfare,
her long conflict, is accomplished, her iniquity par-

doned, and the Lord hath returned unto her double fo
all her sins. That does not mean that Israel will hav
been punished twice as much as her sins deserved. Go
will never do that. When speaking to Job, Elihu ver
clearly says that God will not lay upon man more tha
is right. He will deal with each man according to hi
light and knowledge, and the actual sins that he ha
committed (Job 34). But He will not punish anyon
more than his sins deserve. But this expression, "Sh
hath received of the Lord's hand double for all he
sins," is a commercial one. If a Jew were in financia
difficulties and he turned his home or his farm over t
a creditor in order to meet his debts, a paper woul
be made out giving this full information. One cop
would be kept by the one who placed the mortgag
on the property, and the other would be nailed up o
the doorpost, so that anyone would understand tha
this property was transferred temporarily to another
When the account was settled and everything was paid
the notice on the doorpost would be doubled, tacked u
double, covered over. That indicated it was all settled

When it says, "She hath received of the Lord's han
the double for all her sins," it is as though it said th
account has been fully paid. Nothing more now to suf
fer, because the Lord will have pardoned her iniquity

That is declared in the very beginning of this section
That is the goal toward which the people are to loo
and then later we are told how they reached that goa
And so in the first place now, we have a prophecy tha
relates to the coming of John the Baptist, the voice o
one crying in the wilderness, "Prepare ye the way o
the Lord, make His paths straight."

When certain of the Pharisees asked John the Bap
tist if he was Messiah or the one spoken of by Moses

A prophet shall the Lord your God raise up like unto me, him shall ye hear in all things." John said, "I am not." His questioners asked, "If thou art not Messiah or that prophet, who art thou, and why baptizest thou?"

John said, "I am the voice of one crying in the wilderness; Prepare ye the way of the Lord." Thus he applied to himself these words of Isaiah.

The voice said, "Cry." In sending His messenger God says, "Cry! Cry aloud. Give out My message." And then the question comes back, "What shall I cry?" The answer is, "All flesh is grass . . . and all the glory of man is the flower of grass. The grass withereth, the flower thereof fadeth away, but the word of our God shall stand forever."

What is significant about that to comfort the people of God? "Tell them that all flesh is grass, that they are just poor helpless sinners, there is nothing to glory in. All the glory of man is as the flower of the grass and the grass withereth and the flower thereof fadeth away."

Is there anything comforting in that? It is the first thing we need to know. If we do not learn the lesson of our utter helplessness, we shall never turn to God for salvation. If we think that we can save ourselves we shall not avail ourselves of the provision that God has made for our salvation. So He says, "Tell them that all flesh is grass." But tell them that the Word of the Lord endureth forever. Peter quotes this in the first chapter of his first epistle and gives this significant comment on it: "This is the word which by the gospel is preached unto you." It is the gospel message which comes before us. The Word of the Lord that endureth forever is the good tidings of the gospel.

O Zion, that bringest good tidings, get thee up into the hig
mountain; O Jerusalem, that bringest good tidings, lift up th
voice with strength; lift it up, be not afraid; say unto the citie
of Judah, Behold your God! Behold, the Lord God will come wit]
strong hand, and his arm shall rule for him: behold, his reward i
with him, and his work before him. He shall feed his flock like :
shepherd: he shall gather the lambs with his arm, and carry ther
in his bosom, and shall gently lead those that are with youn;
(verses 9-11).

Immediately following the words, "The word of th
Lord endureth for ever," comes, "O Zion, that bringes'
good tidings . . . say . . . Behold your God!" Goo
tidings—that is the gospel.

Here are not only "the silent glances of Scripture,"
but they are intimately linked with the early chapter
of all the four Gospels, which speak of the Lord's firs
advent, and Matthew says plainly the events given ar
the fulfillment of that which was spoken by Isaiah anc
other prophets. The coming One is Emmanuel, "Go
with us," "the Lord God will come," and then His
character is given as the tender Shepherd.

When the Lord Jesus actually came, He took the ver)
phrase spoken of here by Isaiah. He says, "I am the
good shepherd . . . I lay down My life for the sheep"
(John 10:11, 15). And so as the tender shepherd He is
pictured here in the good news that God brings to
Israel—the shepherd carrying the lambs in his bosom
and gently leading the flock, gently leading those with
young.

Yet this One who comes to us so tenderly as the Good
Shepherd, a real Man, a Man in absolute holiness, kind
compassionate, loving, is the almighty omnipotent God
the omnipresent and omniscient One, the Creator of
the ends of the earth.

God Himself speaks in power and majesty, putting Himself in contrast with the helpless man-made idols of the heathen, to whom many of the people of Israel had turned.

Who hath measured the waters in the hollow of his hand, and meted out heaven with the span, and comprehended the dust of the earth in a measure, and weighed the mountains in scales, and the hills in a balance? Who hath directed the Spirit of the Lord, or being his counsellor hath taught him? With whom took he counsel, and who instructed him, and taught him in the path of judgment, and taught him knowledge, and shewed to him the way of understanding? Behold, the nations are as a drop of a bucket, and are counted as the small dust of the balance: behold: he taketh up the isles as a very little thing. And Lebanon is not sufficient to burn, nor the beasts thereof sufficient for a burnt offering. All nations before him are as nothing; and they are counted to him less than nothing, and vanity. To whom then will ye liken God? or what likeness will ye compare unto him? The workman melteth a graven image, and the goldsmith spreadeth it over with gold, and casteth silver chains. He that is so impoverished that he hath no oblation chooseth a tree that will not rot; he seeketh unto him a cunning workman to prepare a graven image, that shall not be moved (verses 12-20).

The Blessed One, Shepherd of Israel, who is speaking here as the Creator of the heavens, the One of omnipotent power and omniscient wisdom, has resources for faith to lay hold upon. So great is He that no suitable offering could be made to Him. "Lebanon is not sufficient to burn, nor the beasts thereof sufficient for a burnt offering" (vs. 16).

Sin is so terrible an affront to a holy God that no sacrifice, however great, which man could offer would ever avail to put it away. Although the mountains of Lebanon became as a great altar, and all the cedars thereon were hewn down and piled up for one enormous fire, on which were sacrificed the vast herds and flocks that grazed upon the pastures of these wooded hills, yet all together they would not be sufficient to atone for one sin. Only the precious blood of Christ avails to make propitiation for our guilt and to justify us before God.

Have ye not known? have ye not heard? hath it not been told you from the beginning? have ye not understood from the foundations of the earth? It is he that sitteth upon the circle of the earth, and the inhabitants thereof are as grasshoppers; that stretcheth out the heavens as a curtain, and spreadeth them out as a tent to dwell in: That bringeth the princes to nothing; he maketh the judges of the earth as vanity. Yea, they shall not be planted; yea, they shall not be sown: yea, their stock shall not take root in the earth: and he shall also blow upon them, and they shall wither, and the whirlwind shall take them away as stubble. To whom then will ye liken me, or shall I be equal? saith the Holy One. Lift up your eyes on high, and behold who hath created these things, that bringeth out their hosts by number: he calleth them all by names by the greatness of his might, for that he is strong in power; not one faileth. Why sayest thou, O Jacob, and speakest, O Israel, My way is hid from the Lord, and my judgment is passed over from my God? Hast thou not known? hast thou not heard, that the everlasting God, the Lord, the Creator of the ends of the earth, fainteth not, neither is weary? there is no searching of his understanding. He giveth power to the faint; and to them that have no might he increaseth strength. Even the youths shall faint and be weary, and the young men shall utterly fall: But they that wait upon the Lord shall renew their strength: they shall mount up with wings as eagles; they shall run, and not be weary; and they shall walk, and not faint (verses 21-31).

Why, we may well ask, has God thus truly described Himself? It is because those over whom He has such a tender care are faint and weary, without strength, so He turns them to Him as the Source of power, simply to wait upon Him, for this divine God has an interest in everyone.

It is not because of lack of power that God does not give immediate release from trial and tribulation. His understanding is infinite and He is working out His own counsels for our blessing when He permits affliction to fall upon us and continue to oppress us. We must learn the lesson put before Job, that man cannot fathom His plans, so should seek to submit without question to His providential dealings. It is easy, when distress or suffering becomes prolonged, to think that God has forgotten or is indifferent to what one is going through. But this is always wrong. He is ever concerned about His people, and in His own time will give deliverance; and until then His grace is available to sustain and strengthen the soul, that one may endure as seeing Him who is invisible.

"He giveth power to the faint." It was this that enabled Paul to glory in his infirmities, that the "power of Christ might rest upon" him (2 Cor. 12:9). He will supply the needed strength to meet every test He permits us to face.

"They that wait upon the Lord shall renew their strength." Mere natural and physical powers will not avail in the hour when one is called upon to face great mental and spiritual emergencies. But they who have learned to refer everything to God and to wait quietly upon Him will be given all needed strength to rise above depressing circumstances, thus enabling them to mount heavenward as eagles facing the sun, to run their race with patience, and to walk with God with renewed confidence and courage, knowing that they are ever the objects of His love and care.

It is one thing to wait *on* the Lord. It is quite another to wait *for* Him. As we wait on Him we are changed into His likeness. As we wait for Him in patience we are delivered from worry and fretfulness, knowing that God is never late, but that in His own time He will give the help we need.

Someone has suggested that we may apply Isaiah's words, verse 31, as representing Christians or children of God in different ages. The young believers mount up with wings of hope and expectancy as eagles flying into the height of heaven. The middle-aged ones are running with patience the race set before them, while those who have reached old age have come down to a quiet walk with God as they near the portals of the eternal Home of the saints.

CHAPTER FORTY-ONE

THE INFINITELY STRONG ONE

Keep silence before me, O islands; and let the people renew their strength: let them come near; then let them speak: let us come near together to judgment. Who raised up the righteous man from the east, called him to his foot, gave the nations before him, and made him rule over kings? he gave them as the dust to his sword, and as driven stubble to his bow. He pursued them, and passed safely; even by the way that he had not gone with his feet. Who hath wrought and done it, calling the generations from the beginning? I the Lord, the first, and with the last; I am he (verses 1-4).

IN CHAPTER forty-one God is still put in contrast with man's weakness. These are promises made to Israel when they are restored to Him, but they follow the account of the majesty of God, and it is man in his weakness depending on the infinitely Strong One.

But thou, Israel, art my servant, Jacob whom I have chosen, the seed of Abraham my friend. Thou whom I have taken from the ends of the earth, and called thee from the chief men thereof, and said unto thee, Thou art my servant; I have chosen thee, and not cast thee away. Fear thou not; for I am with thee: be not dismayed; for I am thy God: I will strengthen thee; yea, I will help thee; yea, I will uphold thee with the right hand of my righteousness. Behold, all they that were incensed against thee shall be ashamed and confounded: they shall be as nothing; and they that strive with thee shall perish. Thou shalt seek them, and shalt not find them, even them that contended with thee: they that war against thee shall be as nothing, and as a thing of nought. For I the Lord thy God will hold thy right hand, saying unto thee, Fear not;

245

I will help thee. Fear not, thou worm Jacob, and ye men of Israel; I will help thee, saith the Lord, and thy redeemer, the Holy One of Israel. Behold, I will make thee a new sharp threshing instrument having teeth: thou shalt thresh the mountains, and beat them small, and shalt make the hills as chaff (verses 8-15).

To know God and to confide in Him is to be invincible. None can really injure one whose confidence is in the Lord, for He will cause all that seems to be evil to work for the good of those who put their trust in Him. It is thus that fear, that deadly enemy of the heart, is overcome. In due time God will deal with those who seek to injure His people. He will mete out righteous judgment to those who trouble His saints (2 Thess. 1:6, 7). The believer can afford to leave all in His hands and so go on in quietness and confidence, through good or evil report.

Since retribution is in God's hands the enemies of God's people shall soon pass away and be forgotten, but those who do the will of God abide forever. We have the reassuring promise, "Fear not; I will help thee." It is God Himself who has given this word. Faith lays hold of it and the heart enters into rest, content to know that He who loved us enough to give His Son to die for us will never fail those who commit their ways unto Him. These promises come in as an encouraging preface before Jehovah points out the folly of turning to senseless idols who are absolutely unable to help.

The words here, "Abraham My friend," are referred to in James 2:23, where Abraham is called "the friend of God." What a wonderful thing for God to say of any man—"My friend"! The Lord Jesus said to His disciples: "Henceforth I call you not servants; for the servant knoweth not what his lord doeth: I have called you friends." The servant is to do what he is told. It is not for him to ask, "Why should I do this?" But to a friend one unburdens his heart, and the Lord speaks of Abraham as "My friend." He took him into His confidence in regard to Sodom's judgment.

So all the way through, God delights to open up His heart and mind to His friends. That is the object of the prophetic Scriptures. They open up God's truth so that His friends may enter into it and understand that which He is about to do.

The expression concerning Israel that God will make them a "sharp threshing instrument with teeth," points on to the great harvest of the last days when a remnant of Israel restored to the Lord will be used of Him to bring many down before Him in repentance and lead them to put faith in the message that they proclaim.

As servants of Christ we also need to be sharp threshing instruments with teeth. A great deal of preaching has very few "teeth." We should be faithful in pointing out the wickedness of mankind and the exceeding sinfulness of sin that men may realize where they stand before God. So preaching needs to have "teeth," else it may be absolutely powerless and colorless, and saved or unsaved can sit and listen to it and enjoy it.

THE CHOSEN SERVANT

I N CHAPTER forty-two Messiah is brought before us. The forerunner—the voice of one crying in the wilderness—has been spoken of. Now Messiah Himself is presented. This is taken up more fully later, but He is shown here that Israel may have the program of God before them and realize what folly it is to turn away from the living and true God to their senseless idols.

Behold my servant, whom I uphold; mine elect, in whom my soul delighteth; I have put my spirit upon him: he shall bring forth judgment to the Gentiles. He shall not cry, nor lift up, nor cause his voice to be heard in the street. A bruised reed shall he not break, and the smoking flax shall he not quench: he shall bring forth judgment unto truth. He shall not fail nor be discouraged till he have set judgment in the earth: and the isles shall wait for his law (verses 1-4).

This passage is definitely applied to our Lord in Matthew 12:17-21: "He shall not break the bruised reed, nor quench the smoking flax." Wherever there is the least evidence of the heart's desire to turn to God, He quickens and encourages it and leads on into full assurance of faith at last. These things characterized the Lord's ministry here. How far different from us! We are apt to go to extremes; either we do not like to talk to any one about their souls or do any personal work; we pay no attention, no matter what people may say or do, except to preach to them from the platform, or else we are inclined to be very obtrusive and self-assertive and do many things that are hardly in keeping with that Christian culture which we ought to manifest.

This passage helped me greatly when I was a young man. I began my ministry as a Salvation Army officer, and sixty years ago the Salvation Army was a mighty power for good in this country. We used to march the streets of San Francisco in processions of over 1,000, with two or three brass bands, and we won hundreds of souls to Christ, but little by little the organization got away from soul-seeking. It dwindled down from that, and now it is almost merely a great charitable organization. But we were inclined, perhaps, to go to too great extremes in our intense earnestness, and to do things that possibly were not wise. Instead of impressing people for God, it made them think we were unbalanced impressions of ourselves. Personally I was so under the power of legality that I felt guilty if I rode in a street car without immediately rising to give my testimony.

As soon as we left the corner I would get to my feet and say, "Friends, I want to give my testimony for Jesus Christ, and I want to tell you how God saved me." The conductor would come and say, "Sit down. We didn't ask you to come in here to conduct a church service."

Then I was rather rude to him. I said, "Well, I'll sit down if you say so, but you'll have to answer at the judgment-bar of God for preventing these people from hearing the gospel."

I would do the same thing in a railroad train. As soon as we got away from the station, I faced the passengers and began to give my testimony. I felt I had to do it, or be responsible for their souls. I did not realize that this was rude.

The last time that I got up in a railroad train in this way I had just started when a Roman Catholic priest jumped to his feet and said, "What's this? What's this? Do I have to be insulted in this train? Do I have to sit in a Protestant service? Call the conductor!"

The conductor came and said, "Young man, you can't do this—you've no right to interfere with other people's religion when you're riding on a railroad train." And so I had to sit down.

It bothered me. The devil either tries to keep you quiet or makes you think you must do what is unreasonable. What delivered me at last and showed me there was a golden mean between indifference and rudeness was this very passage.

What does it say of the Lord? "He shall not strive nor cry, neither shall His voice be heard in the street." He went through His service here for God in such a restful, quiet way. When people came to Him and wanted to know how to get eternal life, how to be saved, He was always ready to meet them, and He sought out the lost, like the woman at Sychar's well, but you never find Him doing anything boisterous or uncouth. He was truly "God's gentleman."

When I first saw that expression applied to Him I was rather startled. I picked up a little volume, an old History of the World, in London some years ago, published early in 1600. When it came down to the days of the Roman Empire and Augustus Caesar, it said, "In his days, there was born in Bethlehem of Judea that goodly gentleman, Jesus Christ." As I meditated on that, I thought, why should not that epithet be applied to Him?

What is a gentleman? A gentle man, a gracious man. Jesus was all that—always gentle and gracious. Even when rebuking sin sternly He never did anything that was boisterous or made Him seem uncouth.

> I will bring the blind by a way that they knew not; I will lead them in paths that they have not known: I will make darkness light before them, and crooked things straight, These things will I do unto them, and not forsake them (verse 16).

If God explained all His ways with us beforehand we would no longer walk by faith, but by sight. He leads us along strange paths, and through new and peculiar experiences that we may learn how marvelously His grace can sustain, and how blessedly His wisdom can plan. It is not necessary that we should see the road ahead. It is only necessary that we trust our Guide. He knows the end from the beginning, and He never deviates from His purpose of blessing. When, at last, we have reached the city of God and look back over the way we have come, we shall praise Him for all His dealings with us, and we shall understand the reason for every trial.

CHAPTER FORTY-THREE

GOD'S WITNESSES TO HIS FAITHFULNESS

THE Lord's gracious care of Israel is continued. How wonderfully He enters into their sorrows!

> But now thus saith the Lord that created thee, O Jacob, and he that formed thee, O Israel, Fear not: for I have redeemed thee, I have called thee by thy name; thou art mine. When thou passest through the waters, I will be with thee; and through the rivers, they shall not overflow thee: when thou walkest through the fire, thou shalt not be burned; neither shall the flame kindle upon thee. For I am the Lord thy God, the Holy One of Israel, thy Saviour (verses 1-3).

He who led Israel in safety through the Red Sea and the Jordan, and who walked with the three devoted Hebrew youths in the fiery furnace, is still the unfailing resource of His troubled people in every hour of trial, no matter how severe the test. Faith can count on His sustaining grace and blessed companionship in each perplexity or apparent defeat or grave danger. Millions have tested and proven the faithfulness of His promise.

With His gracious care for His people He brings His witnesses to it.

> Ye are my witnesses, saith the Lord, and my servant whom I have chosen: that ye may know and believe me, and understand that I am he: before me there was no God formed, neither shall

there be after me. I, even I, am the Lord; and beside me there is
no saviour . . . Yea, before the day was I am he (verses 10-13).

It is to Israel the Lord says, "Ye are my witnesses,"
and this is true of them whether they are obedient to
Him or disobedient, in the land or out of the land,
whether they are keeping the law or breaking it, because God has given His testimony through Moses and
other prophets showing just how He was going to deal
with His people down through the centuries, the blessings that would be theirs, if they walked in obedience;
the curses and judgments that would come upon them
if they were disobedient. History shows the truth of
what God has declared and, therefore, Israel are God's
witnesses to the truth of His Word.

Frederick the Great who had been listening to Vol-
taire's agnostic ideas once asked one of his court chap-
lains, "If the Bible is true it ought to be capable of very
clear and succinct witness. Generally when I ask if the
Bible is true, I am handed some long scholarly volume
which I have neither the time nor the patience to read.
If your Bible is true, give me the proof of it in one
word."

The chaplain answered, "Sire, Israel."

And Frederick acknowledged that this indeed is a
proof that the Bible is true, the Word of the living God.

But to Israel's witness to the past is added, "And my
chosen Servant." He is the faithful and true witness
to God's faithfulness. In chapter 42:1-9 we were called
to behold Him and the character of His service. The
purpose of this witness is next given: "That ye may
know and believe Me, and understand that I am He:
before Me there was no God formed, neither shall there
be after Me. I, even I, am the Lord; and beside Me
there is no Saviour."

From this time on Jehovah challenges the idolaters to give some evidence of any spirit of prophecy working in them. Tell us what is to come. Tell us things that have never been. Explain the past. Explain the origin of the world. They could not. God alone has done all these things.

CHAPTER FORTY-FOUR

GOD'S UNCHANGING PURPOSES
OF BLESSING

G OD continues this theme in a very precious and
wonderful way.

> Yet now hear, O Jacob my servant; and Israel, whom I have
> chosen: Thus saith the Lord that made thee, and formed thee from
> the womb, which will help thee; Fear not, O Jacob, my servant;
> and thou, Jeshurun, whom I have chosen. For I will pour water
> upon him that is thirsty, and floods upon the dry ground: I will
> pour my Spirit upon thy seed, and my blessing upon thine off-
> spring . . . Fear ye not, neither be afraid: have not I told thee
> from that time, and have declared it? ye are even my witnesses.
> Is there a God, besides me? yea, there is no God; I know not any
> (verses 1-3, 8).

Then comes His promise to pour His Spirit upon
Israel from on high. That has not taken place yet, and
is not to be confused with the day of Pentecost. It is
the prophecy of Joel (2:28, 29) which we have here.

Next comes Jehovah's direct word in regard to
idolatry.

> They that make a graven image are all of them vanity; and
> their delectable things shall not profit; and they are their own wit-
> nesses; they see not, nor know; that they may be ashamed . . . He
> heweth him down cedars, and taketh the cypress and the oak, which
> he strengtheneth for himself among the trees of the forest: he
> planteth an ash, and the rain doth nourish it. Then shall it be for
> a man to burn: for he will take thereof, and warm himself; yea,

he kindleth it, and baketh bread; yea, he maketh a god, and worshippeth it; he maketh it a graven image, and falleth down thereto. He burneth part thereof in the fire; with part thereof he eateth flesh; he roasteth roast, and is satisfied: yea, he warmeth himself, and saith, Aha, I am warm, I have seen the fire: And the residue thereof he maketh a god, even his graven image: he falleth down unto it, and worshippeth it, and prayeth unto it, and saith, Deliver me; for thou art my god. They have not known nor understood: for he hath shut their eyes, that they cannot see; and their hearts, that they cannot understand. And none considereth in his heart, neither is there knowledge nor understanding to say, I have burned part of it in the fire; yea, also I have baked bread upon the coals thereof; I have roasted flesh, and eaten it: and shall I make the residue thereof an abomination? shall I fall down to the stock of a tree? He feedeth on ashes: a deceived heart hath turned him aside, that he cannot deliver his soul, nor say, Is there not a lie in my right hand? (verses 9, 14-20).

The idol-makers are said to be their own witnesses (verse 9) to their own folly. Isaiah satirically pictures a man going out into the forest and finding a noble tree. He cuts it down, takes off all the branches and begins to fashion it with his tools. By-and-by he has the figure of a man, and he gathers up the chips as they fly, the parts that are not wanted to make the image, and he uses them as fuel. He cooks his food and says, "This is fine! I have warmed myself at the fire and have a god to worship, all out of the same tree."

Isaiah's remarkable satire and ridicule show the folly of idolatry. The prophet Jeremiah also uses similar language as to this (Jer. 10).

What folly for the people of Israel, after all that God had done for them, to turn aside to dumb idols! Yet how senseless people are! On different occasions the kings in Chronicles—even when the people of Israel or Judah went out against some of their foes and overcame them—brought back the gods of the nations they had conquered and set up shrines for them and worshiped them though those gods had proved powerless to defend their own worshipers.

Idolatry seems inherent in the heart of man. Today, men do not worship idols of gold and silver, and brass and iron, but every man who turns away from God sets up some kind of an idol in his heart. He either worships himself or some folly, pleasure, or fame.

An esteemed servant of Christ spoke aptly when introduced on one occasion as a "self-made man." He said he regretted he had been so termed, though he appreciated the kindly thought, "for," he said, "I've noticed that these self-made men always worship their own creation." He knew that if men do not know the one living and true God, they set up the great god self, and worship him.

Remember these, O Jacob and Israel; for thou art my servant: I have formed thee; thou art my servant; O Israel, thou shalt not be forgotten of me. I have blotted out, as a thick cloud, thy transgressions, and, as a cloud, thy sins: return unto me; for I have redeemed thee. Sing, O ye heavens; for the Lord hath done it: shout, ye lower parts of the earth: break forth into singing, ye mountains, O forest, and every tree therein: for the Lord hath redeemed Jacob, and glorified himself in Israel. Thus saith the Lord, thy redeemer, and he that formed thee from the womb, I am the Lord that maketh all things, that stretcheth forth the heavens alone; that spreadeth abroad the earth by myself (verses 21-24).

God tells Israel what He has in store for them, the Redeemer who was still to come, the forerunner who would announce His coming, the comfort He has for them who believe His word and put their trust in Him. He has foreseen the dangers and sorrows that Israel must pass through—the deep waters through which they will have to go. But where there is real faith on their part, He has promised to be with them in all their sorrows and all their troubles.

Then in the closing words of the chapter there is an abrupt change, and He speaks of one who was yet to come to be the deliverer of Israel from the power of the Chaldeans, calls him by name, though he has not known Him—that is Cyrus, King of Persia.

That saith of Cyrus, He is my shepherd, and shall perform all my pleasure: even saying to Jerusalem, Thou shalt be built; and to the temple, Thy foundation shall be laid (verse 28).

Isaiah wrote these words long before the Babylonian captivity of seventy years, so that many decades would elapse before Cyrus himself was to appear. He was foretold so long before that when he did come, Israel would know it was the hour of Jehovah's deliverance.

Sometimes the divisions in the chapters and verses come in the wrong places in our English Bible. Its division into chapters and verses is not a question of inspiration. It was simply a matter of accommodation on the part of human editors who thought it would help us to separate the subjects and define certain passages. And while it has been very helpful to have chapters and verses, on the other hand sometimes it is misleading, and may keep us from getting the full content of the passage if it is broken up in the middle. At times the editors seem to have used poor judgment in doing so.

For instance, take the break between John 7 and 8. The last words of John 7 are: "And every man went to his own house." The opening words of John 8 are: "Jesus went to the Mount of Olives." They failed to translate one little word that should have been rendered "but," and the omission has broken a sentence right in two. "Every man went to his own house, *but* Jesus went to the Mount of Olives." He had no house. He was the homeless stranger in the world His own hands had made. And when others went to their comfortable homes that night, He went out to the mountainside, perhaps to the Garden of Gethsemane, and spent the night there, lying upon the bare ground and communing with His Father.

It is very evident here that there should be no break between the last verse of chapter forty-four and the first verse in chapter forty-five.

THE COMING OF CYRUS FORETOLD

Thus saith the Lord to his anointed, to Cyrus, whose right hand I have holden, to subdue nations before him; and I will loose the loins of kings, to open before him the two-leaved gates; and the gates shall not be shut; I will go before thee, and make the crooked places straight: I will break in pieces the gates of brass, and cut in sunder the bars of iron: And I will give thee the treasures of darkness, and hidden riches of secret places, that thou mayest know that I, the Lord, which call thee by thy name, am the God of Israel. For Jacob my servant's sake, and Israel mine elect, I have even called thee by thy name: I have surnamed thee, though thou hast not known me (verses 1-4).

THIS is the passage preeminently given by unbelieving critics as proof that the Isaiah who wrote the first part of the book could not have written these words. But as we have already said, that is simply discounting the whole question of inspiration. If we believe, as every Christian should, that all Scripture is given by inspiration of God, that the prophecy came not in old time by the will of man, but that holy men of God spake as they were moved by the Holy Ghost, there is no more difficulty in understanding that God could foretell the rise of King Cyrus and what he would do for His people than it was to foretell the coming of the Lord Jesus into the world, and the redemption that He would accomplish; His first coming and His second coming and the effects, both of His rejection and of His final acceptance by the people of Israel. All this was foretold ahead of time, and so in the same way, God through Isaiah foretold the rise of Cyrus.

Cyrus the Persian was the nephew of Cyraxares, king of Media. Media and Persia were, as a rule, very closely related. They sprang from the same stock; it was through these kingdoms united together under the leadership of Cyraxares and Cyrus that eventually Chaldea was conquered and Babylon became one of the chief cities of the Persian Empire until its eventual complete destruction. Secular history gives fuller information about its conquest. Herodotus has much to say of it, and other ancient records relate that Cyraxares and Cyrus in alliance marched against Babylon, and Cyrus eventually took it by turning aside the waters of the Euphrates into another channel, and so came in on the river-bed under the two-leaved gates, the gates of the river itself. That is what is indicated here. God foresaw all this. Cyrus was no mere legendary figure. The majestic rifled ruins of his magnificent tomb still stand at Pasargardae in Iran. The original inscription concluded: "Who founded the Persian Empire and was King of Asia . . . Therefore grudge me not this monument."

One reason why Cyrus and the Persians befriended the people of Israel was that the Persians like the Israelites were monotheists. They did not believe in idolatry. They did not worship idols, but abhorred them. They worshiped God under the symbol of the sun, and also believed in a great power they called Ahriman. Ormazd was their name for God. Ahriman was the name for the power of darkness. Some people think of them as dualists as though they believed in two great gods, the god of light and the god of darkness. But it seems more likely that they really believed in one true and living God, but with a great Adversary seeking to impede the carrying out of God's counsels. A people believing in one God, symbolized by the sun (they did not actually worship it) would look with favor upon Israel, when they found that they did not worship idols.

It was because of idolatry that Israel were carried captives to Babylon, its source, but this cured them of idolatry. Soon after their arrival they found that death was the punishment there of refusal to worship an image (Dan. 3:14, 15). Undoubtedly, here and there, there have been Jews who have been idolators because of ignorance, but the nation itself learned to abhor idolatry from what they saw in Babylon. There they suffered for seventy years until its fall under the awful conditions of that idolatrous kingdom. Never again have they been an idolatrous people. To this day, they abhor idols of any description. That is one reason why the Roman Catholic, the Greek Catholic, the Greek Orthodox, and other branches of the Catholic Church, have had difficulty in impressing the Jews, because if a Jew looks inside one of their churches, to him it is just a heathen temple. Here are all kinds of icons and images, and people burning incense and candles and bowing down to them. To the Jew that is abhorrent. He hates and detests it.

It is only when pure Christianity, apart from all that, is presented in loving-kindness to the Jew that any impression is likely to be made upon him. Through the centuries there have been Jews who have been converted to Romanism, but frequently that conversion has been a mere pretence to escape persecution. With outward conformity to the Church of Rome, their hid-

den services were carried on in the synagogue worship
as of old. But where there is a real new birth and a
Jew becomes a true Christian, he turns away from all
this idolatry because it is something that his very soul
abhors.

But God's reiterated warnings and pleadings are not
unneeded. There will be a supreme test for Israel which
is yet to come during the great tribulation. The son of
perdition shall arise to oppose and exalt "himself above
all that is called God, or that is worshipped; so that he
as God sitteth in the temple of God, shewing himself
that he is God" (2 Thess. 2:4). He will persuade men
to make an image, and will have power to give life to
it, that the image shall both speak and cause that as
many as would not worship the image should be killed
(Rev. 13:14, 15). Many in fear of death will fail, with
terrible results (Rev. 14:9-11); others will be victors
over the image and will glorify God's holy name (Rev.
15:2-4). Again let us repeat, God's continued warnings
and pleadings in Isaiah are not unneeded.

God foretold the rise of King Cyrus. He was to open
the way for the remnant to return to Jerusalem. But,
of course, this was to be but a partial return. There
are those who insist that all the prophecies connected
with the return of Israel have been fulfilled already
and, therefore, we are not to look for any future fulfillment of them, but God says in this very book of
Isaiah, "I will set my hand a second time to recover
my people," and that is what He has already begun to
do, as they gather back as a people to their land.

Following this revelation in regard to King Cyrus,
God comes back to the subject that had occupied Him
before, emphasizing man's littleness, his frailty and his

lack of merit, and His own majesty and power and glory, in contrast to the idols to which the people had turned. He continues, and it is:

> I am the Lord, and there is none else, there is no God beside me: I girded thee, though thou hast not known me: That they may know from the rising of the sun, and from the west, that there is none beside me. I am the Lord, and there is none else. I form the light, and create darkness: I make peace, and create evil: I the Lord do all these things (verses 5-7).

That is very striking in connection with the Persian beliefs. In their sacred writings, the Zend-Avesta for instance, they gave the primary place to Ormazd, the god of light, the one true living God. And Ahriman occupies a very large place as the supernatural foe of God, in constant conflict with Him. One is the God of light, the other is the evil spirit of darkness. One is the God of peace and the other the spirit of war. One is the God of goodness and the other the spirit of evil. So here in answer to this, God, as though addressing King Cyrus, says "I am the one true and living God . . . beside Me there is no other. I create peace and I create evil. I create light and I create darkness. There is no other power that can share omnipotence with Me."

"I create peace and I create evil." What does that mean? Extreme high Calvinists insist that God has foreordained everything that takes place on the earth; therefore that man should sin, in order that He might have opportunity to display His redemptive grace. But that is not what is involved here when He says, "I create peace and I create evil." It is evil in the sense of calamity. In other words, if there is a thunderstorm and great damage is done, God says, "I take full responsibility for it"; if everything is fair and beautiful

God says, "This is from Me"; if there is a great earthquake, God is behind that. Whatever it is, "I the Lord create peace, I create evil." And so we read, "Shall there be evil in a city and the Lord hath not done it?" (Amos 3:6).

God takes the responsibility for everything that occurs, but it is not always that He is working directly Himself, but that He permits others to work. For instance, He permitted Satan to try Job. But the point here is that there are not two great powers in the universe in conflict with each other, both of whom are God, a good God and an evil god; but there is *one* God, though there is an evil power working against Him.

Woe unto him that striveth with his Maker! Let the potsherd strive with the potsherds of the earth. Shall the clay say to him that fashioneth it, What makest thou? or thy work, He hath no hands? . . . Assemble yourselves and come; draw near together, ye that are escaped of the nations: they have no knowledge that set up the wood of their graven image, and pray unto a god that cannot save. Tell ye, and bring them near; yea, let them take counsel together: who hath declared this from ancient time? who hath told it from that time? have not I the Lord? and there is no God else beside me; a just God and a Saviour; there is none beside me. Look unto me, and be ye saved, all the ends of the earth: for I am God, and there is none else (verses 9, 20-22).

What a marvelous declaration! God making Himself known in those Old Testament times as a just God and a Saviour, a God who will deal in absolute righteousness with the sin question, and yet who Himself has found a way consistent with His own infinite holiness and the righteousness of His throne, whereby He can be the Saviour of the sinner who turns to Him in repentance and faith. A just God and a Saviour! Long ago in Greece such wise men as Socrates and Plato argued one day as to forgiveness of sin. Socrates turned to Plato saying, "It may be that God can forgive sins but I do not see how."

That is remarkable! This pagan philosopher to a very large extent had his eyes open to divine realities. "It may be that God can forgive sins, but I do not see how." What did he mean by that?

If God is the moral Governor of the Universe and if God is a righteous Judge, and all men are to come before Him to be judged for the deeds done in the body, how can He forgive sins? It is not in the province of the judge to forgive criminals but to pronounce sentence upon evil-doers and see that sentence carried out.

How then could a righteous God forgive sins? Away back here in Isaiah, who lived two centuries and a half before Socrates, God declares in Israel that He is a just God and a Saviour. And in the Epistle to the Romans written nearly five centuries after Socrates, we are told how God can be just and the Justifier of him that believeth in Jesus.

This is a wonderful gospel passage: "Look unto Me, and be ye saved, all the ends of the earth: for I am God, and there is none else."

Now God is revealed in the Lord Jesus Christ, and these very same words can be used in connection with Him, because He said, "I am the Way, the Truth, and the Life: no man cometh unto the Father, but by Me." "There is none other name," says Peter, "under heaven given among men, whereby we must be saved."

"Look unto Me . . . all the ends of the earth: for I am God, and there is none else." What does it mean to look unto Him? God has used such simple terms to show people how easily we may come into direct contact with Him through grace. And yet difficulty is made out of the plain words "believe" and "look." To "look" here simply means to turn our eyes to the only One who can help us, He who bids us to look. It is the Person that makes all the difference. We do not look at ourselves, we know our helpless condition, but turn an expectant, obedient gaze on Him. "Look unto Me . . . for I am God, and there is none else." The invitation is world-wide and with blessed results—"be ye saved." Hebrews 12:2 gives the glorious Person too, "Looking unto Jesus." Isaiah doubtless refers to the dying, serpent-bitten Israelites in Numbers 21:8, 9, who lived when they fixed their earnest gaze on the brazen serpent lifted up by Moses.

Chapters 45-48 are part of one section embracing chapters 40-48, in which we have Jehovah's controversy with idols. He emphasizes His own power and majesty. In one of his printed lectures Col. Robert G. Ingersoll dwelt on this. He said, "What a boaster this God of the Bible is! How often He talks about Himself and what He has done and can do!" One can understand an ungodly man saying this, but who in all the universe has a right to boast save the God who created it? And why does He set forth His own glory and His own majesty and His own power? Why does He emphasize His own wisdom and His own strength and ability? It is that men may realize the importance of living in touch with Him and the uselessness of turning to anyone else.

CHAPTER FORTY-SIX

THE EVERLASTING ONE CONTRASTED WITH IDOLS

GOD is still contrasting Himself with idols and, He says, they can do nothing to save themselves. When Cyrus attacked Babylon and the city fell, the idolatrous priests loaded their helpless gods upon carts to wheel them away and set them up somewhere else. Idols who could not deliver their worshipers had to be delivered by them from absolute destruction.

Bel boweth down, Nebo stoopeth, their idols were upon the beasts, and upon the cattle: your carriages were heavy loaden; they are a burden to the weary beast. They stoop, they bow down together; they could not deliver the burden, but themselves are gone into captivity. Hearken unto me, O house of Jacob, and all the remnant of the house of Israel, which are borne by me from the belly, which are carried from the womb: And even to your old age I am he; and even to hoar hairs will I carry you: I have made, and I will bear; even I will carry, and will deliver you. To whom will ye liken me, and make me equal, and compare me, that we may be like? They lavish gold out of the bag, and weigh silver in the balance, and hire a goldsmith; and he maketh it a god: they fall down, yea, they worship. They bear him upon the shoulder, they carry him, and set him in his place, and he standeth; from his place shall he not remove: yea, one shall cry unto him, yet can he not answer, nor save him out of his trouble. Remember this, and shew yourselves men: bring it again to mind, O ye transgressors. Remember the former things of old: for I am God, and there is none else; I am God, and there is none like me (verses 1-9).

God says, "I am altogether different from these gods who have to be carried by their makers. I undertake to carry you. I have brought you hitherto and I will continue to carry you through, even down to old age will I carry you, when hoar hairs adorn your brow I will be there to carry you, to deliver, to sustain you, and to see you through."

God had satirized the making of gods out of the trees of the forest. Now He ridicules those who make graven images out of the various metals. The goldsmith takes metal, fashions and works over it and then sets it up and says, "This is a god." But it is immovable. It cannot walk. It cannot see. It cannot hear. It cannot do anything, and in time of danger it needs someone to protect it. What a god!

Notice the satire here and the irony, and the wonderful precious promises brought before us. God says, "How differently I have acted toward you, Israel. How could you ever turn aside to such senselessness as idolatry when you have known how wonderfully I have sustained and cared for you through the centuries. Look back over the past and see what I have done. And I promise to care for you just as wonderfully in the future.

CHAPTER FORTY-SEVEN

THE DOWNFALL OF BABYLON

Come down, and sit in the dust, O virgin daughter of Babylon, sit on the ground: there is no throne, O daughter of the Chaldeans: for thou shalt no more be called tender and delicate. Take the millstones, and grind meal: uncover thy locks, make bare the leg, uncover the thigh, pass over the rivers. Thy nakedness shall be uncovered, yea, thy shame shall be seen: I will take vengeance, and I will not meet thee as a man. As for our redeemer, the Lord of hosts is his name, the Holy One of Israel. Sit thou silent, and get thee into darkness, O daughter of the Chaldeans: for thou shalt no more be called, The lady of kingdoms (verses 1-5).

IN THE first part of this book we drew attention to the fact that Babylon was the very fountainhead of idolatry. According to the best records idolatry began there. A famous book, *The Two Babylons*, gives the details and proofs of this.

Babylon, by her sorceries, her enchantments, is said to have bewitched the nations. Nation after nation followed her in the practice of idolatry. She was called, "The Lady of Kingdoms"; her wealth, and her culture surpassed those of any nation around her.

But God, looking far ahead to the time when Cyrus and his army would come against her, says, "Thou shalt no more be called, The lady of kingdoms" (vs. 5). The day was coming when she would be stripped and laid bare, all her treasures destroyed, and everything taken away from her, when God would prove that her idols had absolutely no power, but His word

270

hould stand. He speaks of her folly in turning for
onfidence to the star-gazers, the astrologers, the
nonthly prognosticators.

Stand now with thine enchantments, and with the multitude
f thy sorceries, wherein thou hast laboured from thy youth; if
o be thou shalt be able to profit, if so be thou mayest prevail. Thou
rt wearied in the multitude of thy counsels. Let now the astrolo-
ers, the star-gazers, the monthly prognosticators, stand up, and
ave thee from these things that shall come upon thee. Behold, they
hall be as stubble; the fire shall burn them; they shall not deliver
hemselves from the power of the flame: there shall not be a coal
o warm at, nor fire to sit before it. Thus shall they be unto thee
vith whom thou hast laboured, even thy merchants, from thy
'outh: they shall wander every one to his quarter; none shall save
hee (verses 12-15).

Wherever people turn away from the one, true and
iving God and refuse the Word of God, they are al-
vays ready to turn to other things. It has been char-
cteristic down through the centuries that when men,
;reat leaders, gave up confidence in God and His Word
:hey readily became the prey of all sorts of charlatans.
Even the infamous Hitler had a special astrologer
vhom he consulted as to lucky and unlucky days, and
;uitable times to attack nations. He consulted the map
)f the stars to see what was indicated. That began at
Babylon. Centuries ago they had their astrologers, their
;tar-gazers.

An astrologer and an astronomer must not be confused. Astronomy is an exact science, astrology is a
fraud, a fake. Yet how many people give heed to it.
Many of our newspapers contain astrologers' reports
from month to month, and people are foolish enough
to believe them. Some of the greatest operators on the
Market in New York City, I have been credibly in-

formed, when it comes to making big deals never do a thing without consulting an astrologer. Men still believe in these worse than follies. They turn away from the Word of the living God to turn unto fables.

While in Los Angeles years ago I went down one day on the electric line to Long Beach, just to have a little relaxation on a Saturday. I was all worn out with so many meetings and I had hardly taken my seat when a Bulgarian gypsy came along in a red dress with some spangles across her brow, and long braids of black hair. She sat right down beside me, and took my hand.

Then she said, "Gentleman—gentleman—you cross my palm with silver—25¢—I tell you past, present, future. I am seventh daughter of a seventh daughter. I born with a veil on. I can tell all mysteries."

I said, grabbing her by the hand, "Well, it isn't really necessary—because I've had that all told already."

"But oh!" she said, "I am expert—I know very exact —past, present, future."

"Yes, but I got it from an expert—I have it here in a little book." And I pulled out, with my other hand, my New Testament and turned to the second chapter of the book of the Ephesians. I said, "Here, I've got my past, present and future. Here's the past: 'You hath He quickened, who were dead in trespasses and sins, wherein in time past ye walked according to the course of this world, according . . . to the spirit that now worketh in the children of disobedience.' "

"Oh, what is that, a Bible? I got the wrong man. I got the wrong man. Let go."

"No," I said, "I won't let go, I didn't ask you to come down here and take hold of me. Now that I've got you, you're going to stay here. Now I'll give you the rest of

t. Now I'll give you my present: 'But God, who is rich n mercy, for His great love wherewith He loved us, Even when we were dead in sins, hath quickened us ogether with Christ . . . by grace are ye saved hrough faith; and that not of yourselves: it is the gift of God.'—That's my present."

"That's all right. That's all right. I've got enough. Good-bye."

I said, "Wait a minute. I haven't given you it all yet. Now," I said, "here's my future: 'That in the ages to come He might shew the exceeding riches of His grace in His kindness toward us through Christ Jesus.' "

"Yes, gentleman—I've got enough," and she gave such a pull she was gone. And down the car she went saying, "I got the wrong man—I got the wrong man."

A passenger in a railroad train one day was reading his Bible when a dapper-looking gentleman came along, looked at it and said, "Oh, reading the Bible? Do you believe the Bible? I didn't think that any educated people believed in the Bible any more. You look like a cultured man, and I'm surprised that you're reading that. I believe the day will soon come when people will no more believe in the Bible than they believe in ghosts and witches, like our forefathers."

"My friend," remarked the Bible-reading gentleman, "when people reach the place where they do not believe in the Bible any more, they believe in witches and ghosts again."

That is true. How many have turned away from the Word of God to Spiritism and Theosophy and other occult systems that profess to have to do with the dead. That is Babylonianism, come right down through the centuries.

God has judged it all and He puts it all, as it were, to one side. "Why do men need this? Here am I, infinite in wisdom, power and might, and ready in grace to reveal Myself to the man who seeks My face."

CHAPTER FORTY-EIGHT

GOD'S CONTROVERSY WITH ISRAEL

Hear ye this, O house of Jacob, which are called by the name
of Israel, and are come forth out of the waters of Judah, which
swear by the name of the Lord, and make mention of the God of
Israel, but not in truth, nor in righteousness. For they call themselves of the holy city, and stay themselves upon the God of Israel;
The Lord of hosts is his name (verses 1, 2).

THIS chapter covers God's dealings with the children of Israel. No other nation has suffered like
them, yet they remain nationally intact to this
day, and will do so to the very end. When at last they
have passed through all the afflictions and tribulations
and troubles, they will understand the meaning of
verse 10. God will refine Israel by their troubles and
tribulations, eventually to be to the praise of His glory,
a royal diadem upon His brow, throughout the generations to come.

Behold, I have refined thee, but not with silver; I have chosen
thee in the furnace of affliction . . . Thus saith the Lord, thy
Redeemer, the Holy One of Israel; I am the Lord thy God which
teacheth thee to profit, which leadeth thee by the way that thou
shouldest go. O that thou hadst hearkened to my commandments!
then had thy peace been as a river, and thy righteousness as the
waves of the sea . . . Go ye forth of Babylon, flee ye from the
Chaldeans, with a voice of singing declare ye, tell this, utter it
even to the end of the earth; say ye, The Lord hath redeemed his
servant Jacob . . . And they thirsted not when he led them through
the deserts: he caused the waters to flow out of the rock for them:

he clave the rock also, and the waters gushed out. There is no peace, saith the Lord, unto the wicked (verses 10, 17, 18, 20-22).

Just as in the past God has undertaken for Israel, so He will do also in the days to come. It is He who will refine them by their very sorrows. And those who turn to Him, in repentance, those who receive the Saviour He has provided will be brought into fullness of blessing.

The section ends with the solemn words: "There is no peace, saith Jehovah, to the wicked." Here it is "Jehovah," for He speaks to His people whose peace might have been as a river (verse 18) if they had been obedient. "Jehovah" stands out in vivid contrast with the idols to whom they have turned for succor and help and who have failed them utterly. At the end of the next section it is "my God," for all who are of a contrite and humble heart are included in the promise, "Peace, peace to him that is far off, and to him that is near" (chapter 57:19). The promise and the warning there come to all the hearers, whether of Israel or not.

Now we come to a very precious and important part of the book of Isaiah. The Apostle Peter speaks of "exceeding great and precious promises." Everything in God's Word is precious, even though at first sight it may not always seem so. And it is all important, for "All scripture is given by inspiration of God, and is profitable," but certain parts of God's Word speak to us more loudly, perhaps, than others. And the portion upon which we now enter has a very loud voice for all those who know and love the Lord Jesus Christ, because it brings Him personally before us in such a clear, definite way. We have concluded the first subdivision of the last half of Isaiah.

In this great third division of the book are three sub-divisions. First, as we have already had, Jehovah's controversy with Israel concerning their idolatry, in chapters 40-48, ending, "There is no peace, saith Jehovah, to the wicked."

Jehovah's controversy with Israel concerning their treatment of the Messiah begins with chapter forty-nine and ends with chapter fifty-seven, concluding with the words, "There is no peace, saith my God, to the wicked." See how aptly these endings come in. There is no peace to the one who substitutes anything else for the One True and Living God.

When one turns to any substitute for the true God he can never find peace. Then on the other hand, there is no peace for the one who rejects the Saviour whom God has provided. "There is no peace, saith my God, to the wicked."

CHAPTER FORTY-NINE

MESSIAH DESPISED, GOD'S ANSWER

Listen, O isles, unto me; and hearken, ye people, from far; The Lord hath called me from the womb; from the bowels of my mother hath he made mention of my name. And he hath made my mouth like a sharp sword; in the shadow of his hand hath he hid me, and made me a polished shaft; in his quiver hath he hid me; And said unto me, Thou art my servant, O Israel, in whom I will be glorified. Then I said, I have laboured in vain, I have spent my strength for nought, and in vain: yet surely my judgment is with the Lord, and my work with my God. And now, saith the Lord that formed me from the womb to be his servant, to bring Jacob again to him, Though Israel be not gathered, yet shall I be glorious in the eyes of the Lord, and my God shall be my strength. And he said, It is a light thing that thou shouldest be my servant to raise up the tribes of Jacob, and to restore the preserved of Israel: I will also give thee for a light to the Gentiles, that thou mayest be my salvation unto the end of the earth (verses 1-6).

IN CHAPTER forty-nine Israel is brought before us as Jehovah's servant, but Israel as a nation had failed terribly in that place. And so while it is Israel who speaks and says, "The Lord hath called me from the womb . . . And said unto me, Thou art My servant," it is really the Lord Jesus Christ Himself who takes the place of Israel, the true Israel. The servant here is no longer the nation as such, though it does speak here in these opening verses. But it is the Lord Jesus who takes the place of the nation.

Other scriptures indicate this. In Hosea God speaks of bringing the nation out of Egypt: "Out of Egypt

have I called My Son." That prophecy is referred to the
Lord Jesus Christ Himself, who as a little babe was
carried down to Egypt and brought back to the land
"that it might be fulfilled," Matthew says, "which was
spoken of the Lord by the prophet, saying, Out of
Egypt have I called My Son" (Matt. 2:15). So that in
the first instance the son there was Israel, but it was the
Lord Jesus, the true Israel, who was actually before the
mind of God.

We often use similar language, substituting an individual for the whole people. Louis the Fourteenth, that
proud French monarch, exclaimed on one occasion:
"France must rule the world, and I am France." And
Napoleon Bonaparte said, "The State must be supreme,
and I am the State." If uninspired men use language in
that way, how much more has Christ the right to say,
"I am Israel, the true Israel." The very name "Israel"
meant "A Prince with God," and it was He then who
was manifested as the true Prince, the servant of Jehovah, when Israel, both as a nation and individually,
utterly failed.

Next comes a remarkable prophecy of Christ's rejection by Israel and the calling of the Gentiles. Messiah says, "I have laboured in vain, I have spent My
strength for nought" (verse 4). That is, as far as Israel
is concerned, His work seemed a failure on earth. "He
came unto His own, and His own received Him not."
But He leaves all with Jehovah, and declares, "Though
Israel be not gathered, yet shall I be glorious in the eyes
of the Lord." For He has said unto Him, "It is a light
thing that Thou shouldest be My servant to raise up
the tribes of Jacob, and to restore the preserved of
Israel: I will also give Thee for a light to the Gentiles,
that Thou mayest be My salvation unto the end of the

earth." Through Messiah's rejection by Israel, a greater work would be accomplished. The message would go out to the Gentile world.

Thus saith the Lord, the Redeemer of Israel, and his Holy One, to him whom man despiseth, to him whom the nation abhorreth, to a servant of rulers, Kings shall see and arise, princes also shall worship, because of the Lord that is faithful, and the Holy One of Israel, and he shall choose thee (verse 7).

While in the Old Testament we do not have the present age brought clearly before us, the Old Testament prophet is like a man looking at two mountain peaks, one some distance beyond the other and higher than the first one, and he was therefore unable to see the valley between them. So the prophets testified of the sufferings of Christ at His first coming and of the glories that should follow the Second Coming. But they do not give us any clear teaching and outline as to all that goes on in between.

We know now from the New Testament that God had us in His heart from all eternity to call out from Jew and Gentile a people to His name, who should be the bride of His Son. So that when the Lord Jesus returns to reign in power and glory, He will not return alone. He will have a bride with Him who shall sit with Him upon His throne.

If Isaiah gives no definite instruction in regard to the present day as yet, it is very evident that such a prophecy does cover the present age as well as looking on to the millennium. It will have its fulfillment in millennial days, when all the kingdoms of this world will become the kingdom of our God and His Christ.

Then Jehovah speaks to the One whom man despised, the One whom the nation abhorreth, an expression not too strong for the feeling of Israel toward the Lord Jesus Christ, for terms are used concerning Him in Jewish writings, the Talmud and others, such as the "leper" and the "hanged-one"—the one whom the nation abhorreth. They could not understand. "Had they known," Peter says, "they would not have crucified the Lord of glory." But they did not know.

God will glorify that One whom the nation abhorreth, the kings and princes of the earth will recognize Him and bow down before Him. In a remarkable sense that has been true even during the present age, although unforeseen by the prophets. Because as the gospel went from land to land throughout the early centuries, whole nations were brought to profess, at least, subjection to the Lord Jesus and many kings proclaimed themselves His subjects. Down to the present time among the nations there are rulers who confess the authority of the Lord Jesus Christ. The rulers of Great Britain, of Holland, and of Scandinavia are all professed Christians. That does not mean necessarily that they are all born again, but they are all professed Christians and acknowledge, outwardly at least, the authority of the Lord Jesus Christ.

Many leaders in the United States have taken the same place. Franklin D. Roosevelt was a professed Christian, a warden of an Episcopal Church. And President Truman, after his first press conference, asked for prayer, saying he would need it. He professes the Christian faith and, in that sense, he recognizes the authority of the Lord Jesus Christ.

Queen Victoria was very definite in her confession of faith when a heathen African prince came to Great Britain and was presented to her. He inquired, "Your Majesty, to what do you attribute the great prosperity

of the British Empire?" She handed him a Bible and
said simply, "This Book." He carried this Book back
to his people, to tell them that it was that on which
the prosperity of the British Empire was based.
Toward the end of her life Queen Victoria once publicly
stated, "I am a firm believer in the Second Coming of
the Lord Jesus Christ. And I have sometimes thought
that He has permitted me to reign so long that perhaps
I will never lay down my crown until I lay it down at
His feet, when He comes again." It was a lovely expression of subjection to the Lord. Queen Victoria
evidently knew Christ as her Saviour. She was accustomed every summer to go to Balmoral, a lovely place
in Scotland, and used to visit the Highland women living in the little cottages in the hills around. She became
acquainted with all of them and went from one to another to chat with them. Of course, they were delighted
that the Queen would take such notice of them. Finally,
as she was returning to London, she came to bid one old
cottager goodbye. The old lady said, "Well, your
Majesty, I may never see you on earth again. May I
ask your gracious Majesty a question?"

She said, "Yes; as many as you like."

"Well," she said, "will your Majesty meet me in
heaven?"

The Queen replied, "Yes; through the all-availing
blood of Jesus."

That was a good testimony from the ruler of a mighty
empire. The kings have bowed down before the Lord
Jesus Christ. The nation of Israel rejected Him. They
did not understand, but God has made His name glorious throughout the world. The passage of course looks
on to complete fulfillment in millennial days when all

the kings of the earth will bring their riches and glory into the New Jerusalem.

Thus saith the Lord, In an acceptable time have I heard thee, and in a day of salvation have I helped thee: and I will preserve thee, and give thee for a covenant of the people, to establish the earth, to cause to inherit the desolate heritages; That thou mayest say to the prisoners, Go forth; to them that are in darkness, Shew yourselves. They shall feed in the ways, and their pastures shall be in all high places. They shall not hunger nor thirst; neither shall the heat nor sun smite them: for he that hath mercy on them shall lead them, even by the springs of water shall he guide them. And I will make all my mountains a way, and my highways shall be exalted (verses 8-11).

The two parts of this passage are clearly brought before us in the New Testament. "In an acceptable time have I heard thee." We read in 2 Corinthians 6:2, "Behold, now is the accepted time; behold, now is the day of salvation," so that God applies the words at the present time, while the gospel of the grace of God is going out into all the world.

The latter part of this scripture carries us on to the time of the great awakening when all over the world men will be brought to recognize the Lord Jesus Christ. That is pictured in Revelation 7. After giving us the vision of the 144,000 sealed ones of Israel, John says, I saw "a great multitude, which no man could number . . . clothed with white robes, and palms in their hands"; and they stood before the throne of God and of the Lamb. Many commentators say that these are the martyred saints who will be slain under the rule of the Beast and the false prophet, and that now they are seen up in heaven. But it seems very evident that is an utter mistake; that this is a great multitude who will form the nucleus of the coming glorious kingdom with the Lord Jesus Christ here on the earth, because one of the elders turns to John and says, "What are these which are arrayed in white robes? and whence came they?"

John says, "Sir, thou knowest." And so the other replies: "These are they that come out of the great tribulation,"—literally there are two definite articles there, "They come out of *the* tribulation *the* great one— and washed their robes, and made them white in the blood of the Lamb." Here is a great blood-washed multitude who have come up out of the great tribulation, not ascended into heaven, but they have gone through all that period of trial and been preserved by God. The Lord says of them in Revelation 7:16,17: "They shall hunger no more, neither thirst any more; neither shall the sun light on them, nor any heat. For the Lamb which is in the midst of the throne shall feed them, and shall lead them unto living fountains of waters: and God shall wipe away all tears from their eyes."

The kindred passage in Isaiah will show how exactly the one fits the other. "They shall feed in the ways, and their pastures shall be in all high places. They shall not hunger nor thirst; neither shall the heat nor sun smite them: for He that hath mercy on them shall lead them, even by the springs of water shall He guide them" (verses 9, 10).

The two passages refer to exactly the same group, an earthly group, who will be saved for the glorious millennial kingdom of our Lord Jesus Christ: primarily the remnant of Israel, and associated with them is a great company from among the Gentiles who will be brought to acknowledge the authority of the Lord Jesus

Christ. The once-rejected Messiah now is their Saviour and their Lord.

So the Spirit of God says, as it were, to the Lord Jesus Christ, "It is true the nation did not recognize you, that you seemed to have labored in vain and spent your strength for nought, but a coming day will show that a tremendous harvest will result from your labors of love when you were down here unrecognized and misunderstood."

CHAPTER FIFTY

WHY ISRAEL HAS BEEN SET ASIDE

W E ARE next shown why Israel has been set to one side during the present age. The question is put, "Where is the bill of your mother's divorcement?" Why did God divorce His earthly bride? Israel is spoken of as the wife of Jehovah, but during the present time she is like a divorced wife. God no longer recognizes her as in covenant relation with Himself and the question arises as to Why? Where is the bill of your mother's divorcement? On what grounds did God set her aside? Why was she divorced?

Then the answer comes:

Wherefore, when I came, was there no man? when I called, was there none to answer? Is my hand shortened at all, that it cannot redeem? or have I no power to deliver? Behold, at my rebuke I dry up the sea, I make the rivers a wilderness: their fish stinketh, because there is no water, and dieth for thirst. I clothe the heavens with blackness, and I make sackcloth their covering. The Lord God hath given me the tongue of the learned, that I should know how to speak a word in season to him that is weary: he wakeneth morning by morning, he wakeneth mine ear to hear as the learned. The Lord God hath opened mine ear, and I was not rebellious, neither turned away back. I gave my back to the smiters, and my cheeks to them that plucked off the hair: I hid not my face from shame and spitting (verses 2-6).

What a wonderful passage! Ask any thoughtful Jew to consider this carefully, for here Jehovah says why

He set Israel to one side. "Wherefore, when I came, was there no man?" When who came? we must ask. The rabbi must acknowledge that unquestionably it was when Jehovah visited Israel, when He says, "There was no one to welcome Me. I am the One that clothes the heavens with blackness. I make sackcloth their covering. I dry up the sea, and make the rivers a wilderness." He refers to the time when He dried up the waters of the Red Sea and later the waters of the Jordan for Israel to go through. It is the Eternal God speaking, the God of creation.

There is no change in the Person as He continues to tell how He came down to earth in humiliation. One who says Himself that He clothes the heavens with blackness and dries up the sea, who has creatorial power. Here we have an indication of the Trinity; He says, "The Lord God hath given Me the tongue of the learned," or the disciple, I who clothe the heavens with blackness have come down to earth and taken the place of a disciple. It was the Lord Jesus Christ in infinite grace, coming down here in humiliation, choosing to lay aside, as it were, His rightful claim to full Deity. It is not that He laid aside His Deity—He could not do that —but He refused to act in the power of His own omnipotence, He chose on earth to learn from the Word of God and to be subject to the Holy Spirit. He "increased," we are told, "in wisdom and stature, and in favour with God and man." And He said, "The Lord hath given Me the power of the disciple, that I might learn how to comfort the weary with the Word" (*Leeser's Jewish translation*).

How that fits in with the Saviour's own invitation: "Come unto Me, all ye that labour, and are heavy laden, and I will give you rest."

"We have not an high priest which cannot be touched with the feeling of our infirmities; but [One who] was in all points tempted like as we are," and "is able to succour them that are tempted." He came down to this earth and went through all human experience, apart from sin, entering fully into our sorrows, our griefs, and troubles, thus learning in a practical way how to comfort the weary with the Word. And what treatment did He receive in return?

> I gave my back to the smiters, and my cheeks to them that plucked off the hair: I hid not my face from shame and spitting (verse 6).

That lowly Man in Pilate's judgment-hall is delivered over to the soldiers, who gathered about Him, and in their ribaldry laughed, and smote Him and exposed Him to all kinds of vulgarities and indecencies. This was God manifest in the flesh.

This then tells us why the divorced state, why, for the present, Israel has been set to one side. They rejected their Messiah when He came in lowly grace.

> Behold, all ye that kindle a fire, that compass yourselves about with sparks: walk in the light of your fire, and in the sparks that ye have kindled. This shall ye have of mine hand; ye shall lie down in sorrow (verse 11).

Who has ever suffered, or has ever known greater sorrows nationally than Israel? And we who once rejected Christ too, but through grace have had our eyes opened to receive Him as our Saviour, how our hearts should go out in yearning love and compassion to Israel with their eyes still blinded. How we need to pray for them, but we are so forgetful. When some Hebrew

Christian spoke of his blinded brethren in our prayer-meetings, how his hearers prayed for Israel when he was there. But if he were not, prayer-meeting after prayer-meeting might pass without petitions for them. Prayer ascended for everything else, and everyone else, but no one ever voiced a request for Israel unless special attention was called to it. Yet God has said, "Pray for the peace of Jerusalem. They shall prosper that love thee."

Alas, Israel kindled her own fire! They tried to walk in the light of the teachings of the rabbis, but have found sorrow upon sorrow and will never be released—fully released, rather—until they look upon Him whom they pierced, and they mourn for Him as one mourneth for his only son and as one who is in bitterness for his firstborn.

THE CALL TO AWAKE

IN CHAPTER fifty-one God stresses the disobedience of Israel and their suffering because of it, and also emphasizes the coming day when Messiah will be recognized and granted the fullness of blessing.

Hearken to me, ye that follow after righteousness, ye that seek the Lord: look unto the rock whence ye are hewn, and to the hole of the pit whence ye are digged. Look unto Abraham your father, and unto Sarah that bare you: for I called him alone, and blessed him, and increased him. For the Lord shall comfort Zion: he will comfort all her waste places; and he will make her wilderness like Eden, and her desert like the garden of the Lord; joy and gladness shall be found therein, thanksgiving, and the voice of melody (verses 1-3).

God will fulfill every promise He has made. He says, "Look unto Abraham." God had said to Abraham, "in thee and in thy seed shall all the nations of the earth be blessed." Israel failed in that blessing. But still the promise abides, and the day is coming when they themselves will enter into fullness of blessing through the Son of Abraham and when they will be made a blessing to the whole earth, because they have become like a nation of priests in the coming day and will be used of God to bless all the Gentile nations. The nations that once persecuted them will have to suffer, but after God has destroyed the enemies—those who are taken in red-handed opposition to His Word—the nations that

have never been guilty of these things will find the
Lord as their Saviour and enter into blessing in the
millennial day.

In the rest of this chapter and the first part of chapter fifty-two, we have three calls to awake. First is a
call addressed to the arm of the Lord, "Awake, awake."
Then we have a call addressed to Jerusalem as she now
is with her suffering and sorrow, calling her to arise.
And then there is a call to Zion and to Jerusalem, as
she will be in the coming day, when the Lord leads her
into blessing.

> Awake, awake, put on strength, O arm of the Lord; awake, as
> in the ancient days, in the generations of old. Art thou not it that
> hath cut Rahab, and wounded the dragon? . . . Awake, awake,
> stand up, O Jerusalem, which hast drunk at the hand of the Lord
> the cup of his fury; thou hast drunken the dregs of the cup of trem-
> bling, and wrung them out (verses 9, 17).

In verse 9 Rahab the dragon refers to Egypt; it is
the term here used for that land.

CHAPTER FIFTY-TWO

THE GOOD TIDINGS TO ALL

THEN comes another call in the next chapter:

> Awake, awake; put on thy strength, O Zion; put on thy beautiful garments, O Jerusalem, the holy city: for henceforth there shall no more come into thee the uncircumcised and the unclean. Shake thyself from the dust; arise, and sit down, O Jerusalem: loose thyself from the bands of thy neck, O captive daughter of Zion. For thus saith the Lord, Ye have sold yourselves for nought; and ye shall be redeemed without money (verses 1-3).

These three consecutive calls to awake are very clear and definite. First, it is the call of the people in their sorrow and in their trouble. "Awake, awake . . . O arm of the Lord." Remembering how the arm of the Lord had been manifested on their behalf in ancient times, they cry out from the depths of their heart, "O God, come in and undertake for us! Awake, O arm of the Lord!"

As will soon be shown in chapter fifty-three, the arm of the Lord is a Person. It is the Lord Jesus Christ Himself. So it is really He who is being addressed, though the people do not know it. "Arm of the Lord, awake, awake!" They call on Him to rise for their deliverance, and, thank God, in due time He will. This is one of the first things that will take place. There will be a moving on the part of a remnant of Israel, a recognition of their past failure and sin, and they turn back to the Lord. Here the words apply: "Seek ye the Lord while He may be found, call ye upon Him while He is near . . . Let the wicked forsake his way, and the unrighteous man his thoughts: and let him return unto the Lord, and He will have mercy upon him; and to our God, for He will abundantly pardon."

In response to that cry, "Awake, awake, O arm of the Lord," God addresses Israel in her present broken condition, and says, "Awake, awake, O Jerusalem; arise from the dust; clothe yourself in your beautiful garments; turn from your iniquity, acknowledge your sin, confess your transgressions." And when they do, then deliverance will come.

He goes on to show them that the Lord in His own time will bring them back to Zion, the ransomed of the Lord shall return with everlasting joy upon their heads.

Here God is addressing the restored people when at last the work of repentance has been wrought in their souls, and now that they have turned back to Him, the day of their blessing has come. He says, "Awake, awake, O Zion," calls upon them to sing with gladness as they come forth from the lands of the Gentiles, to enter again into their own land and into happy reconciliation with God and joyful subjection to the Saviour whom He has provided.

How beautiful upon the mountains are the feet of him that bringeth good tidings, that publisheth peace; that bringeth good tidings of good, that publisheth salvation; that saith unto Zion, Thy God reigneth! (verse 7).

The remnant company of the last days go out over the mountains, out to the world to proclaim the gospel of peace, the gospel of the kingdom, but it is not a different gospel from that which we preach today. There is only one gospel. The Apostle Paul says, "Though we, or an angel from heaven, preach any other gospel unto you than that which we have preached unto you, let him be accursed." And he emphasizes this: "As we said before, so say I now again, If any man preach any other gospel unto you than that ye have received, let him be accursed" (Gal. 1:8, 9). There is only one gospel, the gospel of God concerning His Son! But that gospel takes on different aspects at different times, according to God's dispensational dealings. John the Baptist proclaimed the gospel of the kingdom of God, but that doesn't mean that he did not tell sinners how to be saved. It was he who said, "Behold the Lamb of God, which taketh away the sin of the world." But the emphasis of his message was the responsibility of Israel to receive the King, and so enter into the kingdom.

When the Lord Jesus began to preach, He went from city to city proclaiming the gospel of the kingdom, and sent His disciples out to all Israel to preach it, but when the kingdom was rejected, a new thing came in, and now we preach the glorious gospel of the grace of God. The light of the knowledge of it shines in the face of Jesus Christ (2 Cor. 4:6), for grace and truth came by Him. But does that mean that we have to be silent in regard to the King and His kingdom? Surely not, because during the forty days that He appeared on earth after His resurrection we are told that the Lord Jesus spoke to His disciples "of the things pertaining to the kingdom of God." Many years after, Paul abode two years in his own hired house, still preaching the kingdom of God (Acts 1:3; 28:23, 31). We too preach the gospel of the kingdom, but now the emphasis is on the gospel of the grace of God, God's grace to a lost, ruined world. When this age has come to an end, and the Church has been taken home, and God calls out a little company called in Daniel 12:3, 10, the *Maskilim*, the wise—"the wise shall understand!"—they will be those with beautiful feet to go forth proclaiming the glad tidings that the time has drawn near when the Prince of Peace will return, and there will be blessing for all the world through Him.

How fitting it is that these words should come here immediately before Isaiah presents the greatest and most complete Messianic prophecy in all the Old Testament, in which we come to the very Holy of Holies.

CHAPTER FIFTY-THREE

THE SUFFERING SAVIOUR

T HE inspired writer gives us a graphic pen-por-
trait of the suffering Saviour and tells us of the
glorious work He was to undertake in order that
the sin question might be settled forever to the perfect
satisfaction of God, the infinitely Holy One.

This great Messianic prophecy is referred to a number of times in the New Testament, and in each instance is applied directly to our Lord Jesus Christ, as
in Matthew 8:17; Acts 8:32-35; and 1 Peter 2:21-25.

Christ is here presented as the sinless Substitute for
sinful men, to whom our sins were imputed that divine
righteousness might be imputed to us who believe in
Him. His lowly life, His rejection by His own people,
His voluntary subjection to the suffering of the Cross,
His atoning sacrifice, His glorious resurrection and the
triumph of His gospel in the salvation of a great host of
sinners are all foretold here in a clear and concise way.
None but God Himself could have given us this remarkable delineation of the character and work of the Lord
Jesus so long before He came into the world. Isaiah
wrote this prophecy some seven hundred years before
Jesus was born in Bethlehem in order to fulfill all that
was written of Him. God foreknew all that His Son was
to endure, and He gave this message to Isaiah to hand
on to the future generations.

This wonderful passage begins with the 13th verse

of chapter fifty-two: "Behold, My Servant," for the One whom it describes is the same Person of whom he continues to speak in chapter fifty-three.

This is Hebrew poetry in blank verse, as may be seen from various other versions and translations. It is in sections of three stanzas each. The first one (chapter 52:13-15) introduces the Servant of Jehovah whose glory must be equal to the shame He endured.

> Behold, my servant shall deal prudently, he shall be exalted and extolled, and be very high. As many were astonied [astonished] at thee; his visage was so marred more than any man, and his form more than the sons of men: So shall he sprinkle many nations; the kings shall shut their mouths at him: for that which had not been told them shall they see; and that which they had not heard shall they consider (verses 13-15).

Hebrew scholars tell us that the word "sprinkle" here is from the same root as that for "astonied," so that it really means, As many were astonished at Him, so shall He astonish many nations.

Then chapter fifty-three presents God's servant, the suffering Saviour.

> Who hath believed our report? and to whom is the arm of the Lord revealed? For he shall grow up before him as a tender plant, and as a root out of a dry ground: he hath no form nor comeliness; and when we shall see him, there is no beauty that we should desire him. He is despised and rejected of men; a man of sorrows, and acquainted with grief: and we hid as it were our faces from him; he was despised, and we esteemed him not (verses 1-3).

To the question, "Who hath believed our report?" Paul the apostle calls our attention in Romans 10:16 as evidencing the incredulity of Israel, the very people who had waited for the coming of their Messiah for centuries, but who, when He came, fulfilled their own

Scriptures in rejecting Him. They failed to see in Jesus "the arm of the Lord" stretched forth for their salvation, as in the case of the great bulk of mankind today.

Christians often say that in their unconverted days, the Lord was to them as a root out of a dry ground, but now He is the altogether lovely one. But the expression does not imply lack of comeliness or beauty, but that the Lord Jesus Christ grew up before God as a sprout, a root. This is the Man whose name is "the Branch," a root out of the dry ground of formalistic Israel, the one lovely plant that Jehovah gazed down upon with such approval that He could open the heavens above Him and say, "This is My beloved Son, in whom I have found [all] My delight" (*Darby*). This was what the blessed Lord was to God—a tender plant, a plant of renown and beauty, growing out of the dry ground of Israel and of humanity in general. To God He was precious beyond words, but to unbelieving men He had no form, no comeliness, no beauty; that is, men did not recognize the moral loveliness that He ever exhibited. Some Christian teachers have misunderstood the expression, "He hath no form nor comeliness," and have believed that the Lord Jesus Christ as man was positively repulsive in appearance, so that no one would like to look upon Him. But that is not in accordance with other scriptures.

In Psalm 45:2 it is written of our blessed Lord, "Thou art fairer than the children of men," and we have every reason to believe that the Lord Jesus Christ, being the only sinless child that was ever born into the world, came here with a perfect human body and spotlessly beautiful. And as He grew up as a young man and later matured, He would be of lovely, splendid appearance, but those who listened to His teaching but loved their sins, and were angered by Him, saw in Him no beauty that they should desire Him.

It is not a question of physical characteristics; because of the sufferings He endured, His visage became marred more than any man, and His form more than the sons of men. But as Man here on earth, the Second Man, the Last Adam, He was as to His human form, face, and features absolutely perfect. But men looked upon Him with scorn and disdain because His teaching interfered with the lives that they loved to live. They say, "When we shall see Him, there is no beauty that we should desire Him."

So the prophet goes on to say:

He was despised and rejected of men; a man of sorrows, and acquainted with grief: and we hid as it were our faces from him; he was despised, and we esteemed him not (verse 3).

All this was fulfilled in the days of our Lord's ministry here on earth. Before that there is no hint that he was despised and rejected. The little that we are told of Him is that "Jesus increased in wisdom and stature and in *favour* with God and man." Before His ministry began, He must have been acceptable wherever He went; He was evidently a reader in the Nazareth synagogue because He went there and publicly began to read from this very book of Isaiah, so that He was in favor in the eyes of His townsmen.

It was when He went out on His great mission that men turned away from Him—despised and rejected Him—a man of sorrows and acquainted with grief, and we hid as it were our faces from Him; He was despised and we esteemed Him not. Yet He was suffering in our place. Rejected, despised, He endured patiently all the shame put upon Him.

Surely he hath borne our griefs, and carried our sorrows: yet we did esteem him stricken, smitten of God, and afflicted (verse 4).

Men looked upon the sorrows He endured as divine judgments for His own sins, deserved because of what He was in Himself, as though God was angry with Him, whereas He was but entering into our griefs and the sorrows that sin had brought upon the race of mankind. All through His lowly life He saw what misery sin had caused. Men said He had a devil, and called Him a Samaritan—made Him out as a deceiver, and considered that the sufferings that He endured were deserved.

But he was wounded for our transgressions, he was bruised for our iniquities: the chastisement of our peace was upon him; and with his stripes we are healed. All we like sheep have gone astray; we have turned every one to his own way; and the Lord hath laid on him the iniquity of us all (verses 5, 6).

This brings us to the Cross, where He endured vicariously the judgment that our sins deserved in order that through His stripes we might be healed. There on the tree He was the great sin offering and the peace offering, too—there He "made peace through the blood of His cross" (Col. 1:20).

Surely here is substitutionary atonement. Sometimes people object to this on the ground that the word "substitution" is not found in the Bible, but when one is in the place of another, when one is taking what another deserves, that is substitution, and here we have the plain, definite statement, "He hath borne our griefs . . . He was wounded for our transgressions, He was bruised for our iniquities," the chastisement whereby our peace was made fell upon Him with the result: "With His stripes we are healed."

In verse six God, as it were, balances the books of the world—two debit entries and one credit entry. The two debit entries: "All we like sheep have gone astray"—there is the whole fallen human race; "we have turned every one to his own way"—there is each individual's own personal sin; and then the credit entry that clears it all on the books of God if men would but receive it: "Jehovah hath laid on Him the iniquity of us all" (R.V.).

Here we have the entire story of the Bible epitomized: Man's ruin both by nature and practice, and God's marvelous and all-sufficient remedy. The verse begins with *all* and ends with *all*. An anxious soul was directed to this passage and found peace. Afterward he said, "I bent low down and went in at the first *all*. I stood up straight and came out at the last." The first is the acknowledgment of our deep need. The second shows how fully that need has been met in the Cross of Christ. How happy to be numbered among those who have put in their claim and found salvation through the atoning work which there took place!

To me verse six is the most wonderful text in the Bible. I have been trying to preach for sixty years and that is the first text I ever preached on. I was just a boy fourteen years old, and out on the street in Los Angeles with the Salvation Army, I started speaking on that verse, meaning to take five minutes, but a half-hour later the captain leaned over and said, "Boy, we should have been in the Hall twenty minutes ago. You'll have to tell us the rest some other time." I have been trying to tell the rest all through the years since, but it is a text I never get beyond.

The mock trial of the Lord is next foretold.

He was oppressed, and he was afflicted, yet he opened not his mouth: he is brought as a lamb to the slaughter, and as a sheep before her shearers is dumb, so he openeth not his mouth. He was taken from prison and from judgment: and who shall declare his generation? for he was cut off out of the land of the living: for the transgression of my people was he stricken (verses 7, 8).

Taken from one place to another His case was heard but there was no one to speak for Him. It was all contrary to law, yet God permitted it. He said nothing for Himself. Pilate wondered greatly at His silence. Herod tried to make Him speak, yet brought as a lamb to be slain and like a sheep dumb before her shearers, so He opened not His mouth. With no word of complaint He gave Himself into the hands of wicked men to be crucified because there was no other way whereby guilty sinners could be saved.

Then the question comes in: "Who shall declare His generation?" or "Who shall declare His manner of life?" How careful God was to see that His manner of life was declared! Through false evidence he was condemned to die as a felon, as though guilty of sedition against Caesar, head of Imperial Rome; but God saw to it that His manner of life was fully declared, so that actually He was justified before His judges.

Pilate's wife sent him the message, "Have thou nothing to do with that just Man: for I have suffered many things this day in a dream because of Him." Pilate himself publicly took water and washed his hands, saying, "I am innocent of the blood of this just Person."

Then as He hung upon that Cross, left to die as a felon, a thief by His side turned to his fellow and said, "Dost thou not fear God, seeing thou art in the same condemnation? And we indeed justly . . . but this Man hath done nothing amiss."

God saw to it that this declaration was made even on he very cross, "This Man hath done nothing amiss." Yet He was allowed to suffer. Why? Because He was he great Sin Offering. "He was taken from prison and from judgment and who shall declare His generation? or He was cut off out of the land of the living: for the transgression of my people was He stricken." He was hurried from one judgment scene to another until, at last, He was nailed to the Cross, there to endure all that our sins deserved.

And he made his grave with the wicked, and with the rich in his death; because he had done no violence, neither was any deceit in his mouth. Yet it pleased the Lord to bruise him; he hath put him to grief: when thou shalt make his soul an offering for sin, he shall see his seed, he shall prolong his days, and the pleasure of the Lord shall prosper in his hand. He shall see of the travail of his soul, and shall be satisfied: by his knowledge shall my righteous servant justify many; for he shall bear their iniquities (verses 9-11).

They "made His grave with the wicked." This was man's intention. They would have cast His precious body out to be devoured by vultures or jackals, or burned in the fires that destroyed the refuse of the city in the valley of Hinnom. But God saw to it that He lay "with the rich in His death," as a testimony to His absolute holiness and perfection of spirit.

What a wonderful epitome of the whole story of the life and death and mock trial and condemnation of our Lord Jesus is here! The four accounts of the crucifixion taken together give us the full meaning of the work of the Cross. Jesus is presented as enduring the shame and physical anguish inflicted upon Him by man for three awful hours. In that period He gave no evidence of perturbation of spirit. He was in perfect communion with the Father, and manifested a tender concern for others, but there was no word of self-pity or commiseration for His own sufferings. But in the last three hours He was enduring the terrible ordeal of bearing the judgment our sins deserved. His cry of loneliness is the key to the deeper suffering of those hours when God the righteous Judge, had to abandon Him to the inward spiritual suffering as the Surety for sinners. It was then His soul—not merely His body—was made an offering for sin.

Observe, it was Jehovah, God Himself, who dealt with Christ in judgment when He hung upon the tree. It was not His physical sufferings alone that made propitiation for sin, but what He endured in His inmost being when His holy, spotless soul became the great Sin Offering. In other words, it was not what man did to Him that made reconciliation for iniquity, but what He endured at the hand of God, leading to Immanuel's orphaned cry, "My God, My God, why hast Thou forsaken Me?" He was forsaken that we might be received into the divine favor. Because of this, in resurrection, "He shall see His seed . . . and . . . be satisfied." God has raised up Jesus Christ from the dead and made Him the head of the new creation, made up of all who are saved through the work He accomplished on the Cross. Thus both His death and resurrection are depicted here.

The word "travail" refers to but one kind of suffering —birth pangs. Jesus travailed in His soul that millions might be born of the Word and Spirit of God to His eternal joy and satisfaction. The gospel is based upon what He endured on that Cross, and this message goes out to all who have ears to hear.

Therefore will I divide him a portion with the great, and he
shall divide the spoil with the strong; because he hath poured out
his soul unto death: and he was numbered with the transgressors;
and he bare the sin of many, and made intercession for the transgressors (verse 12).

Instead of the offering of His body as a sin offering
ending His days, He shall prolong His days. And He
shall come back from the grave in resurrection life.
How wonderful is that promise, "Therefore will I divide Him a portion with the great, and He shall divide
the spoil with the strong." Evidently the strong one
here refers to Satan as man's great enemy. The Lord
Jesus said, "No man can enter into a strong man's
house . . . except he first bind the strong man." He
used that expression as typical of Satan himself, a
wonderful encouragement here for those who try to
preach the gospel. "He shall divide the spoil with the
strong." Many people have an idea that there will be
far more people in hell than in heaven, but God's Word
does not warrant that. Someone at once thinks of the
question of the disciples, "Are there few that be
saved?" But that was a question which the Lord did
not answer by saying, "Yes, there are only a few that
will be saved." He said, "Strive to enter in at the strait
gate." In other words, Be in earnest about it, because
many will strive to enter when it will be too late.

But what is the testimony of the Scriptures? Will
there be few saved? There will be far more in heaven
than will ever be in hell, because all the little ones will
be in heaven—all the millions who have died in im-
maturity before coming to the years of accountability
—they will all be in heaven. Jesus said, "It is not the
will of your Father which is in heaven, that one of

these little ones should perish," and all those who hav
been mentally defective and never have been capable o
accepting or rejecting Christ will all be covered by Hi
blood. And then in addition, all those who have turne
to Him in repentance and trust in Him as Saviour. S
he divides "the spoil with the strong." God reward
the Lord Jesus according to His own thoughts of tha
which His Son has accomplished. Men may thin
lightly of His glorious work but God never does.

CHAPTER FIFTY-FOUR

THE CALL TO THE REMNANT
TO SING

Sing, O barren, thou that didst not bear; break forth into singing, and cry aloud, thou that didst not travail with child: for more
are the children of the desolate than the children of the married
wife, saith the Lord. Enlarge the place of thy tent, and let them
stretch forth the curtains of thine habitations: spare not, lengthen
thy cords, and strengthen thy stakes; for thou shalt break forth on
the right hand and on the left; and thy seed shall inherit the Gentiles, and make the desolate cities to be inhabited (verses 1-3).

NOW after all the darkness, the gloom, the suffering, and the sorrow of the Cross, the first word
of the next chapter is "Sing!" Yes, after all that
Jesus has done, we sing. The Spirit of God calls upon
the once-unfruitful people to rejoice, here directed to
the remnant of Israel in the last days: "Sing, O barren,
thou that didst not bear." He pictures Israel turning to
the Lord in that day, and being used of God to bring a
great multitude of Gentiles, so that the desolate have
more children than the married wife who has been set
aside for so long. God uses that remnant to bring a
great host to Him in that coming day. And all who are
saved, both in millennial days and now, will be saved
through the glorious work of which Isaiah 53 speaks
so clearly.

So after the call to sing come God's promises:

Fear not; for thou shalt not be ashamed: neither be thou con founded; for thou shalt not be put to shame: for thou shalt forget the shame of thy youth, and shalt not remember the reproach of thy widowhood any more. For thy Maker is thine husband; the Lord of hosts is his name; and thy Redeemer the Holy One of Israel; The God of the whole earth shall he be called. For the Lord hath called thee as a woman forsaken and grieved in spirit, and a wife of youth, when thou wast refused, saith thy God. For a small moment have I forsaken thee; but with great mercies will I gather thee. In a little wrath I hid my face from thee for a moment; but with everlasting kindness will I have mercy on thee, saith the Lord thy Redeemer. For this is as the waters of Noah unto me: for as I have sworn that the waters of Noah should no more go over the earth; so have I sworn that I would not be wroth with thee, nor rebuke thee. For the mountains shall depart, and the hills be removed; but my kindness shall not depart from thee, neither shall the covenant of my peace be removed, saith the Lord that hath mercy on thee (verses 4-10).

What wonderful promises these are! This is God's word to Israel. We Christians are such thieves—we steal so many things that belong to Israel and try to apply them to ourselves. At the head of many of these chapters in Isaiah, our old valued Bagster Bibles read, "Curses on the Jews," "Punishment on the Jews," "Judgment on the Jews." And then when they come to the promises we saw, "Blessings of the Church," "Joys of the Church." All the judgment passages were definitely applied to the Jews but all the glory passages to the Church. But these headings were written by uninspired men, who did not profess to give them as the Word of God.

The promises here refer to Israel's blessing, God will bring them back to Himself. He will not keep His fury forever. He says, "This is as the waters of Noah unto Me," for He promised that never again should the earth be destroyed by a flood. Just as truly He has promised the nation Israel that they will never be utterly destroyed, that some day a remnant will be saved and become a great nation, and Israel shall blossom and bud and fill the face of the whole earth with goodness.

CHAPTER FIFTY-FIVE

THE GREAT INVITATION

Ho, every one that thirsteth, come ye to the waters, and he that hath no money; come ye, buy, and eat; yea, come, buy wine and milk without money and without price. Wherefore do ye spend money for that which is not bread? and your labour for that which satisfieth not? Hearken diligently unto me, and eat ye that which is good, and let your soul delight itself in fatness. Incline your ear, and come unto me: hear, and your soul shall live; and I will make an everlasting covenant with you, even the sure mercies of David. Behold, I have given him for a witness to the people, a leader and commander to the people. Behold, thou shalt call a nation that thou knowest not, and nations that knew not thee shall run unto thee because of the Lord thy God, and for the Holy One of Israel; for he hath glorified thee (verses 1-5).

IF IT WERE not for the truth set forth in chapter 53 of Isaiah, there would be no possibility of this gracious invitation. Throughout this entire section of Isaiah (chaps. 49-57) God is presenting His chosen Servant, our Lord Jesus Christ, as the Redeemer of Israel and of the world, whose rejection at His first coming was foreknown and plainly predicted, but who by His propitiatory work was to open up the way for guilty sinners to find peace with God and pardon for all their transgressions. Because of His work God can send forth the gracious invitation for all men everywhere to partake of His salvation. Isaiah has been called "the evangelical prophet," and he well deserves to be so designated. Nowhere else in the Old Testament is the Person and work of our Lord set forth so clearly and fully as in this wonderful book. Man is shown to be utterly bankrupt spiritually, destitute of righteousness, and with no claim upon God whatsoever. Yet Christ, Jehovah's sinless Servant, is presented as the great sin offering through whose infinite sacrifice all who come to Him in faith will be justified in His sight. His salvation is based upon righteousness. In the Cross the sin question has been settled in a righteous way, and so God can now save all who come to Him in faith.

It is hard for the natural man to appreciate the fullness of God's grace. It is so easy to think of God as a merchantman with something to sell. But the truth is that God is too rich to seek to sell His salvation to anyone, and if He were to put a price upon it we would all be too poor to buy. In each dispensation salvation has been by grace alone. All who were saved in Old Testament times, in the various ages before the Cross, owed everything to the work the Son of God eventually accomplished upon Calvary. There were different degrees of light, and men were placed under various economies as to their responsibilities to God in this world, but no man was ever saved by the animal sacrifices (Heb. 10:4), or "by the deeds of the law" (Rom. 3:20).

So Isaiah, after having set forth so clearly the atoning death the Anointed of God was to die, called upon all needy, troubled souls to appropriate by faith the gracious provision thus depicted. His message to thirsty souls was identical with that proclaimed by the Lord Jesus at a later date (John 7:37), and it is with a similar proclamation that the New Testament draws to a close (Rev. 22:17).

Isaiah here emphasizes not only the grace of God offering the water of life freely to all men, but also stresses the quickening and authoritative power of the Word of God, for it is through believing that Word that men receive divine life.

This gospel message is itself the water of life so freely offered. The Holy Spirit uses the Word as living water to bring life to those dead in trespasses and sins and to refresh and satisfy thirsty souls, who could never find true satisfaction in what this poor world has to offer. We may well be reminded of our Lord's words to the Samaritan woman, "Whosoever drinketh of the water that I shall give him shall never thirst; but [it] . . . shall be in him a well [or fountain] of water springing up into everlasting life" (John 4:14).

Although not mentioned here by name, it is the Lord Jesus Himself to whom reference is made. He is God's witness who was sent into the world to be the Saviour of sinners. For His advent Israel was taught to wait expectantly, but when He came in grace to save, they spurned and rejected His claims upon them.

This clearly predicts the calling of the Gentiles when Israel failed to recognize the Son of David in the Person of the Lord Jesus Christ. Grace then went out to the nations who had hitherto been strangers to the covenants of promise.

Seek ye the Lord while he may be found, call ye upon him while he is near: let the wicked forsake his way, and the unrighteous man his thoughts: and let him return unto the Lord, and he will have mercy upon him; and to our God, for he will abundantly pardon (verses 6, 7).

"Seek ye the Lord while He may be found, call ye upon Him while He is near." Men are responsible to turn to the Lord, and so to find Him as their deliverer. It is not that He is hidden and has to be searched for, but the call is to earnestness of purpose in turning to Him and heeding His voice while He waits to be gracious, lest if He be rejected too often He may no longer exercise the hearts and consciences of those who harden themselves against Him.

"Let the wicked forsake his way" by turning to God in true repentance and the acknowledgment of utter helplessness, thus repudiating the thoughts of the natural heart, and he may be assured that as he turns to the Lord, God waits to "abundantly pardon," for He delights to meet the trusting penitent in grace.

The chapter goes on to show how ready God is to take up those who turn to Him in confession of sin, and trust His love.

For my thoughts are not your thoughts, neither are your ways my ways, saith the Lord. For as the heavens are higher than the earth, so are my ways higher than your ways, and my thoughts than your thoughts. For as the rain cometh down, and the snow from heaven, and returneth not thither, but watereth the earth, and maketh it bring forth and bud, that it may give seed to the sower, and bread to the eater: So shall my word be that goeth forth out of my mouth: it shall not return unto me void, but it shall accomplish that which I please, and it shall prosper in the thing whereto I sent it. For ye shall go out with joy, and be led forth with peace: the mountains and the hills shall break forth before you into singing, and all the trees of the field shall clap their hands. Instead of the thorn shall come up the fir tree, and instead of the brier shall come up the myrtle tree; and it shall be to the Lord for a name, for an everlasting sign that shall not be cut off (verses 8-13).

How Isaiah's own soul must have been stirred as he gave forth this proclamation! And what an encouragement it should be for every servant of Christ to remember that God has declared that His word will accomplish that for which He has sent it.

Sometimes preachers may get a little discouraged

thinking they are talking, as it were, against a brazen wall, but God's Word will never return to Him void. So the prophetic Word will have a complete fulfillment in God's due time.

Chapter Fifty-six

ENCOURAGEMENT TO RIGHTEOUSNESS

THESE following chapters are of such an exceedingly practical nature, that sometimes we may be inclined to look carelessly over such portions and focus our attention upon passages that speak of great events that are to take place in the future or of God's dealings with His people in the past.

But, we repeat, the great object of prophetic ministry is not simply to occupy people with coming events, but so to impress the truths of the future upon the conscience as to enable God's people to live now in the light of the predicted future. It was so of Israel of old and it is so with us, in this present Church age.

Many people have a rather intellectual interest in prophecy, and will flock to hear a series of such messages. They are very important, and any servant of Christ who sets forth the prophetic parts of the Word of God, will find that fewer professed Christians would be lost to orthodoxy if saved preachers gave more attention to the prophetic Word. People go out into other systems because they are hungry to know the future. That is how the "Voice of Prophecy" appeals to so many who hear it over the air, who do not know that it is the radio department of the Seventh-day Adventists. They are specially thrilled when it attempts to open up the future. Then it is suggested that the listeners should take one of their Bible Study Courses. They never announce over the air, "This is the Seventh-day Adventist propaganda." They keep that hidden closely, and not until the student is well on in the Bible Courses does he see what it really is. But thousands of people all over this country have been swept into Seventh-day Adventism annually just because of an interest in prophecy. Properly instructed from the Scriptures, they would not have been in the same danger.

"Jehovah's Witnesses" work on the same principle. They try to hide their real views until little by little hearers listen to their great program for the future. The truth as to the Second Coming of the Lord, particularly in its two aspects, would preserve them from the ridiculous teachings of so-called "Pastor" Russell and Judge Rutherford, that the Lord has already come and has been here since 1874, but is manifesting Himself only to those of special spirituality, and the millennium began in 1914 and we are already in it. Wonderful millennium, is it not? But who that has been well-instructed in clear Bible teaching would be carried away with such vagaries? On the other hand, it is important that with every message something of an intensely practical character should be incorporated lest its hearers be carried away with the glowing pictures of the future and the visions of such prophecies as set forth in Daniel and The Revelation, while very careless and indifferent as to their lives.

Once when I was asked to give some addresses on the Second Coming of the Lord, a speaker sitting beside me remarked as someone entered before the meeting commenced, "There is one of the most godless men in our community and yet he is always on hand if anyone lectures on prophecy. He is so interested in finding out all about the future."

When I got through preaching, this man came up to me. "Brother," he said, "I'm glad to know that you hold the Second Coming—I hold that too." I asked, "Do you? Does it hold you? It is one thing to hold the Second Coming, it is quite another thing to be held by it. The Word says, 'Every man that hath this hope in him purifieth himself, even as He is pure.' Does it have that effect on your heart and life?"

He said, "Who has been talking to you about me?"

Clearly something was wrong. Many people want to know all about the horns of Daniel and the beasts of Revelation; they do not want you to probe their consciences.

But we get prophetic ministry in the proper proportion in a book like this of Isaiah. Again and again after giving pictures of the future, the prophet comes down to the actual condition of the people at the time when he was speaking.

In chapter fifty-six Isaiah begins a very practical section. He points out the importance of living in a godly way in the then present, and also that in the future it is as the nations learn to seek after righteousness that the blessing of the kingdom will be theirs.

Thus saith the Lord, Keep ye judgment, and do justice: for my salvation is near to come, and my righteousness to be revealed (verse 1).

That gives exactly the same principle. "Keep judgment and do justice" because these things are soon to take place. In other words, live *now* in the light of *then*.

Blessed is the man that doeth this, and the son of man that layeth hold on it; that keepeth the sabbath from polluting it, and keepeth his hand from doing any evil. Neither let the son of the stranger, that hath joined himself to the Lord, speak, saying, The Lord hath utterly separated me from his people: neither let the eunuch say, Behold, I am a dry tree. For thus saith the Lord unto the eunuchs that keep my sabbaths, and choose the things that please me, and take hold of my covenant; even unto them will I give in mine house and within my walls a place and a name better than of sons and of daughters: I will give them an everlasting name, that shall not be cut off (verses 2-5).

He goes on to show that no one need fail of the coming blessing if he is sincere in turning to God. Certain ones were prohibited from having any part in the services of the Lord in Old Testament times; a eunuch could not have any part in the priesthood and the stranger had no place there. But in the future, no matter what one's physical condition, or nationality, if his earnest purpose of heart is to seek the Lord and to do the will of God, he will have the same place in the kingdom that anyone else can have. It will be open for everyone. So this chapter emphasizes the importance of practical righteousness.

Also the sons of the stranger, that join themselves to the Lord, to serve him, and to love the name of the Lord, to be his servants, every one that keepeth the sabbath from polluting it, and taketh hold of my covenant; Even them will I bring to my holy mountain, and make them joyful in my house of prayer; their burnt offerings and their sacrifices shall be accepted upon mine altar; for mine house shall be called an house of prayer for all people (verses 6, 7).

These are the words of the Lord Jesus Christ, when He drove the money-changers out of the temple. "Is it not written, My house shall be called of all nations the house of prayer? but ye have made it a den of thieves" (Mark 11:17).

Our Lord thus gives us the key to the practical application of this passage. It was God's word not only to Israel but to assure the Gentiles that they, too, might come into blessing if they would seek His face and take hold of the Abrahamic covenant: In thee "and in thy seed shall all the nations . . . be blessed." As long as the Jewish dispensation lasted, in the days of the great tribulation, and on into the millennium, the observance of the Sabbath will be an outward sign of allegiance to the Lord and the recognition of His authority.

We, today, do not recognize the Jewish Sabbath. Why? Because it was part of that Law which was done away for us in the Cross of Christ. The Lord took it out of the way, nailing it to His Cross. So the Word says, "Let no man therefore judge you in meat, or in drink, or in respect of an holyday, . . . or of the sabbath days: which are a shadow of things to come; but the body is of Christ." The light of God of old was shining upon Christ, and Christ cast His shadow before He came—and the Sabbath was one aspect of this shadow —rest at the end of a six-day period of labor. The Lord Jesus was the glorious fulfillment when He said, "Come unto Me, all ye that labour and are heavy laden, and I will give you rest."

Instead of the Jewish Sabbath we now have the Lord's Day. Some object to applying the term "Lord's Day" to the first day of the week. Where John in The Revelation says, "I was in the Spirit on the Lord's day" they insist that the "Lord's day" and "the day of the Lord" are the same thing. And we might take it for granted that the two expressions mean the same—the day of the Lord and the Lord's day. Now if it were thus exactly translated, then that might be so, but the term "Lord" is not in the possessive case there, but an adjective is used, formed from the word for "Lord."

It is the Lordian Day—just as you have an adjective formed from the word "Christ," when we speak of a "Christian" spirit, a Christian church, a Christian atmosphere.

It has been translated "lordly," which does not give the thought since that suggests a superior day to others. It is the Lordian day—the day that brings before us the resurrection of our blessed Lord from the dead. The early Christians knew better than we in the twentieth century the meaning of some of those cryptic expressions in the book of Revelation. All down through the centuries from the earliest days, the first day of the week was recognized by Christians as the Lord's Day, the Lordian Day. The only name that the Greeks have for it is *kuriakos*, the Lord's Day; the Latins called it the Dominical Day, the Lord's Day, which is the same thing. And it has been so known down through the centuries. If we were in the White House and looking at its furniture, and the guard said, "That is the President's chair," or, "That is the chair of the President," the words would mean the same thing. But if we speak of the "Presidential Chair" there is something altogether different.

The "Lordian Day" is that which the Christian Church, from the very beginning, has kept and—mark this—voluntarily, voluntarily, in memory of the resurrection of our Lord Jesus Christ. Its very voluntariness gives it value in the sight of the Lord.

If some loving friend gives you a birthday present its special value is that it shows his kindly thought. If you had written to say, "I am going to have a birthday and will expect a present from you," it would lose all its value. So the Seventh-day Adventists challenge us, "Show us a commandment in the New Testament telling us to observe the first day of the week." We say, "There is no commandment. We are under grace, not law." They ask, "Why do you do it?"

"Because of the gratitude of our hearts to the Lord Jesus who rose from the dead on the first day of the week."

The first day of the week has been given a special place in the Book of the Acts, and the First Epistle to the Corinthians. That special place has been marked from the beginning of Christianity to the present time.

As Israel of old by their recognition of the Sabbath manifested their love to Jehovah, their reverence to His name, so by the observance of the Lord's Day we manifest the same thing. Christians should be very careful about the use of the Lord's Day, and never should allow themselves to treat it just as a common day, and be indifferent to its claims. Suppose it were taken away from us. Suppose this country became like Russia and every day was a secular day and there were no special privileges such as we have enjoyed. How we would miss them! How bitterly we would rue the memory of ever having treated that day carelessly.

We have a spiritual lesson out of this—that for Israel of old it was absolutely legal—we are told that the righteousness of the law is fulfilled in us who walk not after the flesh but after the Spirit. While we are dead to the law in the body of Christ, yet every righteous requirement of the law will be fulfilled in us as we walk in the power of the Holy Spirit.

CHAPTER FIFTY-SEVEN

STRANGERS AND OUTCASTS GATHERED

C HAPTER fifty-seven begins with special comfort for those who while seeking to be faithful to the Lord suffer at the hands of others even unto death.

> The righteous perisheth, and no man layeth it to heart: and merciful men are taken away, none considering that the righteous is taken away from the evil to come. He shall enter into peace: they shall rest in their beds, each one walking in his uprightness (verses 1, 2).

There is always a danger of thinking of those who die before the fulfillment of promises of future blessing as having lost them. The Thessalonians too were concerned that some of their number died before the Second Coming of Christ. So Paul wrote: "I would not have you to be ignorant, brethren, concerning them which are asleep, that ye sorrow not, even as others which have no hope" (1 Thess. 4:13). He went on to show that they would have their part in the rapture with the rest and would share in the glory when the Lord Jesus Christ descended to take the kingdom.

So here, there were those in Israel who would think the promises are for the future, and as one after another died their fellow believers feared they would not enter into their blessing. When times of persecution came and many were put to death, they would feel they had missed so much, and would not be here for the kingdom at all. But "the righteous are taken away from the evil to come," and though taken away from here, God has provided something for them. Everyone shall rest in his uprightness before God—they will have their place of blessing. There is no need to grieve for those who have gone before; they are under the care of the blessed Lord; they have gone Home to be with Him.

Then he goes on to stress again the importance of godliness.

> For thus saith the high and lofty One that inhabiteth eternity, whose name is Holy: I dwell in the high and holy place, with him also that is of a contrite and humble spirit, to revive the spirit of the humble, and to revive the heart of the contrite ones (verse 15).

This is the only place in our Authorized Version where we get the word "eternity." The Hebrew word here so rendered is found in many other places, but here alone our English translators have used the word.

"Thus saith the high and lofty One that inhabiteth eternity," that inhabiteth the ages. In Psalm 90 we read, "From everlasting to everlasting, Thou art God." And it might have been rendered, "From eternity to eternity, Thou art God," but here we have the word standing out clearly and definitely, "Thus saith the high and lofty One that inhabiteth eternity." God dwells in all the ages, for that is what eternity is, a succession of ages. Sometimes in trying to picture eternity, preachers speak of it as an unchanging period. In one sense that is true. They use the expression in Revelation 10:6, "There shall be time no longer," and think of this as embracing the ages through which mankind goes on earth. And then when at last men leave this world or the ages of time expire, suddenly they go out into time where there are no more ages. But that is not true. Ages past, before this world came into existence—and there have been the ages of time since—there will be the age of the ages and ages of ages throughout the great day of God, the eternal day of God.

Throughout eternity one great age after another unfolds, manifesting even more wonderful things in connection with the wisdom, grace, love, and power of our wonderful God. And He inhabits all the ages, He is the God of eternity, and yet He dwells in the heart of him that is humble and of a contrite spirit and that trembleth at His Word. That is why prophetic truths should be borne home to the conscience—it is one thing that often makes men tremble—it ought to exercise people before God. The truth of the Coming of the Lord for His Church surely ought to exercise every Christian heart and lead to the question, "Am I so living that I would be happy and glad and ready to welcome the Lord Jesus at any moment?" Many of us make plans and have associations of which we would be ashamed if the Lord should suddenly come.

Years ago, before the First World War, Professor Stroeter, a well-known prophetic teacher in Germany, used to go through the country giving lectures, and using charts to unfold the dispensations. His lectures attracted the attention of the German Emperor, Kaiser Wilhelm, who in spite of his many idiosyncrasies, was quite a Bible student, and used to preach in the palace chapel on many occasions.

The Kaiser invited Professor Stroeter to his palace to give him an idea of what he was lecturing upon. The professor was taken into the library and spread a roll of his charts out on the table. The Kaiser followed him as he pointed out various things in the dispensations until the Second Coming of the Lord. After a lengthy conversation the Kaiser said, "Do I understand you aright? Do you mean to say that Jesus Christ is coming back literally, and that when He returns all the kingdoms of the world are going to be destroyed and He will set up His kingdom on the ruins of them all?"

And Professor Stroeter said, "Exactly, your Majesty, exactly."

"Oh, no," said the Kaiser, "I can't have that! Why that would interfere with all my plans!"

The Kaiser's plans were interfered with. And there are many who, if honest, would have to say, "The Coming of the Lord would interfere with all my plans." But if we are walking with God as we should be, if we are of a contrite heart and we tremble at the Word, then we shall be in that attitude of soul where we can welcome the return of the blessed Lord. So Isaiah impresses the importance of this spirit of waiting and readiness upon the people of this day.

This chapter fifty-seven ends with, "There is no peace, saith my God, to the wicked." In the previous section, that from 40-48, was God's controversy with Israel concerning idolatry. That ends with, "There is no peace, saith Jehovah, to the wicked."

Then chapters forty-nine through fifty-seven give God's controversy with Israel concerning the Messiah. And that ends with, "There is no peace, saith my God, to the wicked."

Chapter Fifty-eight

FASTS AND SABBATHS PLEASING TO GOD

THIS chapter begins the last section of this book. In chapters fifty-eight through sixty-six we have —in the main—visions of the coming glory, the prophet setting before us the wonderful things that will take place at the coming of the Lord. But God still deals with practical things. A call to the nation to heed the voice of God and get right with Him that judgment may be averted and blessing ensured.

> Cry aloud, spare not, lift up thy voice like a trumpet, and shew my people their transgression, and the house of Jacob their sins. Yet they seek me daily, and delight to know my ways, as a nation that did righteousness, and forsook not the ordinance of their God: they ask of me the ordinances of justice; they take delight in approaching to God. Wherefore have we fasted, say they, and thou seest not? Wherefore have we afflicted our soul, and thou takest no knowledge? Behold, in the day of your fast ye find pleasure, and exact all your labours (verses 1-3).

So chapter fifty-eight commences with the words, "Cry aloud, spare not, . . . shew my people their transgression," and then the prophet goes on to emphasize the sins of Israel. The great sin that he stresses is their reliance upon a mere formal observance of ritual and ceremony when the heart was far from God.

Isaiah takes up particularly the question of fasting. The Jews had a great number of fasts which they observed punctiliously, and there was a definite fast set forth in Leviticus 23 in connection with the appointed times of the Lord. But in addition to these, they brought in other things and added other fasts. They boasted in abstention from food and drink at certain hours and on certain days, taking it for granted that this pleased God, whereas He commends those who fasted from far different motives in order that their minds, taken away from other things, might be able to give attention to the things of the Spirit. So there is no praise but reproof for these merely formal fasts.

> Behold, ye fast for strife and debate, and to smite with the fist of wickedness: ye shall not fast as ye do this day, to make your voice to be heard on high (verse 4).

They used the fast to cover up other offenses. Some people today misuse that text: "Charity shall cover the multitude of sins." "Well," they say, "if I give some money to charity that makes up for other things." That is not what the Lord meant at all.

Israel fasted for strife and debate, to cover up other sins, and thought they were doing it by the careful observance of the fasts.

> Is it such a fast that I have chosen? a day for a man to afflict his soul? is it to bow down his head as a bulrush, and to spread sackcloth and ashes under him? Wilt thou call this a fast, and an acceptable day to the Lord? Is not this the fast that I have chosen? to loose the bands of wickedness, to undo the heavy burdens, and to let the oppressed go free, and that ye break every yoke? Is it not to deal thy bread to the hungry, and that thou bring the poor that are cast out to thy house? when thou seest the naked, that thou

cover him; and that thou hide not thyself from thine own flesh?
(verses 5-7).

In His fasts God called upon them to recognize the
importance of self-judgment. The fasts gave them opportunity to come before Him to meditate upon His
dealings with them, and upon their own failures and
sins, to confess them, and then carry out practically
the compassions of God toward those who are needy.
In other words, the mind of God was not simply that
they should deny themselves a little food but that they
should be constantly living lives of self-denial, dividing
what God gave them with others, and sharing with the
poor and the needy.

The Lord Jesus speaks of the same thing. He says,
"Moreover when ye fast, be not . . . of a sad counte-
nance . . . That thou appear not unto men to fast"
(Matt. 6:16-18).

The people would look at them and say, "That's a
godly man—he hasn't eaten anything since three o'clock
yesterday afternoon." But the Lord says, "When you
fast, let it be between you and God, and have a cheer-
ful, bright and happy countenance among the people."

The Lord Jesus really is in full harmony with Isaiah;
the same Spirit spoke through both. And then the Lord
promises, both through Isaiah and Matthew, that if
there is reality, He will reward.

Then shall thy light break forth as the morning, and thine
health shall spring forth speedily: and thy righteousness shall go
before thee; the glory of the Lord shall be thy rereward. Then shalt
thou call, and the Lord shall answer; thou shalt cry, and he shall
say, Here I am . . . then shall thy light rise in obscurity, and thy
darkness be as the noonday: And the Lord shall guide thee continually (verses 8-11).

What a reward is this!

Then the subject of the sabbath is continued. We have seen that for the Christian the first day of the week has voluntarily taken the place of the sabbath, the covenant sign for the Jew. But the blessing attending their appointed day may be ours abundantly.

If thou turn away thy foot from the sabbath, from doing thy pleasure on my holy day; and call the sabbath a delight, the holy of the Lord, honourable; and shalt honour him, not doing thine own ways, nor finding thine own pleasure, nor speaking thine own words: Then shalt thou delight thyself in the Lord; and I will cause thee to ride upon the high places of the earth, and feed thee with the heritage of Jacob thy father; for the mouth of the Lord hath spoken it (verses 13, 14).

It is of all importance to realize that men are more to God than forms and ceremonies, even of His own devising. "The sabbath was made for man, and not man for the sabbath" (Mark 2:27). He who is "Lord . . . of the sabbath" is pleased when we use His holy day to bless and help those in trouble, and to relieve the afflicted, so far as we are able to do so. Truly to keep the first day of the week holy to the Lord is to use it for rest, worship, and ministry to others. To think only of relaxation, and spend this day in pleasure-seeking, is to misuse it and fail to enter into the purpose God has had in mind in preserving its privileges for us. "I get so weary with all the burdens of business throughout the week," said a Christian, "that I must have rest and exercise on Sunday. So I use the Lord's Day afternoons visiting in the hospital and seeking to comfort and help the friendless." He returned to work on Monday refreshed and ready for another six days of toil.

Let us cherish our privileges and neither despise them, on the one hand, nor hedge them about with legal enactments, on the other, for which there is no biblical authorization.

CHAPTER FIFTY-NINE

ADDERS' EGGS AND
SPIDERS' WEBS

HERE we have a very solemn word, God calling the people to repentance and then giving wonderful promises of blessings that are to take place under Messiah's reign. He begins:

Behold, the Lord's hand is not shortened, that it cannot save; neither his ear heavy, that it cannot hear: But your iniquities have separated between you and your God, and your sins have hid his face from you, that he will not hear. For your hands are defiled with blood, and your fingers with iniquity; your lips have spoken lies, your tongue hath muttered perverseness (verses 1-3).

He goes on to explain why when they sought the Lord, He did not seem to answer or hear, for there was unjudged sin that needed to be dealt with. The Psalmist had written long before, "If I regard iniquity in my heart, the Lord will not hear me." They were covering up their sins and hoping to please God by observance of outward form and attendance to ritual, but he says of them "They hatch cockatrice' (or the adder's) eggs and weave the spider's web."

None calleth for justice, nor any pleadeth for truth: they trust in vanity, and speak lies; they conceive mischief, and bring forth iniquity. They hatch cockatrice' eggs, and weave the spider's web: he that eateth of their eggs dieth, and that which is crushed breaketh out into a viper. Their webs shall not become garments, neither shall they cover themselves with their works: their works are works of iniquity, and the act of violence is in their hands. Their feet run to evil, and they make haste to shed innocent blood: their thoughts are thoughts of iniquity; wasting and destruction are in their paths (verses 4-8).

This portion is taken up in the third chapter of the Epistle to the Romans: "Their feet are swift to shed blood."

Here is pictured a people who professedly are the Lord's. They go on with all the outward forms of religion, attending the service of the temple, offering their sacrifices, fasting before men, hoping thus to provide a righteousness which will be satisfactory to God. But He says it is just like hatching out adders' eggs—the preachings, the teachings were false, they were poisonous. "He that eateth of their eggs dieth." When people took up with this false teaching, it brought eternal ruin to them. "They weave the spider's web," but he says, "Their webs shall not become garments, neither shall they cover themselves with their works."

The spider's web is just foam, and proceeds from the spider himself. It looks very beautiful. Many preachers like those spiders spin the webs out of themselves, out of their own heads. They do not bring them from the Word of God. And people who try to clothe themselves with their own righteousness are like those who might try to make garments out of spiders' webs. It has been tried, but found impossible. What a contrast there is between a spider's web and a silk cocoon, though both come out of the creature itself, one from the spider and one from the silkworm. Yet the cocoon furnishes the material that makes the most beautiful and lasting

othing for kings and princes while the other is a bit
f foam that soon disappears.

Some years ago there came to Los Angeles, the great
₁etropolis of Southern California, a so-called "human
y." It was announced that on a given day he would
limb up the face of one of the large department store
uildings, and long before the appointed time thousands
f eager spectators were gathered to see him perform
he seemingly impossible feat.

But slowly and carefully he mounted aloft, now cling-
₁g to a window ledge, anon to a jutting brick, again
o a cornice. Up and up he went, against apparently
₁surmountable difficulties. At last he was nearing the
op. He was seen to feel to right and left and above his
ead for something firm enough to support his weight,
o carry him further. And soon he seemed to spy what
ᴐoked like a grey bit of stone or discolored brick pro-
ruding from the smooth wall. He reached for it, but
t was just beyond him. He ventured all on a spring-
ike movement, grasped the protuberance and, before
he horrified eyes of the spectators, fell to the ground
₁nd was broken to pieces. In his dead hand was found
₁ spider's web! What he evidently mistook for solid
tone or brick turned out to be nothing but dried froth!

Alas, how many are thinking to climb to heaven by
ₑffort of their own, only to find at last that they have
ᵥentured all on a spider's web, and so are lost forever.

Christ, and Christ alone, can save. His gospel is un-
ᵃiling and peace-giving. It is no adder's egg nor spi-
₁er's web, but the "power of God unto salvation to
ₑvery one that believeth."

Here you have the "garment of salvation," "the best
ᵣobe," "the robe of righteousness," provided by God

Himself through the death of His Son for all who ow
their guilt and trust His grace. "He gives the garme
of praise for the spirit of heaviness."

How futile are human efforts to fit the ungodly f
the divine Presence. Spiders' webs will not avail
cover the moral nakedness of Christ-rejecting sinner
"Their webs shall not become garments, neither sha
they cover themselves with their works." Whoeve
heard of a dress woven from the web of the spider?

But how different is the produce of another tin
creature, the silkworm! This marvelous little bein
spins a thread of such strength that it is readily wove
into cloth of the utmost beauty and made up into gai
ments of glory. But the silkworm must die that th
floss may thus be utilized. Is it too much to say tha
here we have in nature more than a hint of Him wh
in the depth of His humiliation could exclaim, "I am
worm and no man," and who gave His life that w
might be clothed in glory?

Then we have the omniscient One giving deliverance

And he saw that there was no man, and wondered that ther
was no intercessor: therefore his arm brought salvation unto him
and his righteousness, it sustained him . . . And the Redeeme
shall come to Zion, and unto them that turn from transgression i
Jacob, saith the Lord. As for me, this is my covenant with then
saith the Lord; My Spirit that is upon thee, and my words whic
I have put in thy mouth, shall not depart out of thy mouth, nor ou
of the mouth of thy seed, nor out of the mouth of thy seed's seed
saith the Lord, from henceforth and for ever (verses 16, 20, 21).

Yes, "the Redeemer shall come," for all hope fo
guilty man, for Israel as well as for the nations, is i
the Man at God's right hand.

It is the Lord Jesus Christ who speaks here. Ther

s no intercessor, no deliverer, so "His own arm
ought salvation." It is for His coming the people will
it. He came in grace the first time to settle the sin
estion on the Cross. He is coming again to bring in
e glory.

CHAPTER SIXTY

GOD GLORIFIED IN THE REMNANT

Arise, shine; for thy light is come, and the glory of the Lor is risen upon thee (verse 1).

AFTER that call the prophet goes on to show then the need for that light. It is the darkness.

For, behold, the darkness shall cover the earth, and gross dark ness the people: but the Lord shall arise upon thee, and his glor shall be seen upon thee. And the Gentiles shall come to thy light and kings to the brightness of thy rising (verses 2, 3).

Restored Israel is brought to the forefront of God' plan and blessing for the whole earth. The kings of th earth will bow down to them, the nations that onc persecuted them come and acknowledge that God i with them, and they will seek to enter into fellowshi and communion with them. This is to be taken literally God will deal thus with His people Israel and bring th nations that once antagonized and persecuted them int this blessed harmony in the last days.

And the sons of strangers shall build up thy walls, and thei kings shall minister unto thee: for in my wrath I smote thee, bu in my favour have I had mercy on thee . . . Whereas thou has been forsaken and hated, so that no man went through thee, I wil make thee an eternal excellency, a joy of many generations . .

he sun shall be no more thy light by day; neither for brightness
hall the moon give light unto thee: but the Lord shall be unto thee
n everlasting light, and thy God thy glory. Thy sun shall no more
o down; neither shall thy moon withdraw itself: for the Lord shall
e thine everlasting light, and the days of thy mourning shall be
nded (verses 10, 15, 19, 20).

What a day that will be for Israel after the long
enturies of suffering and their days of mourning! This
carries us on through the millennial glory and into the
eternal state, for God will never give up this people.
They will always have a separate place in His mind, as
he Church too will have hers. God has various groups,
all of whom have their own place in His counsels—all
redeemed alike by the precious blood of the Lord Jesus
Christ.

CHAPTER SIXTY-ONE

THE ANOINTED SERVANT AND HIS MINISTRY

IN CHAPTER sixty-one we have the portion to which the Lord Jesus directed His hearers' attention when He went into the synagogue at Nazareth. After His baptism in the Jordan and His temptation in the wilderness He came up through Judea—He gave the Word in Judea—into Galilee and entered into the city where He had been brought up—Nazareth. There, we are told, that as His custom was on a Sabbath day, He went into the synagogue. That is very significant. As already remarked, we have but little information as to the early days of the Lord Jesus Christ, and men have tried to imagine what may have taken place between His childhood and His thirtieth year, when He went forth to be baptized by John, as He consecrated Himself to His great work.

In connection with this, all sorts of vain imaginations have been indulged in. Some years ago, a Russian wrote a book purporting to be a translation of a record that he found in a Lama monastery in Tibet, and supposed to be a record of the journeys of Issah. It was taken for granted that Issah was to be identified with Jesus, and that he came from Palestine through India to Tibet, and among the lamas learned secrets that enabled him to perform miracles. Eventually he went ack to Palestine to begin his work, but was suspected by the Jewish leaders of trying to subvert their teaching and at last was crucified. Many hailed this at first as a wonderful discovery which might add to our knowledge of Jesus, but finally the author confessed that it was a forgery, and that he had written it himself.

People have tried to imagine what Jesus may have done during those years, but Scripture says that when some of His townspeople came to hear Him, they said: "Is not this the carpenter?" They had known Him as a carpenter. And Luke says that He went as His custom was on the Sabbath day into the synagogue. It shows that the Lord Jesus not only submitted Himself to the obedience of the laws divinely given, but also to the ordinary regulations of the rabbis, and attended the synagogue service and apparently took part in it. They would recognize Him as one who had a right to go up to the dais and read from the Holy Scriptures. In that synagogue at Nazareth was handed to Him the book of the prophet Isaiah; this book, the last part, too, of this book—and it is called the prophet Isaiah.

The Spirit of the Lord God is upon me; because the Lord hath anointed me to preach good tidings unto the meek; he hath sent me to bind up the brokenhearted, to proclaim liberty to the captives, and the opening of the prison to them that are bound; To proclaim the acceptable year of the Lord (verses 1, 2a).

Then He closed the book. He read to the middle of the sentence but then He closed the book. Why did He not go on with Isaiah's words? Because those verses tell what He came to do at His first coming. His first and His second comings are intimately linked together

in this chapter of Isaiah. He came to preach deliverance
to captives, to give sight to the blind, to open the
prisons of those that are bound, to proclaim the accept
able year of the Lord. There He stopped at what we
would call a comma. He put this whole dispensation in
which you and I live into that comma. It is the accept
able year of the Lord still. We have not moved one iota
beyond that point where He closed the book. Why did
He close it there? Because the rest of the sentence
would carry us on into the day of the Lord after this
present age has come to an end. So now is the accepted
time, now is the day of salvation. Speaking metaphori-
cally, when He comes again He will open that book once
more to the rest of this passage and it will all be fulfilled to the letter.

And the day of vengeance of our God; to comfort all that
mourn; To appoint unto them that mourn in Zion, to give unto them
beauty for ashes, the oil of joy for mourning, the garment of praise
for the spirit of heaviness; that they might be called trees of righteousness, the planting of the Lord, that he might be glorified
(verses 2b, 3).

It is a wonderful linking of the first and second comings. He came to proclaim the acceptable year of the
Lord, He is coming again to declare the day of vengeance of our God. When God destroys those who are in
red-handed opposition to Himself, and the enemies of
His people Israel, it will be the time of the Lord's
vengeance.

Then our Lord will bring comfort and blessing to
those who have suffered so much. "To comfort all that
mourn." This glorious prophecy will be fulfilled literally
for all Israel after the judgments of the day of the
Lord have been poured out upon the wicked. Meantime,

ach individual soul who trusts in Christ may enjoy the
blessings here enumerated. Christ gives the wedding
garments of praise in place of the funereal attire of the
mourner of which the ashes and the garment of heaviness speak. Those who have sought in vain for peace
and satisfaction in the world and whose fondest hopes
have failed may find fullness of joy and satisfaction in
Christ, who is glorified in all His saints and who finds
His joy in their eternal blessing.

Our English word "comfort" is from two Latin roots,
con, to be with, and *fortis*, strong. It literally means
"to strengthen by companionship." A child, with a long
walk before him on a dark night, may be filled with
fear. But if his father is with him to take his hand, all
fear is gone as they walk together through the gloom
of the night. So God would have us realize the blessed
reality of His presence with us as we face the trials
and griefs to which all are exposed while passing
through the changing scenes of time and sense. It is
this that will keep the heart in peace and free the spirit
from fear. Nothing can come to those who know the
Lord but what His love allows and which He will use
for our blessing as we go through it all in subjection to
His holy will and implicit dependence upon Himself.

Beauty for ashes, the oil of joy for mourning, the
garment of praise for the spirit of heaviness. The
figures suggest a funeral and a wedding. At a funeral
service Jews put ashes upon their heads and mourn and
lament; at a wedding, they wear beautiful bridal
wreaths and garments of praise. Israel's long centuries
of mourning will be over and she will enter into
the joyousness of her marriage to Jehovah with all
the blessings attendant upon it.

We are living now in the parenthesis between the

sixty-ninth and seventieth weeks of Daniel, betwee[n] the beginning of the acceptable year of the Lord an[d] the day of vengeance of our God.

Other passages contain the same thought. For in[-] stance, the Apostle Peter speaks of those who woul[d] see good days, who seek peace and ensue it, for th[e] face of the Lord is against them that do iniquity. H[e] stops there. The Old Testament continues, "to cut of[f] the remembrance of them from the earth." That da[y] has not yet come. God's face is still against wickednes[s] and corruption, but the day has not come when He wil[l] cut off the remembrance of evil-doers from the earth[.] We can still preach the gospel of the grace of God an[d] offer salvation to the worst sinner. To the vilest sin[-] ners, those who have done the very worst, God is offer[-] ing His grace. We are living in this period between th[e] first coming of Christ and His second coming, the on[e] having to do with the fulfillment of these early proph[-] ecies and the other with the later ones—all linked u[p] with the restoration of Israel and the blessing of th[e] whole Gentile world.

> But ye shall be named the priests of the Lord: men shall cal[l] you the ministers of our God: ye shall eat the riches of the Gentiles, and in their glory shall ye boast yourselves (verse 6).

The nation of Israel then will be a nation of priests, who will go into God's presence on behalf of all the other peoples of the earth, and also be God's messengers to them.

> I will greatly rejoice in the Lord, my soul shall be joyful in my God; for he hath clothed me with the garments of salvation, he

hath covered me with the robe of righteousness, as a bridegroom decketh himself with ornaments, and as a bride adorneth herself with her jewels. For as the earth bringeth forth her bud, and as the garden causeth the things that are sown in it to spring forth; so the Lord God will cause righteousness and praise to spring forth before all the nations (verses 10, 11).

How much these wonderful promises should mean to God's earthly people, and how we should be interested in them! Our blessings are heavenly. Theirs, to a great extent, will be earthly, and yet their salvation is just the same as our salvation. "He hath clothed me," they will be able to sing in that day, "with the garments of salvation, He hath covered me with the robe of [His] righteousness." Is not that true of us today? We who at one time were trying to piece out a covering for ourselves with the filthy rags of our own unrighteousness have cast that to one side and can say, "He hath clothed me with the garments of salvation, He hath covered me with the robe of [His] righteousness."

God has provided a righteousness for men and women who have none of their own. And in that coming day, Israel will learn this precious truth—they will give up all pretense of their human righteousness and rejoice in the righteousness of God which will be bestowed upon them.

The prophet Jeremiah referring to this time says, "This is His name whereby He shall be called, [Jehovah-tsidkenu] the Lord our Righteousness." And then a little farther on in his prophecy, speaking of Jerusalem and its restoration, he says, "This is the name whereby she shall be called, [Jehovah-tsidkenu] the Lord our Righteousness," recognizing that she has no righteousness of her own, but the day will come when the people of Israel will find their righteousness in the Lord God Himself. What a blessed thing it is when we have learned that lesson even now! So many people have never learned it.

Years ago it was no easy thing when a colored school was first started in Dallas. There was no help financially, and as we vainly tried to interest people, I began to wonder if it was worthwhile to do anything for these colored people. After the third year as I was in Dallas to lecture I went to the school to give an address there one night. I said to my son, "It costs so much to run this and you are giving your very life for it, and I don't know whether it is really worthwhile." He looked at me rather strangely, and then said, "Why don't you ask the men what they think about it?"

So before speaking that night, I said, "I would like to know what you men think of it. Is it a worthwhile investment? Are you getting enough out of it?" For many minutes there was not a sound. They sat there with downcast faces and no one said a word.

Finally one man got up and said, "I've been wondering if I heard aright. Did I understand that this school may be closed? If this school is closed, then I shall feel that the last bit of light for us poor colored people in Dallas has gone out, and we are just to be left in the dark. Let me tell you how I was in the dark. I was a pastor of a church for thirteen years. I didn't know the gospel. I didn't know how sinners were saved. I preached. The people came together and I baptized them and they joined the church—and they shouted and they went on. I thought if I put on plenty of 'arousements' and got them all going, that that was the power of the Holy Spirit. I heard about this school, but I was kind of prejudiced when I heard a white man was running it. I thought there must be something queer about it. But finally I came one night." He turned to me and went on, "Your son was speaking that night on the first three chapters of the Epistle to the Romans. It took away from me all the religion I'd been building up for thirteen years. I just sat there in a daze as he tore off one filthy rag after another until I stood there naked before God. I had no righteousness of my own and I thought I had so much. I thought I was doing so well. I went out of the class that night and went home and said, 'What am I going to do? All that I've tried to do to fit myself for heaven is gone. I haven't anything left." I could hardly wait for the next class two nights later. That night he began in the middle of the third chapter of Romans and he went on to show that God had a righteousness for men who had none of their own. Oh, I can't tell you what that meant to me! I found out that night I didn't have to provide my own righteousness, God had provided one, and if I just trusted the Lord Jesus Christ, I was made the righteousness of God in Him. From that day to this I've been preaching the righteousness of God, and my people have been learning to see this great truth. Brother, don't close up this school—it's the only place I know where they open up these things to us colored folks."

Many people try to build up a righteousness of their own—and poor Israel is doing that. The Apostle Paul says, "They being ignorant of God's righteousness, and going about to establish their own righteousness, have not submitted themselves unto the righteousness of God" (Rom. 10:3).

In this coming day everything will be changed. Their

eyes opened, they will see in Christ their Redeemer and be able to sing with gladness, "He hath clothed me with the garments of salvation . . . covered me with the robe of righteousness."

CHAPTER SIXTY-TWO

PROCLAMATION TO THE REMNANT

For Zion's sake will I not hold my peace, and for Jerusalem's sake I will not rest, until the righteousness thereof go forth as brightness, and the salvation thereof as a lamp that burneth. And the Gentiles shall see thy righteousness, and all kings thy glory: and thou shalt be called by a new name, which the mouth of the Lord shall name. Thou shalt also be a crown of glory in the hand of the Lord, and a royal diadem in the hand of thy God (verses 1-3).

HOW PRECIOUS this is! These words, even to-day, would naturally fill the heart of every redeemed Hebrew as he thinks of his people still wandering in the darkness of unbelief, and he prays for the peace of Jerusalem and looks forward to the day when all will be brought into this knowledge. So at the very beginning of the tribulation period a remnant will be called out to carry this message to all their brethren and be an intercession to God, looking to Him to hasten the day when Jerusalem will be made a praise throughout all the earth.

The chapter goes on to tell of the Lord in His grace restoring Israel to Himself and bringing them into all the blessing of the Abrahamic Covenant.

I have set watchmen upon thy walls, O Jerusalem, which shall never hold their peace day nor night; ye that make mention of the Lord, keep not silence, And give him no rest, till he establish, and till he make Jerusalem a praise in the earth. The Lord hath sworn by his right hand, and by the arm of his strength, Surely I will no more give thy corn to be meat for thine enemies; and the sons of the stranger shall not drink thy wine, for the which thou hast laboured: But they that have gathered it shall eat it, and praise the Lord; and they that have brought it together shall drink it in the courts of my holiness. Go through, go through the gates; prepare ye the way of the people; cast up, cast up the highway; gather out the stones; lift up a standard for the people. Behold, the Lord hath proclaimed unto the end of the world, Say ye to the daughter of Zion, Behold, thy salvation cometh; behold, his reward is with him, and his work before him. And they shall call them The holy people, The redeemed of the Lord: and thou shalt be called, Sought out, A city not forsaken (verses 6-12).

The days shall be when all this will be fulfilled. The words hardly need comment—they are so clear, so plain.

CHAPTER SIXTY-THREE

THE WARRIOR CONQUEROR
FROM EDOM

HERE we have the wonderful picture of Israel's Redeemer with garments red with the blood of their enemies, coming up from the East—from whence their enemies generally came. Syria was pressing upon them at this time and Assyria would come to them through the lands of Moab and Edom, and so, looking to the last days, to the time of their great trial in the tribulation period, Isaiah depicts Him as a conqueror coming toward the land, driving His foes before Him, taking vengeance on Israel's adversaries in order to redeem His chosen people. He had looked for someone to help. There was no one, and so He came Himself. Just as He came Himself to die for their sins on the Cross, so He is to be their final deliverer from their foes.

Remembering the salvation here is from their enemies, deliverance from every power that has oppressed them, bringing them into blessing in their land, this majestic passage should be noted carefully.

Who is this that cometh from Edom, with dyed garments from Bozrah? this that is glorious in his apparel, travelling in the greatness of his strength? I that speak in righteousness, mighty to save. Wherefore art thou red in thine apparel, and thy garments like him that treadeth in the winefat? I have trodden the winepress alone; and of the people there was none with me: for I will tread them in

mine anger, and trample them in my fury; and their blood shall be
sprinkled upon my garments, and I will stain all my raiment. For
the day of vengeance is in mine heart, and the year of my redeemed
is come (verses 1-4).

This passage has often been misapplied. The words,
"I have trodden the winepress alone," have often been
used of our blessed Lord going through the agony of
Gethsemane's Garden, and there is a sense in which one
might think of Him there as "treading the winepress,"
but the whole context here shows it is treading the
winepress in judgment on the foes of Israel. It links
with Revelation 14:15-20, where we have the vintage,
and the vine of the earth is fully ripe and is cast into
the great winepress of the wrath of God. It is the
Eastern figure. They gathered their grapes, threw them
into a great winepress, and then, taking off part of
their garments, with bare feet the young men stepped
into the winefat, trod out the fruit, and became spat-
tered with the red blood of the grapes. It was always a
time of great rejoicing. Among the Greeks this was a
festival in honor of the god Bacchus, or Dionysius,
but among the Hebrews, too, there was the annual
treading of the grapes, and the picture here is God
putting into the winepress all the enemies of Israel, all
who have sought to destroy His chosen people, and then
looking for someone to tread that winepress. There was
no one. "I looked . . . there was none." So He came.
"I have trodden the winepress alone; and of the people
there was none" to help me.

He says, "I will stain all my raiment." His garments are looked upon as stained with the blood of
of Israel's foes. In Revelation 19 we have the wonderful
vision of the Lord descending from heaven, pictured
as a mighty warrior astride a great white charger.

There it is said He was clothed with a vesture dipped in blood, His own precious blood, the blood that poured from the wound in His side and would naturally stain His vesture. It is the symbol of His love for His people. But here in Isaiah His garments are stained with the blood of His enemies—it is the day of vengeance of our God.

When that day comes, all those who are found in opposition to God will be destroyed. Look carefully into the prophetic Word, and link it up with the book of Revelation, and it will be evident that there are two different characters of judgment upon the world at the time of the Lord's second advent. There is the warrior judgment, when the nations will gather together and the Lord will descend in power from heaven and destroy them—that is the treading of the winepress which we have here. Then there is what might be called the sessional judgment when the Son of Man shall come in His glory and all His holy angels with Him. Then shall He sit upon the throne of His glory, and before Him shall be gathered all nations, and He shall separate them one from another—the shepherd dividing the sheep from the goats (Matt. 25).

There He is not dealing with the nations that have been maintaining a vicious attitude toward God and His people, but those who will be judged in that day according to their attitude toward His messengers of Israel as they have gone through the world proclaiming the coming of the King.

These two aspects of one judgment may be distinguished but not separated. The Lord Jesus is revealed in flaming fire taking vengeance on those that know not God, those that obey not the gospel, who have had every opportunity to be saved and have turned away and taken the place of enemies of God and His people.

In the sessional judgment it is the nations as such, to many of whom the gospel message had never before gone, who are judged according to their attitude toward His people. The sheep, for instance, are not saved because of what they did to His people, nor are the others lost because of their bad treatment of them. It is a question in either case of whether they had faith in Christ or not. If there was real faith, it was manifested by their treatment of His messengers. Where there was no faith, it would be manifested by their indifference to them.

Judgment is always according to works and so He speaks of their attitude in each instance toward those who have carried the message. "Inasmuch as ye have done it unto one of the least of these My brethren, ye have done it unto Me . . . Inasmuch as ye did it not to one of the least of these [My brethren], ye did it not to Me."

In Isaiah 63 the treading of the winepress is the warrior judgment when all found in definite, open opposition to God and His people will be destroyed when the Lord Jesus is revealed from heaven in flaming fire.

And I looked, and there was none to help; and I wondered that there was none to uphold: therefore mine own arm brought salvation unto me; and my fury, it upheld me. And I will tread down the people in mine anger, and make them drunk in my fury, and I will bring down their strength to the earth. I will mention the lovingkindnesses of the Lord, and the praises of the Lord, according to all that the Lord hath bestowed on us, and the great goodness toward the house of Israel, which he hath bestowed on them according to his mercies, and according to the multitude of his lovingkindnesses. For he said, Surely they are my people, children that will not lie: so he was their Saviour. In all their affliction he was afflicted, and the angel of his presence saved them: in his love and in his

pity he redeemed them; and he bare them, and carried them all the
days of old (verses 5-9).

This precious portion applies to God's care over all
His people in any dispensation, but here He is primarily dealing with the suffering saints of the last days,
and also with those that might be suffering for the
truth's sake in Isaiah's own day. Yet it may be taken
to heart by God's afflicted people in any time, because
He is always concerned about His saints. Weymouth's
beautiful translation of 1 Peter 5:7 is, "Casting all
your care upon Him, for it matters to God about you."
So here "in all their affliction He was afflicted, and the
angel of His presence saved them."

God is not an unmoved spectator as He gazes upon
the sufferings of His saints. His heart of compassion
goes out to every one of them, and if He permits the
suffering to go on, it is because He sits as a refiner of
silver, waiting to purge them from all dross, that His
own countenance may be fully manifested in them.
What a comfort a passage like this will be to the remnant of Israel in the last days when suffering terribly
under the Beast and the false prophet but waiting for
the manifestation of the King. He will come and their
sufferings will end, and they will enter into all the
blessings that He has predicted.

THE HEART-CRY OF THE REMNANT

THE last three chapters of the book (chaps. 64, 65, 66) are all intimately linked together. In chapter sixty-four we have what might be called the heart-cry, the prayer, of the remnant in the last days, whilst suitable for God's people at any time of trial or affliction, who feel the need of divine intervention. In actual prophetic application it opens up to us the hearts of the people of Israel in the last days, suffering under the Beast and the Antichrist. They cry to the Lord to come down on their behalf.

Oh that thou wouldest rend the heavens, that thou wouldest come down, that the mountains might flow down at thy presence. As when the melting fire burneth, the fire causeth the waters to boil, to make thy name known to thine adversaries, that the nations may tremble at thy presence! When thou didst terrible things which we looked not for, thou camest down, the mountains flowed down at thy presence. For since the beginning of the world men have not heard, nor perceived by the ear, neither hath the eye seen, O God, beside thee, what he hath prepared for him that waiteth for him (verses 1-4).

The Apostle Paul quoted these words from the Septuagint Version in the Epistle to the Corinthians, "Eye hath not seen, nor ear heard . . . the things which God hath prepared for them that love Him" (1 Cor. 2:9, 10). But he immediately adds, "But God hath revealed them unto us by His Spirit." An added revelation has been given, of which Isaiah knew nothing, something that God had reserved for a future day. People often quote the words as if they stand today as in Isaiah's time. They forget Paul immediately gives the added revelation, "But God hath revealed them unto us by His Spirit . . . But we have the mind of Christ" (verses 10, 16).

How fitting will be the cry for help on the lips and from the hearts of the exercised remnant of Israel in the last days. They call upon God to intervene, they see no help in man, as the nations are gathering together. God has said in the book of Zechariah, "I will gather all nations against Jerusalem to battle" (Zech. 14:2). The remnant see that ominous gathering and cry, "O God, wilt Thou not intervene? Wilt Thou not rend the heavens and come down? Wilt Thou not deal with these nations Thyself and give the deliverance for which our hearts crave?"

But we are all as an unclean thing, and all our righteousnesses are as filthy rags; and we all do fade as a leaf; and our iniquities, like the wind, have taken us away. And there is none that calleth upon thy name, that stirreth up himself to take hold of thee: for thou hast hid thy face from us, and hast consumed us, because of our iniquities. But now, O Lord, thou art our father; we are the clay, and thou our potter; and we all are the work of thy hand (verses 6-8).

The remnant take the place of confession, of self-judgment, of repentance before God, realizing that if God will undertake for them, they must take their rightful place in His presence. They know of the patience of God so often shown to Israel, so there is no self-justification. They do not ask God to intervene because of their merits or their faithfulness. They say, "Our iniquities, like the wind, have taken us away." We understand why we and our fathers have been suffering through the centuries. "We are all as an unclean thing, and all our righteousnesses are as filthy rags." It is not merely filth contracted by dragging garments in the streets, but contaminated by filth from within. They are all as an unclean thing because of the corruption of the heart. But they turn to God because He has promised definitely, "He that covereth his sins shall not prosper: but whoso confesseth and forsaketh them shall have mercy" (Prov. 28:13).

David cried out in Psalm 25:11, "O Lord, pardon mine iniquity, for it is great." "Great!" We might have expected him to say, if he had been like some of us, "O Lord, pardon mine iniquity, for after all it is not very great. I didn't really mean to do wrong. I failed, but I am sorry, but I did not mean to be bad." That is the way people talk today. But he says, "O Lord, pardon mine iniquity, for it is great." Only a great God can pardon great iniquity. And so the remnant here do not try to justify themselves, nor cover up, but make full, frank confession of their sin and iniquity and acknowledge that they have no righteousness of their own to plead. All their own fancied righteousnesses are but contaminated rags in the sight of a holy God. When we take this attitude we may count on God's answer in blessing.

Chapter Sixty-five

NEW HEAVENS AND A
NEW EARTH

I am sought of them that asked not after me; I am found of them that sought me not: I said, Behold me, behold me, unto a nation that was not called by my name. I have spread out my hands all the day unto a rebellious people, which walketh in a way that was not good, after their own thoughts: A people that provoketh me to anger continually to my face; that sacrificeth in gardens, and burneth incense upon altars of brick; Which remain among the graves, and lodge in the monuments, which eat swine's flesh, and broth of abominable things is in their vessels; Which say, Stand by thyself, come not near to me; for I am holier than thou. These are a smoke in my nose, a fire that burneth all the day (verses 1-5).

GOD is explaining—if I may use the word, since God does not have to explain; but He does here —thus meeting the remnant in grace and making clear to them why these judgments have been upon the people, because of all these sins—some open, some hidden. They had set aside His own holy law, and brought in the practices of the heathen round about them; dwelling "among the graves" for an Israelite was an unclean thing. It pictures the uncleanness into which the people had fallen. Because of all this, God's face was averted; He could not deal with them as otherwise He would have desired. The Lord calls upon His people today to separation from the evils around them, "Come out from among them, and be ye separate, saith the Lord, and touch not the unclean thing" (2 Cor. 6:17). And speaking of the unequal yoke: "Be ye not unequally yoked together with unbelievers: for what fellowship . . . hath light with darkness? . . . Christ with Belial? or . . . he that believeth with an infidel?" (2 Cor. 6:14, 15). It is a call to complete separation from fellowship with those who are walking in avowed disobedience to His Word. This done He immediately says, "And I will be a Father unto you . . . saith the Lord Almighty." Surely God is the Father of all His people, but He is not always free to be a father unto us in the way He desires.

A loving father delights to give his children one manifestation after another of his loving interest in them, and God, our Father, wants to do that. That is implied in being a Father *unto* us. He is a Father of every one of us, but if we walk in disobedience the holiness of His own nature hinders Him from doing the things for which His heart yearns.

Israel of old had become contaminated by their association with the nations and like the heathen around them, and "evil communications corrupt good manners." The reason that God calls upon His people to come out from the world and be separate is because they cannot go on with the world and maintain their Christian testimony.

Many think that the way to win the world is to be "hail-fellow-well-met" with them. It is like the boys who caught two baby linnets and made little cages for them, and as the linnets grew they meant to teach them to sing. They had a canary which sang very beautifully, so they put the linnets' cages on each side of that of the canary, thinking that never having heard others and listening only to the canary's sweet notes they would learn to sing like it. For some time there were no results. And then one day they said, "Oh, listen, our canary is cheeping like a linnet!" Instead of the linnets learning the canary's long-cherished lovely song it was cheeping like them.

That is the result when God's people have fellowship with the ungodly. Instead of the ungodly learning the ways of Christ, the children of God soon follow the ways of the ungodly.

Separation certainly involves the marriage relation; Scripture has made it very clear that a child of God and an unsaved person should not contemplate marriage. An old Puritan quaintly said, "If you are a child of God and you marry a child of the devil, you can expect to have trouble with your father-in-law."

Then, too, how many a Christian, hoping to make more money, has gone into partnership with an unsaved man in some business venture, soon to find that he has put himself under an unequal yoke? That unsaved man feels perfectly free to do many things in business that a conscientious Christian cannot. He either has to stand against his partner or go with him, and if he does the latter he will lose his Christian testimony.

The same thing occurs in connection with association with all kinds of societies. Two scriptures should keep us out of them all. The first is this: Jesus said "In secret have I said nothing." Therefore He could not have been a member of any secret society or lodge.

The other scripture, that already referred to, is: "Be ye not unequally yoked together with unbelievers." In these Orders there are saved and unsaved people, and if we want to have a bright testimony for Christ, we must walk apart from that unequal yoke. Paul's reference is to that Old Testament scripture: "Thou shalt not plow with an ox and an ass [yoked] together." The ox was a clean beast and could be offered to God in sacrifice. The ass was looked upon as ceremonially unclean, and the two were not to be yoked together.

When Israel in disobedience mingled with the nations and began to practice their evil doings, God had to pour out His judgment upon them. But when they turned back to Him, confessing their sins, God in His infinite grace was ready to give deliverance.

Thus saith the Lord, As the new wine is found in the cluster, and one saith, Destroy it not; for a blessing is in it: so will I do for my servants' sakes, that I may not destroy them all. And I will bring forth a seed out of Jacob, and out of Judah an inheritor of my mountains: and mine elect shall inherit it, and my servants shall dwell there. And Sharon shall be a fold of flocks, and the valley of Achor a place for the herds to lie down in, for my people that have sought me (verses 8-10).

As all that one might see in a vineyard is one large bunch of grapes which seems good for nothing, yet God says: "Destroy it not . . . a blessing is in it." He will not destroy His people completely, but take out of them a nucleus of the coming nation, the restored nation, in the last days.

He will make the valley of Achor a means of blessing to them. That was the place where Achan and his family were stoned to death, because of their sin when the people first entered the land. Achor, meaning "trouble," speaks of the troubles that we bring upon ourselves by our own willfulness, yet God can so work in grace that He can make those very sorrows an eventual means of blessing for us.

So all of Israel's waywardness of the past will be used of God to correct and bless them, even as Jeremiah said, "Thine own wickedness shall correct thee, and thy backslidings shall reprove thee." God overrules even the failures of His people when they turn in heart to Him and thus learn lessons which can be of help and blessing to them in the days to come.

For, behold, I create new heavens and a new earth: and the former shall not be remembered, nor come into mind. But be ye glad and rejoice for ever in that which I create: for, behold, I create Jerusalem a rejoicing, and her people a joy. And I will rejoice in Jerusalem, and joy in my people: and the voice of weeping shall be no more heard in her, nor the voice of crying (verses 17-19).

Then comes the fulfillment of the promises to the obedient in the land, promised for such obedience under the law.

There shall be no more thence an infant of days, nor an old man that hath not filled his days: for the child shall die an hundred years old; but the sinner being an hundred years old shall be accursed. And they shall build houses, and inhabit them; and they shall plant vineyards, and eat the fruit of them. They shall not build, and another inhabit; they shall not plant, and another eat: for as the days of a tree are the days of my people, and mine elect shall long enjoy the work of their hands. They shall not labour in vain, nor bring forth for trouble; for they are the seed of the blessed of the Lord, and their offspring with them. And it shall come to pass, that before they call, I will answer; and while they are yet speaking, I will hear. The wolf and the lamb shall feed together, and the lion shall eat straw like the bullock: and dust shall be the serpent's meat. They shall not hurt nor destroy in all my holy mountain, saith the Lord (verses 20-25).

Yes, God will undertake, and He brings before us here this glimpse of the new heavens and the new earth. There is no description of this, no instruction given as to what will take place at that time. He simply says, "I will create new heavens and a new earth," and then He adds, As surely as I do this, I will "create Jerusalem" a place of rejoicing. Just as surely as He brings in new heavens and a new earth, so He will fulfill every promise made to Israel, and make Jerusalem a center of joy and blessing to the whole world.

Again the rebellious were warned because when God called they did not answer, when He spoke they did not hear; but with those in millennial days God has promised that before they call He will answer, while they are yet speaking He will hear. This is a promise that abides. God's people can claim it today because it has to do with that which is spiritual. Blessed with all spiritual blessings in heavenly places in Christ, we can appropriate and act upon everything spiritual in the Old Testament, but we are not at liberty to take over the promises that have to do simply with temporal things.

Chapter sixty-five gives the Lord's answer. His indignation has been aroused against many because of their idolatry, the abominations they have committed, and their unreality. But He also assures the faithful remnant, those who truly turn to Him, that He is about to intervene on their behalf.

Chapter sixty-six again brings before the rebellious part of the nation the sins that have moved God's heart and caused Him to turn them over to the power of the enemy, and again assures those who trust in Him, that not one of His promises will fail, He will bring them into fullness of blessing.

We have compared the Old Testament prophet to a man looking upon a mountain range, upon one great peak, and then the clouds rise and a higher peak is seen beyond. In chapters 65 and 66 the prophet lifts his telescope a little higher, and looks beyond that second great peak and gets a momentary glimpse of what God has in store for His people for all eternity. He sees the new heavens and the new earth. These two passages are referred to by the Apostle Peter when he speaks of the passing of the day of the Lord and the bringing in of the day of God, when everything that man has been building up through the years will collapse and the heavens and the earth will melt with fervent heat. "Nevertheless," the apostle says, "we, according to His promise, look for new heavens and a new earth, wherein dwelleth righteousness" (2 Pet. 3:13). That promise is given here through Isaiah in chapters 65 and 66 and nowhere else.

In the book of Revelation, John in vision looks beyond the millennial glory and says, "I saw a new heaven and a new earth . . . and there was no more sea . . . former things are passed away." The new creation would have come in absolute perfection and he gives us some description of the blessedness of the redeemed in the eternal state.

We are not told in so many words that the eternal abode of the redeemed of Israel who have been with the Lord in millennial glory will be upon the new earth, but as we consider what is said in these two chapters we naturally come to that conclusion.

The Church, the Body of Christ, with all Old Testament saints and those who will have died down through the centuries, right up to the beginning of the millennium will have their place in the new heavens, and there will be a wonderful intimate link between the two groups; heaven and earth as it were will be as one. Scripture seems to suggest that distinction—the Church as the bride and the friends of the bridegroom will be the heavenly saints with Christ above, while renewed Israel are with Christ here upon the new earth.

When that day comes, we may all find that we have had very imperfect conceptions of things. We have the guidance of the Spirit of God in the direct statements He has given us, but we are prone to misunderstand. If before the Lord came the first time one had tried to get clearly in mind the succession of events in connection with His advent, perhaps one would have been much perplexed and confused and probably have come to very wrong conclusions. But when the Lord actually came, and one event after another took place as predicted, it would be seen that the prophets had foretold all these things, but might have misunderstood the order of their occurrence. The prophets themselves, we are told, after writing, searched what or what manner of time the Spirit of Christ that was in them did prophesy, when He testified beforehand the sufferings of Christ and the glories which should follow.

In studying Isaiah the prophet, did you ever think that Isaiah studied Isaiah the prophet? After he had written what God gave him by divine inspiration, he sat down over his own scrolls and studied carefully what God had inspired him to write, that he might try to see clearly the succession of events, the order in which things would take place, and then it was revealed to him, as to the other prophets, that it was not yet the time for a full understanding, that much of this was to be reserved for a future day, and they learned that not unto themselves but unto us they made these things known. And now they are opened up by the Holy Ghost sent down from heaven (1 Pet. 1:10-12). So of those things which are still unfulfilled, still in the future, we should not speak too dogmatically.

CHAPTER SIXTY-SIX

THE END OF THE LORD
MANIFESTED

IN THIS last chapter again we find that God stresses
the failures of His people, and then closes by telling of the wonderful conditions that will prevail
in the days of the kingdom, and gives another glimpse
of the new heavens and the new earth.

Thus saith the Lord, The heaven is my throne, and the earth
is my footstool: where is the house that ye build unto me? and
where is the place of my rest? For all those things hath mine hand
made, and all those things have been, saith the Lord: but to this
man will I look, even to him that is poor and of a contrite spirit,
and trembleth at my word . . . Hear the word of the Lord, ye that
tremble at his word; Your brethren that hated you, that cast you
out for my name's sake, said, Let the Lord be glorified: but he shall
appear to your joy, and they shall be ashamed (verses 1-3, 5).

Once more it is emphasized that He who fills heaven
and earth cannot be confined to any house here, yet
deigns to dwell in the heart of the lowly and the contrite. "To this man will I look, even to him that is poor
and of a contrite spirit, and trembleth at my word," he
who walks carefully fearing lest he might go contrary
to the word of God. And those that tremble at the
Word may have the assurance that He himself will ever
undertake for them. He is not looking for great ability
nor wonderful eloquence on the part of His servants,

365

but for a heart subject to His truth. And when H finds that He will intervene on behalf of His peopl But those who are merely formalists, who do not kno the realities of spiritual things, will look down upo them with contempt, think of them, perhaps, as fana ics and accuse them of all kinds of folly. So here H says, "Your brethren that hated you, that cast you ou for My name's sake, said, Let the Lord be glorified. But God says it is for His name's sake.

So the remnant of Israel will be despised and looke down upon by those who do not take their place of repentance before God, but the Lord shall appear t their glory and their enemies shall be ashamed.

Chapter sixty-six gathers together the threads of God's ways of holiness and grace. Heaven is His thron yet He dwells with him who is of a contrite and humbl spirit (chap. 57:15). The offerings of those who hav only a form of pleasing Him are an offense. They hav chosen their own ways, but God will choose too, an bring their fears upon them, because when He calle and spoke they did not answer nor hear, but did evi and chose what did not please Him (chap. 65:12). Ye those who heard His voice heard the promise: "Befor they call, I will answer; and while they are yet speak ing, I will hear" (chap. 65:24).

Jehovah had said to His people that He would giv them peace like a river, and speaking as God the Crea tor He said there would be peace, peace to him that is far off, and to him that is near (chap. 57:19). But the solemn assurance is twice given also: "There is n peace, saith the Lord [my God] unto the wicked" (chaps. 48:22; 57:21).

As one whom his mother comforteth, so will I comfort you; an ye shall be comforted in Jerusalem (verse 13).

Compare chapters 40 and 61 for God's plan and design for His people. The Hebrew word translated "comfort" in this verse is from a root meaning "to sigh!" It might be rendered, "As one whom his mother sighs with, so will I sigh with you." We know how a loving mother enters into the sufferings of her children. Taking the little one in her arms she sighs with him as he sobs out his grief upon her bosom. So does God feel for us in our trials. Of old He said concerning Israel when they were in Egyptian bondage, "I have surely seen the affliction of My people . . . I know their sorrows; and am come to deliver them." He is ever the same in His concern for His afflicted children. His great heart of love is moved with compassion as He beholds the ravages that sin has made and the sufferings that it has entailed upon all minkind. Yet we are so slow to refer our troubles to Him, thinking of Him as a stern Judge rather than a tender, loving Father.

For, behold, the Lord will come with fire . . . to render his anger with fury . . . For by fire and by his sword will the Lord plead with all flesh . . . I know their works and their thoughts: it shall come, that I will gather all nations and tongues; and they shall come and see my glory (verses 15, 16, 18).

The whole book of Revelation bears witness to this.

And I will set a sign among them, and I will send those that escape of them unto the nations, to Tarshish, Pul, and Lud, that draw the bow, to Tubal, and Javan, to the isles afar off, that have not heard my fame, neither have seen my glory; and they shall declare my glory among the Gentiles. And they shall bring all your brethren for an offering unto the Lord out of all nations upon horses, and in chariots, and in litters, and upon mules, and upon swift beasts, to my holy mountain Jerusalem, saith the Lord, as the children of Israel bring an offering in a clean vessel into the house of the Lord. And I will also take of them for priests and for Levites, saith the Lord. For as the new heavens and the new earth which I will make, shall remain before me, saith the Lord, so shall your seed and your name remain. And it shall come to pass, that from one new moon to another, and from one sabbath to another shall all flesh come to worship before me, saith the Lord. And they shall go forth, and look upon the carcases of the men that have transgressed against me; for their worm shall not die, neither shall their fire be quenched; and they shall be an abhorring unto all flesh (verses 19-24).

In chapter 65:22 we read of the longevity of the people in the millennium: "as the days of a tree shall be the days of My people." If one dies at one hundred years of age, he shall be counted as a child, and yet the presence of death and the curse would indicate that death will come only to any who definitely rebel against the King, who sin against Him. And then those who are in the place of blessing will see from time to time the dead bodies of those who are slain, where "their worm dieth not, and the fire is not quenched." The Lord Jesus quotes Isaiah's words again and again when referring to the final estate of the eternally lost (Mark 9:43-48).

And so the book ends with God's holiness and glory manifested and magnified as well as His divine compassions.

> "Here Thy bright character is known,
>   Nor dare a creature guess
> Which of His glories brightest shone—
>   The justice or the grace."

Meanwhile it is true for us as for God's ancient people,

"Upon the wings of every hour
We read Thy patience still."

"Blessing, and honour, and glory, and power, be unto Him that sitteth upon the throne, and unto the Lamb for ever and ever" (Rev. 5:13).